797,885 Books

are available to read at

www.ForgottenBooks.com

Forgotten Books' App
Available for mobile, tablet & eReader

ISBN 978-1-333-11219-6
PIBN 10469848

This book is a reproduction of an important historical work. Forgotten Books uses state-of-the-art technology to digitally reconstruct the work, preserving the original format whilst repairing imperfections present in the aged copy. In rare cases, an imperfection in the original, such as a blemish or missing page, may be replicated in our edition. We do, however, repair the vast majority of imperfections successfully; any imperfections that remain are intentionally left to preserve the state of such historical works.

Forgotten Books is a registered trademark of FB &c Ltd.
Copyright © 2015 FB &c Ltd.
FB &c Ltd, Dalton House, 60 Windsor Avenue, London, SW19 2RR.
Company number 08720141. Registered in England and Wales.

For support please visit www.forgottenbooks.com

1 MONTH OF
FREE
READING

at
www.ForgottenBooks.com

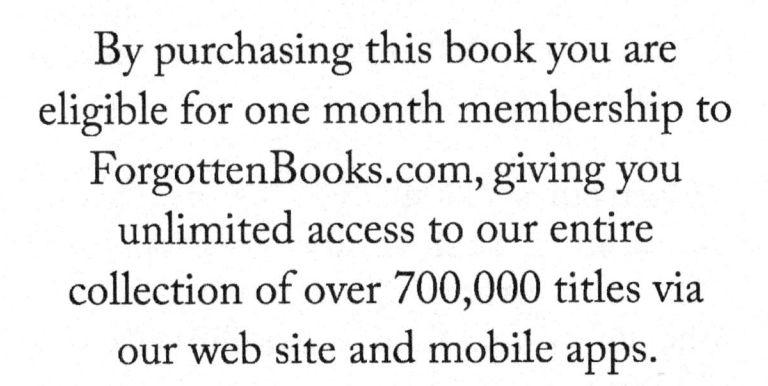

By purchasing this book you are eligible for one month membership to ForgottenBooks.com, giving you unlimited access to our entire collection of over 700,000 titles via our web site and mobile apps.

To claim your free month visit:
www.forgottenbooks.com/free469848

* Offer is valid for 45 days from date of purchase. Terms and conditions apply.

English
Français
Deutsche
Italiano
Español
Português

www.forgottenbooks.com

Mythology Photography **Fiction**
Fishing Christianity **Art** Cooking
Essays Buddhism Freemasonry
Medicine **Biology** Music **Ancient Egypt** Evolution Carpentry Physics
Dance Geology **Mathematics** Fitness
Shakespeare **Folklore** Yoga Marketing
Confidence Immortality Biographies
Poetry **Psychology** Witchcraft
Electronics Chemistry History **Law**
Accounting **Philosophy** Anthropology
Alchemy Drama Quantum Mechanics
Atheism Sexual Health **Ancient History**
Entrepreneurship Languages Sport
Paleontology Needlework Islam
Metaphysics Investment Archaeology
Parenting Statistics Criminology
Motivational

The Folk-Lore Society,

FOR COLLECTING AND PRINTING

RELICS OF POPULAR ANTIQUITIES, &c.

ESTABLISHED IN

THE YEAR MDCCCLXXVIII.

Alter et Idem.

PUBLICATIONS
OF
THE FOLK-LORE SOCIETY.

IX.

Officers of the Society.

PRESIDENT.
THE RIGHT HON. THE EARL BEAUCHAMP, F.S.A.

VICE-PRESIDENTS.
A. LANG, M.A.
W. R. S. RALSTON, M.A.
EDWARD B. TYLOR, LL.D., F.R.S.

COUNCIL.

EDWARD BRABROOK, F.S.A.
JAMES BRITTEN, F.L.S.
DR. ROBERT BROWN.
HENRY CHARLES COOTE, F.S.A.
SIR W. R. DRAKE, F.S.A.
G. L. GOMME, F.S.A

HENRY HILL, F.S.A.
ALFRED NUTT.
PROFESSOR A. H. SAYCE, M.A.
EDWARD SOLLY, F.R.S., F.S.A.
WILLIAM J. THOMS, F.S.A.
W. S. W. VAUX, M.A.

DIRECTOR.—WILLIAM J. THOMS, F.S.A

TREASURER.—SIR WILLIAM R. DRAKE, F.S.A.

HONORARY SECRETARY.—G. L. GOMME, F.S.A., 2, Park Villas, Lonsdale Road, Barnes, S.W.

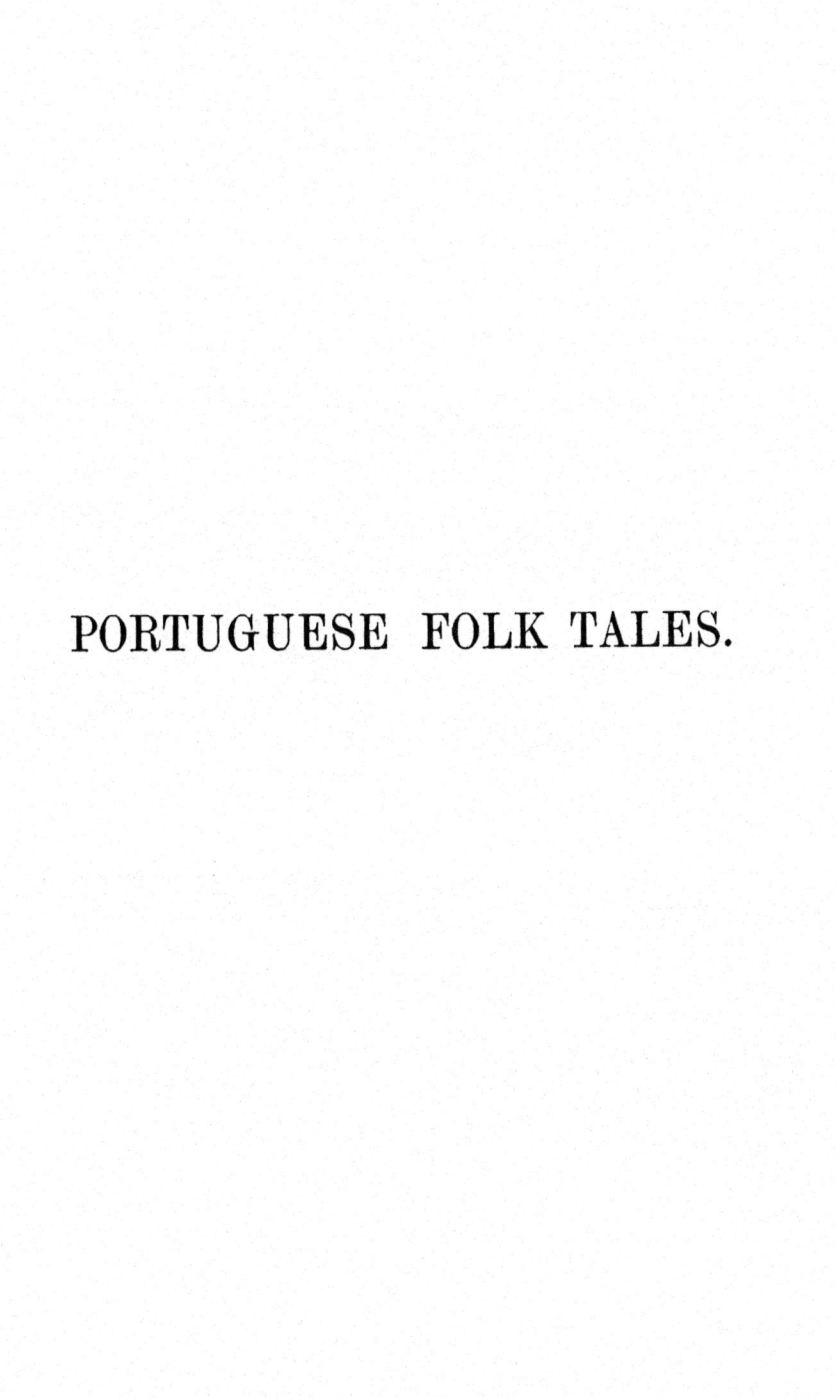

PORTUGUESE FOLK TALES.

PORTUGUESE FOLK-TALES

COLLECTED BY

CONSIGLIERI PEDROSO,

AND

TRANSLATED FROM THE ORIGINAL MS.

BY

MISS HENRIQUETA MONTEIRO.

WITH AN INTRODUCTION BY W. R. S. RALSTON, M.A.

LONDON:
PUBLISHED FOR THE FOLK LORE SOCIETY BY
ELLIOT STOCK, 62, PATERNOSTER ROW.

1882.

WESTMINSTER:
PRINTED BY NICHOLS AND SONS,
25, PARLIAMENT STREET.

CONTENTS AND STORY LIST.

PA

Introduction, by W. R. S. Ralston, M.A.	
Introductory	
The Vain Queen	
The Maid and the Negress	
The Three Citrons of Love	
The Daughter of the Witch	1
May you vanish like the Wind	2
Pedro and the Prince	2
The Rabbit	2
The Spell-bound Giant	3
The Enchanted Maiden	3
The Maiden and the Beast	4
The Tower of Ill Luck	4
The Step-Mother	4
Saint Peter's Goddaughter	5
The Two Children and the Witch	5
The Maiden with the Rose on her Forehead	6
The Princess who would not marry her Father	6
The Baker's Idle Son	7
The Hearth-Cat	7
The Aunts	7
The Cabbage Stalk	8
The Seven Iron Slippers	8

The Maiden from whose Head Pearls fell
The Three Princes and the Maiden
The Maiden and the Fish
The Slices of Fish
The Prince who had the head of a Horse
The Spider
The Little Tick
The Three Little Blue Stones
The Hind of the Golden Apple

INTRODUCTION.

The thirty stories which Prof. Consiglieri Pedroso has selected from his collection of five hundred inedited Portuguese Folk-Tales have this great merit —they are evidently genuine. Just as it is easy to decide in the case of certain tales which their collectors profess to have gathered from rustic lips that they have been submitted to literary manipulation, so is there no difficulty in recognising the justice of the claim made by these Portuguese stories to be considered as "popular" in the technical sense of the word. Their occasional clumsiness and obscurity, their frequent forgetfulness of their original meaning, and some of their other peculiarities, may be objected to by lovers of neat and trim fairy-tales, but those characteristics will be accepted by more serious students of folk-lore as trustworthy evidence in favour of Prof. Consiglieri Pedroso's conscientiousness as a collector and a reporter.

As he has postponed for a time his comments on the stories he has published, it may be useful to say a few words here as regards their principal themes. The group of folk-tales, which is most largely represented in the present collection, is that which treats of a supernatural spouse who is temporarily condemned to assume an unattractive appearance. For the sake of convenience it is often designated the Beauty and the Beast, or the Cupid and Psyche, group. To it belong five tales. No. 10, "The Maiden and the Beast," resembles that form of the story with which we are best acquainted, except in its termination; for in it the forgotten Beast dies, and soon afterwards the penitent Beauty does the same. No. 26, "The Prince who had the Head of a Horse," has remained more faithful to its leading idea, which is that of a transformation terminated by a wife's self-sacrificing pertinacity. The best-known form of the story is probably the Countess d'Aulnoy's "Prince Marcassin," an adaptation of one of Straparola's tales: one of the most interesting of its variants is the Calmuc legend of the Bird-husband, which forms the seventh of Jülg's *Kalmükische Märchen*. No. 20, "The Cabbage Stalk," resembles the Cupid and Psyche variant of the same theme, its supernatural hero being obliged to fly when he is looked at by candle-light at night, and three drops of grease fall upon him. Its main features bear a strong resemblance to those of the Sicilian "Re d'Amuri" (Pitre, No. 18), but it is also closely akin to such tales, current everywhere, as the Norse "King Valemon, the White Bear," and "East o' the Sun and

INTRODUCTION. iii

West o' the Moon." In Nos. 27 and 28 the Beast is not the husband but the wife, there being, as is usual, a feminine as well as a masculine form of the story. In the one case, a young man, in the most improbable manner, without the slightest compulsion, marries a spider; in the other, a youth weds something "which felt very cold and clammy," and which turns out to be "a little tick." In both of these stories the idea which lent an air of comparative probability to their eastern originals has been forgotten or misunderstood. In most of the Indian stories of this class, and their variants in other Asiatic lands, there exists the notion that a celestial being may be condemned to live on earth, generally cased in a bestial husk, but having the power of, at times, laying that husk aside, until the spell under which the fallen divinity labours is brought to an end by the destruction of the husk during the temporary absence of its celestial tenant.

The story of Cinderella occurs twice, Nos. 18 and 24, or three times if the "Katie Woodencloak" form of the tale in No. 16 is included. In the first and second of these the heroine is styled "the Hearth-Cat," because "she was fond of assisting the servant in the kitchen." In neither of them is it stated that she was assisted, as no doubt was the case, by her dead mother. In No. 18 a cow protects her, and in No. 24 a fish, which she had rescued from the frying-pan;

but the narrator was evidently unaware that these creatures had a maternal interest in the Hearth-Cat. The troubles of Maria do Pau, the heroine of No. 16, are very much the same as those of the German Allerleirauh, the Norse Katie Woodencloak, the English Catskin, the Scotch Rashie-Coat, and all the rest of her sister sufferers in divers lands—mysterious maidens of high degree, who to escape from an incestuous marriage voluntarily envelope themselves in a rough husk, represented in the present instance by a dress made of wood

The widely-spread story to which the name of " The Supplanted Bride" may be given, in which the real bride is set on one side, and sometimes even put to death by a step-sister, or serving-maid, or some other impostor who assumes her place, appears four times. No. 2 begins with the Rapunzel's hair-ladder opening. The impostor is a negro woman, who transforms the heroine into a bird by running a pin into her head. No. 3 is the same narrative with a different opening, being the strange story of the three citrons, out of each of which when opened emerges " a most lovely maid," who immediately dies if she is not supplied with water to drink. The story is familiar to the South of Europe, and has even made its way to the North, being No. 66 of Asbjörnsen's Norse Tales (" Tales from the Fjeld," No. 25). In No. 9 the supplanted bride loses not only her husband but her eyes. These, however, she recovers, obtaining them as the price of a nosegay. In No. 22 the supplanted heroine is a girl, whose mother, when dying, gives her a towel and a comb, on the application of which to her head pearls fall therefrom. Her supplanter contrives to have her thrown, in a state of trance, into the sea, where she is swallowed by a whale, from which, after a time, she emerges unhurt. In the first two variants there is a characteristic touch of ferocity at the close. When the true bride was asked what the prince ought to do to the impostor, "the maiden replied that he should kill her, and with her bones make bed-steps for her to climb into her bed, and with her skin to make a drum."

Another group of narratives, describing undeserved suffering, tell the story of what may be called "The Calumniated Wife," the innocent mother who is accused of having killed, and sometimes eaten, her beloved children. A specimen of this group occurs in No. 29. One of its characteristic features is the mention of three little blue stones, which bear witness to the truth of the victim's asseveration of innocence. A confidant somewhat resembling these blue stones is the stone talisman to which the heroine of No. 15, "The Maiden with the Rose on her Forehead," tells the story of her wrongs,—how she has been killed, and hidden away in an iron chest in a secret chamber of the Bluebeard story type, and scorched all over with a hot iron, after having been brought back to life and the light of day, to the temporary destruction of her beauty. This tale seems to be a mixture of several story-scraps.

Enchantment is, of course, the leading feature of many of these stories. No. 1, which is like No. 15, a medley, tells how a vain queen tried to kill a girl who surpassed her in beauty, and how the girl escaped and took refuge in a swineherd's hut, and how, all of a sudden, "it was transformed into a palace, the man who had sheltered the girl was turned into a powerful emperor, the pigs into dukes, the maiden into a beautiful princess." No. 7 deals with a prince who is under a spell, and No. 8 with a "spell-bound giant" The well-known story of the wicked step-mother, who illtreats the girl whom she first cajoles into asking her father to marry again, as in the opening of "the three little men in the wood" (Grimm, No. 13), occupies the whole of No. 12, and the opening of No. 16. Nos. 11 and 25 contain the well-known account of the hag who succeeded in killing, or at least bewitching, the elder brothers of a family, but who was at last overcome by the youngest brother, who rescued his dead or entranced relatives. In these two stories each of the brothers is protected by a horse and a lion, but the hag induces her victims to tie them up with one of her hairs, which acquires irresistible strength when she calls upon it to do so. In the Russian variants of the story the witch usually petrifies her victims. No. 14 contains the widely-spread story of the ogress who intended to bake her human guests, but was baked herself instead. One of its incidents, the testing of the tenderness of her prisoners, closely resembles a passage in the Norse story of "Boots and the Troll." The "Three Spinsters" (Grimm, 14), who attribute their ugliness to the amount of work they have done, and thereby rescue a girl in whom they are interested from a life of industry, figure here in No. 19. "The Seven Iron Slippers" of No. 21 are the counterparts of "The Shoes which were danced to pieces" (Grimm, No. 133). No. 17, "The Baker's Idle Son," is a variant of a tale which is popular everywhere, but especially in the East of Europe. In Russia it is generally known as the story of "Emilian the Fool," or "By the Pike's Will" (Afanasief, *Skazki*, v. No. 55, vi. No. 32, vii. No. 31). The opening is the same as that of the German story of "The Fisherman and his Wife" (Grimm, No. 19), in which a fish, in return for its life being spared, enables its sparer to obtain everything which he wishes. In the variant in Hahn's *Griechische Märchen* (No. 8) the hero is a

Portuguese of my stories, a commentary upon which will constitute a separate volume. In respect to the process by which these present stories were collected, and the method which I have followed in this collection, in order that they should lose none of their popular features, my readers may consult my opuscule lately published, and which bears the title *Estudos de Mythographia Portugesa*. In the next publication, which will constitute the second part of this work, I will communicate to my co-associates of the Folk-Lore Society a summary of Portuguese popular mythology, a work which for some years I have been occupied in reconstituting, and which perhaps I may soon have occasion to present to the same Society.

Later on, when the plan of my researches shall have been completed, the Society may in a special publication, and in a separate volume, assist in bringing forward a Portuguese popular Mythology the existence of which for years, even in Portugal, has been unknown.

Consiglieri Pedroso.

Lisbon, December 1880.

I.—THE VAIN QUEEN.

There was a very vain Queen who, turning towards her maids of honour, asked them, "Is there a face more beautiful than mine?" To which they replied that there was not; and on asking the same question of her servants they made the same answer. One day she turned towards her chamberlain and asked him, "Is there a more beautiful face than mine?" The chamberlain replied, "Be it known to your august majesty that there is." The queen, on hearing this, desired to know who it could be, and the chamberlain informed her that it was her daughter. The queen then immediately ordered a carriage to be prepared, and placing the princess in it ordered her servants to take her far away into the country and there to cut off her head, and to bring back her tongue. The servants departed as the Queen had ordered them, but, on arriving at the place agreed upon, they turned towards the princess and said, "Your highness is not aware for what purpose we have brought you here; but we shall do you no harm." They found a small bitch and killed her, and cut her tongue off, telling the princess that they had done this to take it to her majesty, for she had commanded them to behead her, and to take her back the tongue. They then begged of the princess to flee to some distant part and never to return to the city, so as not to betray them. The maiden departed and went on walking through several lonely wild places until she descried at a distance a small farm-house, and on approaching it she found nothing whatever inside the hut but the trail of some pigs. She walked on, and, on entering the first room she came to, she found a very old chest made of pinewood; in the second room she found a bed with a very old straw mattress upon it; and in the third room a fire-place and a table. She went to the table, drew open the drawer, and found some food, which she put on the fire to cook. She laid the cloth, and when she was beginning to eat she heard a man coming in. The maiden, who was very much frightened, hid herself under the table, but the man, who had seen her hiding away, called her to him. He told her not to be ashamed; and they both afterwards dined at the table, and at night they also supped together. At the end of supper the man asked the princess which she would prefer, to remain as his wife or as his daughter. The princess replied that she should like to remain as his daughter. The man then arranged a separate bed for himself and they each retired to rest. They lived in this way very happily. One day the man told the maiden to go and take a walk to amuse herself. The maiden replied that the dress she wore was too old to go out in, but the man opening a cupboard showed her a complete suit of a country-woman's clothes. The maiden dressed herself in them and went out. When she was out walking she saw a gentleman coming towards her. The maiden immediately turned back very much alarmed, and hid herself at home. At night when the man returned home he asked her if she had enjoyed her walk, to which she replied that she had, but this she said in a timid tone of voice. The next day the man again sent her out to take a walk. The maiden did so and again saw the same gentleman coming towards her, and as before she fled home in great fright to hide herself. When the man saw her in the evening and asked her whether she had enjoyed her walk the maiden replied that she had not, because she had seen a man approach as though he wished to speak to her, and therefore she did not wish ever to go out again. To this the man made no reply. The gentleman was a prince, who, on returning twice to the same place, and failing to meet the maiden, fell love-sick. The wisest physicians attended him; and they gave an account of the illness the prince was suffering from. The queen immediately commanded a proclamation to be issued to the effect that the country lass who had seen the prince should at once proceed to the palace, for which she would be recompensed and marry the prince. But as the maiden now never left her home she knew nothing of the proclamation. The queen, seeing that no one presented herself at the palace, sent a guard to search the place. The guard went and knocked at the door, and told the maiden that her majesty sent for her to the palace, and that she would be well rewarded if she came. The maiden told the guard to return next day for her answer. When she saw the man again in the evening she related to him all that had passed. He told her that when the guard should return for the answer she was to tell him that the queen must come to her as she would not go to the queen. When the guard returned next day for the answer, the girl told him that she did not dare inform him of her decision. The guard told her to say whatever she liked, that he would repeat it to the queen. The girl then told him what the man had advised her to say. When the guard arrived at the palace he also feared to give the girl's answer; but the queen obliged him to do so. The guard then recounted all that the girl had said. The queen was very angry, but as at that very moment the prince was attacked with a severe fit of convulsions, and the queen feared he might die of it, she resolved to go. She ordered a carriage to be brought and she went to see the maiden; but as she was approaching the house it was transformed into a palace, the man who had sheltered the girl was turned into a powerful emperor, the pigs into dukes, the maiden into a beautiful princess, and all the rest into wealth and riches. When the queen saw all this she was very much astonished, and made many apologies for having summoned the girl to the palace. She told the maiden that seeing that her son the prince was so greatly in love with her she begged of her, if such was pleasing to her, to consent to marry the prince, as otherwise he would most certainly die. The maiden was willing and acceded to the request of the queen, and the marriage was celebrated with great pomp, and they all lived very happily.

II.—The Maid and the Negress.

There was once a maiden who was imprisoned in a tower. She was very much attached to a prince, who used to come every afternoon to speak to her. This girl would let down her hair from the tower, and by this means the prince was enabled to come up and hold a conversation with her. One day, just as a witch happened to be passing that way, she saw the prince ascend. What should she do? She came next day to the place, earlier than the prince was in the habit of doing, and, imitating the prince's voice and speech, she called out to the girl. The girl threw down her hair as usual, and the witch caught hold of the long tress and ascended. She then commenced to tell the maiden not to care for the prince, and to discard him, and in fact gave her much bad advice; and when she found that it was near the hour when the prince would arrive as usual at the tower, she again laid hold of the girl's hair and slipped down to the ground. As soon as the maiden saw the prince she recounted to him all the witch had said to her, and how she had deceived her in order to ascend the tower. When the prince heard this he at once ordered a carriage in order to run away with the maiden. Before the girl left the tower she took leave of everything in it, but she forgot to take leave of the besom and the broomstick. She took away with her a glass with water, a little bag with stones, and another with sand, and she ran away. A little while after the witch came again to the foot of the tower, and began calling out to the girl as she had done the day before. To this the table and the chairs replied, "The maiden is very ill." But the broomstick and the besom which had remained, very much hurt and angry on account of the girl not having taken leave of them, came to the window and said to the witch, "What they say is not true; the girl ran away with the prince!" As soon as the witch knew this, she began to run to overtake her. The girl, who felt distrustful of the consequences, put her head out of the carriage to look out, and when she saw the witch following she emptied the bag of sand she had with her, and immediately a sand waste was formed. The witch found great difficulty in getting over the sand, but she managed to pass it, and still continued to run after the carriage. When the maiden saw that the witch was nearly overtaking her, she threw out the stones she carried in the other bag, and instantly a great wall rose up. The witch found great difficulty in getting over this wall, but succeeded in clearing it, and continued running to reach the carriage. But when the maiden saw that the witch had succeeded in getting over the wall, and was nearly upon her, she threw out the water she carried in the glass, and instantly a large wide river was formed; this time, however, the witch was unable to pass.

When the prince arrived at the gates of the city, he said to the maiden, "You must remain here on the top of this tree whilst I go and summon my court together, for I cannot make my public entry without them;" and he gave her his word that he would return for her. The maiden remained on the top of the tree, which grew close to a fountain, and whose branches fell over it. A little while after a negro woman came with a pitcher for water: she saw the reflection of the girl's face upon it, and, thinking it was her own figure. she saw, she cried out, "Oh! beautiful negress! break the pitcher!" She knocked the pitcher against the fountain and broke it. She then went away, but came back with another pitcher. She looked upon the limpid water, and seeing the girl's reflection upon it, she repeated, "Oh!

beautiful negress! break the pitcher!" and again she broke the pitcher. The negro woman departed, and a third time returned with a tin jug. She looked towards the fountain, and again seeing the reflection of the maiden's figure, she said, "Oh! beautiful negress! break the pitcher!" But, as the pitcher was made of tin, she could not succeed in breaking it as she knocked it against the fountain. The negro woman, already very angry because she could not break the jug, said to herself, "Oh, what manner of a beautiful negro woman must this be that cannot break the pitcher!" She looked up to the tree, and, on seeing the maiden, she said, "Oh, poor girl! you are up there quite by yourself; would you like me to stay with you?" And she also went up the tree. She inquired of the maiden what she was doing there, and then said to her, "Oh, my girl! what a beautiful head of hair you have got! Would you like me to comb you?" Saying this, she pierced her head with a long pin. The girl at once became transformed into a dove, and flew about. When the prince returned he was much surprised at this, and said, "What ails you, my girl, who were so beautiful, and now you are so black?" "What would you have?" replied the black woman; "you left me here exposed to the heat of the sun, and I became sunburnt." The prince had certainly doubts about the truth of this, as he was convinced that this negress was not the girl he had left there; yet, as he had given his word to the maid, he took her to the palace and married her.

Every day a beautiful dove came to the garden which would coo, "Oh, gardener, how does the prince fare with his black Maria?" and the gardener replied, "Pretty well; be off." When the gardener met the prince coming into the garden, he related what had taken place. The prince told him that when the dove should come on the following day he was to lay a snare of ribbon to catch her. The next day the dove returned. "Oh, gardener, how does the prince fare with black Maria?" she cried.

The gardener then threw at her the lasso of ribbon, but the dove merely replied, "Ha! ha! ha! Snares of ribbon were not made to catch me!" and flew away. When the prince came to inquire what had occurred, the gardener told him what the dove had said. The prince then said, "To-morrow throw over her a snare made of silver." The dove returned again and said, "Ha! ha! ha! Snares of silver are not made for me!" and flew away. And when the prince heard this, he ordered the gardener to lay a golden snare; and the little dove this time was caught. The gardener then took her to the prince. But when the black woman saw the dove she began telling the prince to kill it; the prince however would not, because he had already grown very fond of the little dove, and esteemed her more and more. One day as the prince was petting her he discovered a pin stuck in her pretty head which he at once extricated, and instantly the dove was transformed into the maiden. She then related to the prince all that had taken place, and he told her he would marry her. After this the prince asked her what she wished him to do to the black woman. The maiden replied that he should kill her and with her bones make bed-steps for her to climb into her bed, and with her skin to make a drum.

III.—The Three Citrons of Love.

There was once a king who had a son passionately fond of hunting. And as he was one day going through some fields he met an old woman in great affliction, and who was nearly starved with hunger. The prince had no money with him, but carried some food which he had brought with him to eat whilst he should be out. He called his servants to him and ordered them to serve her with every thing he had brought for himself. The old woman eat and drank, and when she had satisfied her wants she thanked the prince very much, saying that she had no other way of showing her gratitude to him as she did not possess anything, "Yet here are three citrons which I give you as a mark of my gratitude." At the same time she recommended him never to break them open except when standing by a fountain, and that when he did so he should cut them open lengthways and not across. The prince kept the citrons, took leave of the old woman, and continued his journey.

When he had proceeded on his way for some length of time he thought he would open one of the citrons, but forgot to open it at the foot of a fountain, as the old woman had enjoined him; the instant he opened one a most lovely maid came out of the citron, who said to him, "Give me water to drink, if not I shall die." As there was no water there the poor girl died. The prince was struck very sad indeed, but as he had still two more citrons he became more consoled and reconciled to his loss, and continued his journey. Further on he opened another, but again forgot that he should do it at the foot of a fountain, and at the moment he did so a most beautiful girl made her appearance, who said to him, "Give me water or else I shall die." As there was no water there the poor girl died. The prince was extremely sad at the event, and now he did not dare open the third citron fearing lest the same thing should happen again. However, he had such a great wish to see what was inside it that, looking out for a spot where there was a fountain, he opened the third citron. That moment a most lovely maid stepped out from the citron, much more beautiful than any of the others, who also said to him, "Give me water to drink, or I shall die." The prince, who had brought a shell with him, filled it with water and gave the maiden to drink, who was greatly refreshed; but, as she was very delicate and very thin and spare, the prince, fearing to take her as far as the palace, which was yet very distant, lest the journey should be more than she could bear, told her to go up a tree which stood there, whilst he went for a carriage for her. The maiden did so, and the prince departed. A short while after a negro woman made her appearance, who was very ugly, and had come to draw water for her master. The black woman began to look at the water which, as it was very clear and limpid, reflected the maiden's face in it. The black woman believing that it was her own face, began to say, " What, little black woman, who art so very beautiful, do you come for water? Break, break the pitcher!" And she began to strike the ground with the pitcher, but as the pitcher was made of copper it would not break. The negress again looked at the water, and seeing the maiden's face reflected, repeated, " Little negress, who are so beautiful, how is it that you come to draw water? Break, break the pitcher," and she again struck the ground with it. All this time the maiden was very much amused at what she saw and heard, and felt inclined to laugh, but feared to do so lest the black woman should hear and see her, but at last, unable to contain herself, she laughed outright. This made the negress look on every side, but she was unable to discover any one, until at last looking up she saw the maiden in the tree. She then began to ingratiate herself with her by all manner of affectionate and endearing expressions and caresses, and asked her to come down the tree, but the maiden refused, saying that she was there waiting for the prince. But the negress, being a witch, began to renew her caresses, and said to her, " Come here, my girl, and let me at least clean your pretty little head." The witch said and did so much that at last the maiden decided to come down from the tree. As soon as the witch seized the girl she began to pretend to clean her hair, and ask her many questions about the prince, which the maiden answered her with all truth; and when the negress knew all she wished to know she drew out a large pin which she had upon her, and stuck it into the girl's head. At that moment the maiden was transformed into a dove and flew away. The negress now went up the tree instead of the girl, and there waited for the prince, who arrived before long. He looked up the tree and was much surprised that, after having left such a beautiful girl there, he should find an ugly black woman instead. He began to grow very angry, but the negress commenced to cry and say that it was all owing to an unfortunate spell which pursued her, and that she was as beautiful at one moment as she was an ugly black woman the next. The prince, believing all she said, took compassion upon her, and told her to come down from the tree, and then he took her to the palace. Next day he rose up very early in the morning and went to the garden to take a walk; shortly after he saw a beautiful dove who flew close up to the gardener and said, " Gardener of my own garden, how does the prince get on with his negress, the black, ugly, and evil-eyed bitch?" As she finished speaking she flew away. The gardener made no reply but went up to the prince and told him what the dove had said, and inquired of him, " What does your highness wish me to say in answer to the dove's question?" " Tell her that I live happily and lead a good life," replied the prince. Next day the dove returned and said, " Gardener of my own garden, how does the prince fare with his negress, so black, ugly, and squinting?" The gardener replied, " He lives happily, and leads a good life." The dove then said, " Poor me! who fly about lost and without aim in life." The gardener then went and informed the prince of what the dove had said in answer. The prince ordered him to set up a snare of ribbon to see if they could entangle her leg and catch her, because he liked her very much. Next day the dove returned again and made the same speech as before and the gardener replied as he had done before, and when the dove looked towards the snare laid for her she gave a loud laugh and said, " Ha! ha! ha! A snare of ribbon was never meant for my leg," and she flew away. The gardener again went and told the prince what had occurred this time with the dove; and the prince ordered him to lay a snare of silver cords. The dove came, repeated what she had said before, looked towards the snare laid, and laughingly said, "Ha! ha! ha! Snares of silver cord were not made for my leg." The gardener now repeated to the prince what the dove had said, and the prince ordered a snare of gold cord to be prepared for her. The dove came again next day, said the same words as before, and, looking towards the snare, said, as she laughed, "Ha! ha! ha! Snares of gold were never made for me," and again flew away as she had done each time. When the gardener told the prince what the dove had said he was very angry indeed, and, being resolved to catch her in desperation, ordered a snare of brilliants to be laid for the dove. When next day the dove appeared, she had hardly seen the expensive snare when she flew right into it, saying, "Yes, this snare is the one fit for my leg," and allowed herself to be caught. The moment that the black woman saw that the little dove had been caught, she began to say that she felt very ill and wished a broth to be made with the dove. The prince in deep distress at this said that the dove was not to be killed, and commenced to caress and fondle her, and as he stroked her pretty head he found a pin buried in it which he drew out. That very instant the dove was transformed into a lovely maiden, and the very same form that the prince had left on the tree. The prince was much astonished to see her so suddenly before him; and the maiden related to the prince all that the black woman had done to her. The prince then commanded the woman to be killed, and a drum to be made of her skin and with her bones steps for the maiden to get to her bed. He then married the maiden and they were very happy.

IV.—The Daughter of the Witch.

There was once a witch, and she had a daughter called Guiomar, who was much attached to a certain prince. Her mother did not wish her to marry him, but the maiden told the prince to dress himself like a poor man, and some day, when her mother was not at home, to come begging, for she would open the door for him. The prince did as he was told, and the girl made him stand behind the door, and instructed him that when her mother came home he should say that he was a poor man, and to ask her to give him shelter for the night. When the witch returned home, she said, " I smell royal blood." " No, mother," said the girl, " it is a poor man who asks alms, and who would be glad to have shelter given him, as he has no place to go to." " Well, then, let him remain," replied the witch; " but he must present me to-morrow with a potful of guano of little birds." The prince, distressed to tears, asked the girl to tell him how he could possibly procure the guano. The girl, who knew something of witchcraft, replied, " Do not distress yourself about that, for I will show you how you are to do that." She then told him to go and place an earthenware pot at the foot of a certain great wall, which she indicated to him, and that he was to go at night for it, and he would find it full of little birds' guano; but she enjoined him very particularly not to mention to her mother what she had told him, as it was she who had instructed her. The prince did as the girl told him, and placed the earthenware pot at the foot of the wall, and at night he found the pot full of guano of little birds; and he then gave it to the mother. When the witch saw the pot, she said, " Ha! ha! ha! Guiomar has had a hand in this." But the prince said that she had not. The witch then said, " To-morrow you must plant a number of vines, and at night you must bring me a basket full of grapes from them." The prince, weeping, again went to the girl, and recounted all that the mother had ordered him to do. The girl told him not to be distressed, but to go and plant the vines, and that at night he was to go to the spot and he would find the vines full of grapes. The prince did so: he planted the vines, and at night he returned to the spot and found the grapes, and gave them to the mother. When the witch saw them, she said, " Ha! ha! ha! Guiomar has had a hand again in this." But the prince again assured her that she had not; and he went away contentedly to tell the girl the result. They afterwards agreed to run away on the following day, when the mother should go out. Next day, when they found that the mother had gone out of the house, they arranged everything for their flight. The girl spat three times on the ground at the threshold as she left the house, and they then ran away. When the witch returned and knocked at the door, one of the spits answered, " Who is there?" The witch replied, " Open to me, Guiomar." The other spit then said, " Guiomar has ran away." The witch asked, " With whom?" And the third spit answered, " With a young man." The witch then told the girl's father to go and run after them, for he might yet catch them. The father set to running; and the girl, when she was half way on the road, looked back and saw her father. She then said to the prince, "There comes my father; what shall I do?" He replied, in great fright, "Indeed, what shall we do!" But the girl said that she would arrange everything satisfactorily, and then continued saying, " Let my boy be converted into a public road, and myself into an old man with a sack on his back." And so it all took place. The father then coming up to the spot, and seeing the old man, he said, " Pray, my little neighbour, have you seen a girl, with a young man, on this road?" The old man replied—

> "I sell nuts, and buy garlics;
> I buy garlics, and sell nuts.
> I sell nuts, and buy garlics;
> I buy garlics, and sell nuts."

The father, annoyed at the answer, turned back towards home. The witch had scarcely caught sight of him when she asked, "Well, did you meet with Guiomar?" "No, I did not; I met an old man with a sack on his back, and I asked him if he had seen a girl with a young man pass that way; and he replied to my inquiries thus—

> 'I sell nuts, and buy garlics;
> I buy garlics, and sell nuts.
> I sell nuts, and buy garlics;
> I buy garlics, and sell nuts.'

and, feeling much annoyed at the stupid answer, I came away." The witch then said, "Lo! catch her, for it was Guiomar you saw!" And she hurried him back in pursuit of the girl, telling him that should he find the old man again with the sack on his back, to lay hold of him, for it was no other than Guiomar. The father renewed his pursuit; and when the girl saw him she said to the prince, "Let my lad be turned into a hermitage, and I into a hermit." When the father arrived at the spot, he asked, "Oh, my good uncle, did you happen to see a girl with a young man on this road?" The hermit replied—

> "Tinkle, tinkle, tinkle,
> The bell goes for mass,
> Quick! for the priest is at the altar.
> Tinkle, tinkle, tinkle,
> The bell goes for mass,
> For the priest is at the altar."

"I am not inquiring for this," said the father; "but I wanted to know if your reverence has seen on this road a girl accompanied by a young man." The hermit gave the same answer as before—-

> "Tinkle, tinkle, tinkle,
> The bell goes for mass,
> Quick! for the priest is at the altar.
> Tinkle, tinkle, tinkle.
> The bell goes for mass,
> For the priest is at the altar."

The father, weary and annoyed, turned back home, and when he arrived he related to the witch what had taken place. "Lo! Catch her, for the hermit is no other than Guiomar! And since you are not clever and discriminating enough for the purpose I shall myself go there." When the girl had nearly come to the end of her journey she looked back and said, breathless and in great trepidation, " Oh! there comes my mother! I have saved myself from my father, but now I do not know how to escape from my mother!" But, after a short pause, she said, " My lad, be transformed into a river, and I into an eel!" When the mother arrived she at once found her daughter out; she came close to the edge of the river and called out three times, " Guiomar, come here!" whilst the eel replied significantly every time with her tail that she would not come. The witch then said, " The curse which I invoke to fall upon you is, that when the prince arrives at his own palace, the first person that shall give him a kiss shall make him forget you." And saying this she went away. They now returned to their original form and continued to walk on. The girl said to the prince, " Be on your guard that no one gives you a kiss, for my mother's imprecations never fail to take effect." The prince on entering the palace was on his guard that neither his mother or his sisters should give him a kiss. As he arrived very tired he laid down to sleep. One of the sisters who was passing through his room, seeing that he was quietly asleep, gave him a kiss. When the prince awoke and Guiomar spoke to him he did not know her. And when the girl perceived it she remembered her mother's imprecation and went to live in a separate house which stood in front of the palace; and every day she dressed and adorned herself very well, and sat at one of the windows looking out. One day, as three of the chamberlains were at the palace window, they said one to the other " Who can that girl be, opposite to us ? I have a mind to go and ask her if she will allow me to speak to her." The chamberlain went and passed under her window and asked the girl to allow him to have a chat with her. The girl replied that she was quite willing and appointed him to come at four o'clock in the afternoon. When the chamberlain entered in and saw the girl he sat down to converse with her, until it was nearly dark; and then the girl said, " It is now almost night and my servant does not come to light a candle for me." The chamberlain said that he would go and do it for her. He tried to strike fire with the steel and flint, but do what he would he could not succeed in lighting the tinder, whilst his fingers were hurt and bleeding. He left the house very much mortified and vexed at what had happened to him, and returned to the palace. The girl had done all this to fascinate the prince by means of witchcraft, and to induce him, as will be seen, to come and speak to her. The chamberlain related what had happened to him, and one of the other three chamberlains said, " I lay a wager that I shall go there to-morrow and that she will not treat me in the same way." He therefore passed under her window next day, asked her if he could have a chat with her, and she answered that he might come when he liked. The chamberlain entered and commenced to converse with the girl; and when they had been chatting for some time the girl said, " I am very thirsty, but my servant does not come to give me water." The chamberlain said he would go and get it for her. He took up a glass and from a jar on the table commenced to pour out water, but the water instead of being poured into the glass went over him, so that he was thoroughly drenched. He left the house vexed and mortified, and returned to the palace. He recounted what had happened to him, and then the third chamberlain said, "I lay a wager that if I go and see the girl she will not treat me in this way." Next day he passed under her window and asked the girl if she would allow him to come up and have a chat with her, and the girl said "Yes." When they were deep in conversation, a great wind began to rise, and the girl said to the chamberlain, "Oh! there is so much wind in the room, and the servant does not come to shut the window." The chamberlain immediately offered to shut the window himself; but the window began to slam and to beat him in the chest, and the more he tried to shut it the more did the window beat against him, and to such a degree that he began to spit blood profusely.

The prince found all three chamberlains very bitterly complaining of pain and vexation, and he asked them what was the matter, and they told him what had happened to them. The curiosity of the prince being roused, he said, "I also shall go to see the girl and try if the same thing will happen to me." He passed under the girl's window and asked her when he could go and speak to her. "At once," replied the girl, "and the sooner the better." The prince entered the house, and at the same time the girl threw a spell over him, so that he might remember what had passed on the highroad when they ran away from her mother's house. The prince went up the stairs, pushed open a door he came to, and he there found a public road along which an old man with a sack on his back was trudging along. He asked him the way to the queen's room, and the old man replied,

"I sell nuts, and buy garlics,
I buy garlics, and sell nuts.
I sell nuts, and buy garlics,
I buy garlics and sell nuts."

The prince went further on and he found another door, and pushing it open he there saw an hermitage and a hermit. He asked the hermit the way to the queen's room, and the hermit answered him,

> "Tinkle, tinkle, tinkle,
> The bell goes for mass,
> Quick! for the priest is at the altar.
> Tinkle, tinkle, tinkle,
> The bell goes for mass,
> Quick! for the priest is at the altar."

At this the prince commenced to recollect that he had heard that before. He went on further and he came to another door, and inside he found that there was a river and the eel. That moment he recollected everything that had been dismissed from his mind, and falling upon his knees he begged the girl's pardon for his forgetfulness of her. The girl transformed herself back into her natural state, married the prince, and they lived happily ever after.

V.—MAY YOU VANISH LIKE THE WIND.

There was once a king who had a daughter whom he dearly loved. The princess had the habit of combing herself, and on being ready dressed would go to the garden for a flower to place in her hair. But when she was there she invariably heard a voice which said, "When will you have your troubles, when you are young or when you are old?" This happened several times, and the princess, full of curiosity and tired of hearing always the same question, went one day into the palace and said to her maid of honour, "Do you know what has happened to me the last few days? I hear always a voice which says to me, when I go and gather a flower, 'Which will you do, go through your troubles in your youth or in your old age?'" The maid of honour replied, " Listen, royal lady; for my part I should say that I prefer having my troubles when young; with my old age I would acquire more power." The princess combed and dressed herself next day, and went to the garden. She heard the same voice which always spoke to her, and when it asked her the usual question the princess replied that she would rather go through her troubles in her youth than in her old age. Then the voice rejoined, " Take leave here of every thing that is yours." The princess took leave of the palace, of her father, of her mother, and of the servants. After this the voice led her through the air, and placed her on the top of a windmill. The owner of the windmill said that he missed the flour, and he began to throw stones at the princess. Next day the voice came for her at the same hour as the day before, and again took her through the air, and went and placed her on the banks of a river where some washerwomen were washing their clothes. The washerwomen began to say one to the other, " Just see, there goes the thief who steals the clothes which we have missed." And they all commenced to throw stones at her. The next day the same voice came for her at the same hour, and again led her through the air, and placed her at the gate of a garden. The gardener had hardly seen her when he began to say that it was she who was in the habit of stealing his fruit, and went in and began to pelt her with stones. Next day at the same hour the voice came back for her and took her through the air, and placed her at the door of a beautiful garden close to a palace. The voice then asked the princess if she remembered the time when she used to go to the garden. She replied that she did not recollect. A while after the cook looked out of a window of the palace, and seeing there a maiden that appeared to him to be very beautiful, in spite of her being now so unrecognizable, went in and told the prince that there was a most lovely maiden in the garden. The prince bade him call her in, but the princess said she would not go in, because she was waiting that the voice should come for her as it always did. The prince again said, "Go and call her, for she will recognise me!" The princess then remembered a lover she had had, and she said, "Perhaps it is he;" and, rising quickly, she entered the palace. When the prince saw her he said to her, "Do you not recollect how one day you said to me, 'May you vanish like the wind.' It is that you might know what troubles I went through that you have now passed through the same, but I was fortunate because I became enchanted. It was not I in person, but it was my voice that spoke to you in the garden." The princess replied, "It is true that I often wondered to hear a voice without seeing any one, but I soon found out that it was enchantment." The prince then asked her, "Now, tell me, do you wish to return to your father's house?" The princess replied, "No, now I shall remain in your company." "But listen," said the prince, "I shall not marry you before twenty years' time, because if I marry before then I shall dispel my enchantment." "I shall wait for you even if it should be thirty years," said the princess; and she asked him what he did all the time, and he answered that he eat, and walked, and sauntered about. The prince then said, "It is now three years since you left your father's house. The day after to-morrow we must go there, for he and your family are badly off. Here you have this pin; do not lose it or give it to any one, for you would break my enchantment." The day arrived when they were to take their departure, and they proceeded through the air to their destination. The prince went and placed her in the very same spot from whence he had sought and carried her away, and said to her, "Now bear in mind that you are only to stay here two days." When the princess was about to ascend the stairs of the palace, her father was then sitting at table. She gave a rap at the door, and asked if they required a maid to dress the queen. The king, who was sitting down, imagined that he heard the voice of his daughter, and on rising, as he was very weak, he fell and broke his head. The princess, in great distress, said, deliberately and slowly, "Oh, pin! help me here." That moment the voice appeared to her, which was the lover in enchantment, and he said to her, "What is the matter?" The princess told him what ailed her father. The voice then said, "It is better that you should come away with me;" and he took her through the air. When the princess arrived at the palace she received news that her father had died.

One day the prince said to her, "Remember, that to-morrow is to be the day of our marriage." "Then to-morrow it will be twenty years since I came here?" asked the princess. "Yes, that is so," replied the prince. After this he ordered all the kings to be invited, whilst the father of the princess was also asked, and came. The father had hardly set his eyes upon the princess when he said, "Is this the way you have repaid me, you ungrateful girl? On your account I broke my head, and you left me and went away." "Yes, my father," said the princess, "I came away because I did not wish to break the prince's enchantment, and you had already seen the pin, and you broke your head on purpose, so that I should remain longer than the two days, and the spell should be broken." The father said that it was not so; and then he gave her a walnut. "Here you have this walnut, do not break it open before your husband." The princess replied, "I shall neither break it open, nor shall I eat it." The father, much annoyed, hurriedly went away from the palace. After the marriage the prince ordered another palace to be built in another spot. The princess had the walnut which her father gave her always well guarded; but when everything was taken away from the palace they were in, to remove to the other one newly erected, the princess, who had the walnut in her hands, allowed it to fall to the ground. At that moment the palace was set on fire, and everything was burned. Being very much alarmed, she went and told everything to the prince. " Do you see now, yourself, how your father wished to harm us all ?" The princess was with child, and the prince said that what the father wished was to kill the child.

After a time the princess gave birth to a prince—a very pretty boy. A great banquet was given, and the prince was on the point of inviting the father to it, but, fearing that he should kill the child, did not do so. One day, when the child was older, they took it out for a walk. As they proceeded through a certain road, they met a servant of the princess's father. " Where are you going to?" asked the princess to the servant. " I came to kill the child," answered the servant. The prince then asked him who it was had sent him, and the servant confessed that it was the princess's father. She asked him not to kill the child, but go and be her servant; and he therefore joined them to go to the palace. The princess now returned home, and every river they crossed presented a different appearance to her,—the first was a river of milk, the next one further on was of water covered with a mist, and further on still she came to another filled with blood. The princess, very much alarmed, asked the prince, " What can all this mean ?" The servant answered her question instead, " It is the blood of the child you see." The prince on hearing this said, " Then it shall be yours!" . . . and aiming at him, fired, and shot him dead; then turning round to the princess he said,

> " I went out shooting, I made a good bag,
> Instead of shooting little birds
> I killed a bird of prey."

VI.—Pedro and the Prince.

There was once a king who had an only son, and opposite to the palace lived a man who had a son named Pedro, of the same age as the prince. One day the prince said to the king that he was very desirous to take a journey, but that he would like to go with Pedro. The king then said, " Then my son do you wish to go with Pedro instead of proceeding with your retinue?" The prince replied that it was so. The king then ordered two of the best and finest horses in the army to be got ready, one for the prince and the other for Pedro. They travelled much, they saw many beautiful lands, and when they arrived at a certain place they dismounted. The prince told Pedro to mind his horse whilst he should go to drink some water. Meanwhile the prince disappeared. Pedro, very much distressed, ran everywhere seeking him; but not finding him he returned to the city, and as he was passing by a pond where there were many washerwomen who were witches, he heard much laughing among them, and they were saying, " How foolish he is, he thought he was going to accompany the prince, and that he would be recompensed by the king for his services! Now go and disenchant him from where he is!" Pedro went up to the washerwomen and entreated them to tell him where the prince was to be found. One of them, taking compassion upon him, bade him go to an old palace which was close by. Pedro did so, went in, but did not see anything but orange and lemon trees, and did not meet with any one. Full of rage he commenced to pluck the oranges and lemons, and to throw them on the ground. Each lemon and orange that he threw on the ground was a prince and a princess, who had been until then under a spell, whilst his own prince became disenchanted. Full of joy Pedro entreated him to return with him to his own country; but the prince saw one of the princesses who had been disenchanted and fell in love with her.

He told Pedro that he wished to take her with him; they therefore proceeded on their journey, taking the princess with them. They were much fatigued after a time, and as they could not find a house where they could remain and rest Pedro told them that they could take shelter and pass the night in a shed which stood in a court-yard which he had discovered. The prince and princess accepted the offer very willingly, for they were very tired and travel-worn, and instead of lying down Pedro remained as sentry to keep watch, well armed to defend them. In the middle of the night he heard the witches on the top of the shed in fits of laughter, and he heard one of them say, "What a foolish man he is! he thought that he was going to accompany the prince and princess home! but the first thing that will happen to the princess will be that she will find a handsome little mule, and she will take a great fancy to ride upon it. On her riding it, it will break down, and whoever shall hear this and repeat it shall be turned into marble." Another witch replied to this, "From this mishap she shall be delivered, but she will see a pear tree with very good pears upon it which she will desire much to taste; as she eats them she will be poisoned, but whoever shall hear this and shall repeat it into hard marble shall be turned!" To this one other witch replied, "From this danger she will be delivered, but she will come to a fine bridge, and she will desire to cross it; as she crosses it the bridge will break down, but whoever shall hear this and shall relate it, into hard marble will be converted!" At last to this the fourth witch replied, "Of this she shall be delivered, but on the night of their marriage I shall take the guise of a phantom, and I shall enter their room through the window and behead her as well as the prince, but whoever shall hear this and relate it shall inevitably be turned into hard marble." As she finished saying this the witches took their departure. Shortly after the day dawned, and Pedro was in great distress of mind. They continued their journey, and when they reached a certain spot there appeared a very handsome mule, and the princess immediately coveted to ride upon it as she felt very tired. The instant Pedro heard her say so he ran before her and killed the animal. The prince was very much surprised at this act of Pedro, but as he was fond of him said nothing about it. They went further on and saw a pear tree. The princess longed to taste a pear, but Pedro ran before them and buried the pears. The prince here manifested his annoyance at the act. They proceeded on further and Pedro saw a bridge at a distance; he ran in front and paid some workmen to destroy the bridge that the princess should not be able to cross it. The prince was very angry and reprehended Pedro, but he replied that later on he would give his highness a satisfactory reason for acting as he did.

On their arrival at the palace there was much rejoicing in the capital on receiving the prince and the princess. Their marriage was solemnised and Pedro said that he must perforce sleep in the same room on the first night as the bride and bridegroom. The prince urged that it was impossible, but Pedro remained firm and said that it must be; and he remained armed standing by the window. Far into the night he saw the witch, like a phantom, come in sword in hand in order to behead the princess and the prince. Pedro raised his sword and wrestled with the phantom, but without any such intention he struck the princess's face and drew blood. The princess awoke with a start and commenced to cry out that Pedro was a traitor who wanted to behead her. The prince was very wrathful and said that Pedro must die. He however said to the prince that he did not mind that, but that before he was put to death he would ask the king to give a banquet to all his court, as he had something to declare.

The king acceded to his petition, gave a great banquet to the court, and Pedro on the occasion sat at the royal table. At the end of the banquet Pedro took occasion to narrate all he had heard the witches say on the night when they remained and took shelter under a shed. As he narrated the part which referred to the mule his legs began to harden into stone. As he began to recount what the second witch had said he was already turned into stone as far as his knees. The Prince seeing which asked Pedro not to continue any further to relate what he had heard the witches say, as he had already commuted the sentence of death passed upon him, satisfied of his innocence. But Pedro determined to declare all he had heard the witches say, and as he finished narrating what the last one had said he was turned completely into a marble statue. The prince, much distressed, ordered the statue of marble to be placed under the bed in his room.

At the end of the year the princess had a boy; and when the prince was once in his room, sometime after the event, alone with the child, the witch appeared and said to him, "You are a great friend and patron of Pedro, but you are not capable of killing your son and bathing the marble statue with his blood; did you do so, the marble statue would turn again into Pedro himself." The prince was in great affliction about what was required of him and his poor son, but before long he took into consideration that his son was yet very young, and that Pedro's life was more necessary, as he might yet save many lives and persons from danger; he therefore drew first a very small drop of blood from the boy's arm, and poured it over the stone. Pedro began to move! and the prince, seeing that he was alive, took courage and killed the boy. He then proceeded to bathe the statue with its blood, and immediately the stone was turned again into Pedro. When the princess returned to the room the prince told her that the little boy her son had fallen from the

bed to the floor and had died. The princess in great affliction
and grief ordered a beautiful mausoleum to be erected in the
garden to place the child's corpse in it. The following day
when they were all celebrating with a great feast the event that
Pedro had come to life again, the little boy also returned to life.
He was found playing in the garden with some little stones.
Great was their joy, and they all lived very happily and contentedly.

VII.—The Rabbit.

A man used to go about the streets crying out, "Who'll buy
troubles?" And as he passed by the king's palace, the queen,
looking out of window, saw that he was selling flowers; and
turning towards her maid of honour she told her to buy them.
The maid bought the flowers and planted them in the garden,
and the queen went every day to watch their growth and tend
them. One day, as she was taking a walk in the garden, she saw
a rabbit running past, and she told her maid of honour to try and
catch it. The maid seized it, and then fastened it up with her
garter. They then continued their walk, and, whilst they were
giving a turn round the garden, the rabbit escaped with the
garter round its neck. The princess was very sorry to lose it,
and the following day, at the same hour, took another turn round
the garden, and she again saw the same rabbit running. She
told her maid to catch hold of it, which she did, and this time
she fastened it up with a handkerchief. They took another turn
round the garden, and whilst they did so the rabbit escaped with
the handkerchief. When the princess, with her maid of honour,
returned to the spot where they had left the rabbit, she was

grieved to find that the little animal was gone. Next day, at the same hour, the princess took her usual walk in the pleasure ground, and again saw the rabbit. She then threw down the gold necklet with the king's portrait which she wore, and told her maid to fasten the rabbit with it, as they could now take their walk without anxiety, because the little animal thus secured would not be able to run away. But the moment they turned round to take their walk, the rabbit went away with the necklet and portrait. When the queen returned, and missed the rabbit in its place, she went into the palace and fell ill from sorrow. The court physicians came, and said that what her highness suffered was from being in love, and gave orders that she was to be taken out for walks and amused. Many persons were called in to relate the most beautiful stories known to the princess, but she paid no heed to them.

There were two old women living together who were sisters; and one day one of them said to the other, " Oh! sister, I feel quite equal to going up to the palace with my stories, and try if I can amuse the princess with them." The sister endeavoured to dissuade her by saying that the princess was sure to have much prettier stories than she could relate. But the old woman remained obstinate, and said, " Never mind, any way I shall go to the palace with mine!" and started off, taking with her some Indian corn loaves and some roasted sardines. After that she saw an ass with gold panniers come out from under the milestone which she sat upon; and saw hands that led the ass, but could see no one. The old woman waited for the donkey to return, and when it did so she held on by the panniers, and descended some steps until she reached a palace of great splendour. There was a table laid with every good thing, and the woman sat down to it, and partook of everything. When she had finished her repast she began to look about her, and she saw many hands doing the work, but she could see no one, nor anything else whatever; she could only see hands. When night set in she laid down; and, very early in the morning, she saw a rabbit enter from the garden. The rabbit went and bathed in a tub, and became transformed into a handsome prince; he went to the looking-glass and began combing himself, and repeated:

> "Oh! comb that smooths my hair,
> Oh! ribbons which bind my tresses,
> Would that you could shew me
> She who pines in love for me."

He then again bathed himself in the tub, and once more became changed into the rabbit, and it departed.

The old woman then had her breakfast, and, when she saw that the ass with the golden panniers was going out, she held on by them and went out with the ass also. When she found herself in the high road she walked on to the palace of the princess, and on arriving there she said that she wished to see the princess, to relate a story to her which she was sure would amuse her. The princess was reposing on a couch, and when she saw the old woman she turned towards the wall. The old woman paid no heed to that, but began her story. The princess had scarcely commenced to hear the story about the rabbit than she instantly sat up, asked for some broth to take, and told the old woman to continue. When the story was finished, the princess said to the old woman that she would go with her to see the palace and the rabbit she had seen. Her health then began to improve, and one day, when she had perfectly recovered from her attack, she went with the maid of honour and the old woman to where the milestone was, and waited there to see if the ass with the golden panniers would come forth from whence the old woman had sat before. Shortly after this the ass made its appearance; they all three held on to the donkey, and down they went descending, whilst the princess was greatly astonished to find and behold so much splendour, and to see the hands busy doing all the work without any one being seen. More and more surprised at what she saw, she went further into the palace, until she had seen every part of it, and all it contained. They came to a house, and when the maid was entering she suddenly uttered a scream and ran out; the princess asked her what made her scream, and the maid replied that it was the sight of a dead man. The princess told her to go in and not to mind it, but the maid would not because she felt much frightened; and the princess, finding that she would not, went in herself; she threw water over the corpse and commenced to pray, and suddenly the dead man returned to life and transformed himself into a very handsome prince, and was the same one that the old woman had seen transform himself into a rabbit. In an instant all the hands took the form of persons, and were those that composed the magnificent court which were spell-bound. The prince expressed his grateful acknowledgments to the princess for having broken the spell he was under. The princess asked him for what purpose were all these preparations and work in the palace. The prince replied that it was for the marriage of the princess of Naples; in great surprise, she said, "I am the princess of Naples!" "Then you are destined for me," replied the prince. The princess, in great delight and filled with joy, said that she would marry him. The marriage was solemnized with great pomp, and they all remained in the same palace, living very happily together. The old woman was held in much esteem by all, but she went about looking very sad; and, when they asked her what ailed her, she said that she wished to return to her own home. They loaded her with many riches, and sent her back accompanied by a page. The old woman left the palace, and on arriving at her home she said:

"Oh! my house, my own little house;
There's no place like my own little home;
So let go to the devil my lady queen! ho!"

VIII.—The Spell-bound Giant.

There was a widow who had three sons. They lived in great poverty; and the eldest son said one day, " Oh! mother, things cannot go on any longer in this manner; I am old enough now to do something; so I shall go through different countries seeking a livelihood." The mother, not wishing him to go, began crying; but the son, keeping his resolve, endeavoured to persuade her to consent, until at last, one day she prepared his outfit, and he departed at day-dawn on his journey. He travelled on, and on arriving at a certain country he inquired if any one there required a servant. He was told that a magician, who lived in that part, was always wanting servants, and that he had better apply at the house. The young man went to the house, and inquired if a servant was required to wait upon them. " You have come at an opportune time," replied the magician, " and this very day you may enter my service;—you shall earn one coin a-day, but you will have to accompany me wherever I go." The young man was delighted to earn so much, and said, " Oh, Sir, I am ready to go with you to the very ends of the world, and anywhere you wish." " Very well," replied the magician, " let's go now and get our horses ready to depart." They filled several bags with provisions, and all they could require; they prepared and harnessed two good horses with wallets, and whatever else they might want for the journey, and at midnight the master and his servant left the house and began to travel through dismal places and dark roads. The young man, who was unaccustomed to long journeys, began to get very tired, and did nothing else but ask, " Oh! Sir, have we not yet arrived?" But the magician always answered him by saying, " Don't be troubled, we are sure to get there sometime or

D

another." Thus they journeyed on all the night, and at day-dawn they sighted a very high mountain, and the magician said, "Do you see that mountain? it is there where we have to go." They arrived at the foot of the mountain before long, when the magician told the young man to dismount, and said to him, "Now you must fire a shot at the belly of your horse." The lad, very much frightened, replied, "Oh! Sir, that is just what I shall not do!" "Well, then," rejoined the magician, "I must fire the shot at you instead." The lad, full of fear and terror, fired at the horse. The magician took out the entrails of the horse, filled a bag with them, and then told the lad to get inside the empty belly of the horse, and he put in several bags as well. He then took out a book and commenced to read, and the horse began to ascend the mount until the lad reached the top. The lad came out of the horse, while the magician from the foot of the mount cried out to the boy, "What do you see?" "I see much gold, much silver, many brilliants, many precious stones, and many bones," replied the lad. "Well, then, fill all the bags you have with all those riches," said the magician, "and send the horse down here with them, and I shall send the horse back for you." The lad did as he was told, took out the bags from the horse's belly, filled them with all the richest things that were strewed there, and sent the horse laden with the bags down the hill to his master. When the magician had got the horse safe at the bottom of the hill, he started off with it, leaving the lad quite alone on the top of the mountain. The moment the boy found himself forsaken he commenced to cry, and to seek for some herbs to eat, as he felt very hungry. When he had rambled about for some time, he found a little herb which grew very luxuriantly, and had very large roots, which made it very difficult for him to root up. But when he had succeeded in rooting up some, he found in the hole which was left a massive iron ring of great size and thickness. The lad, curious to know what it was, began to pull it out; and when the ring was pulled out he saw some steps, which were strewed with gold coins and many rich things. The lad, astonished at what he saw, went down the stairs, and at the bottom of the stairs found himself in a magnificent palace. He saw a table loaded with the most delicious viands, and, as he felt very hungry, he sat down at once to eat. He then left the dinner table and proceeded to another apartment; and as he was about entering the chamber, he saw a giant lying down; and the moment he drew near to him, the giant cried out, " Who has authorised you to enter here?" The lad, terrified, fell upon his knees at the giant's feet, and begged him to pardon him; and he then recounted all that had happened to him. " Well, then," said the giant, when the boy had ceased to speak, "your master is the cause of my being spell-bound. You had not the good fortune to kill him; and so long as he lives I shall not get out of this. But you have still one way of saving me: to-morrow before sunrise you must hide behind that tank; after that, three doves will come—a white one, a grey one, and one cinnamon-coloured. If you succeed in catching the white one, you will bring about mine and your happiness." The lad, in his excitement, never laid down to sleep, but spent the night concealed behind the tank. When day began to dawn, the doves appeared; they bathed themselves in the tank, and when the lad tried to catch them, two of their feathers remained in his hand and the birds flew away. The lad, feeling very sad, went to the giant, and said to him, " Oh! sir, the proof that I did my best is, that here I bring two feathers in my hand, but I promise you that they shall not escape me to-morrow." He procured some ribbon, and the following day prepared a snare in the tank, and concealed himself to wait for the doves' return. Day had scarcely dawned when the doves appeared, bathed themselves, and when the white dove was about to fly away she fell into the snare. The lad, very pleased at this, went to put his hands upon her; but at that very instant the dove transformed itself into a lovely maiden. The maiden felt very much ashamed at finding herself in the young man's hand. He then took her to the giant, who was very pleased to see her, and said, " Now, were the magician to die, my enchantment would cease!" Hardly had the maiden approached the giant, than many servants and maids appeared to wait upon her, and bringing many robes of the richest materials for her to wear. Yet the palace remained enchanted,

The young man's brothers, seeing that he did not return, said one day to their mother, " Oh! dear mother, we have never heard any news of our brother; it would be as well if one of us were to go and search for him." The mother replied, " Very well, let one of you go." The youngest of her sons went out in search because he was considered more sharp-witted. He travelled and journeyed on until he arrived at the same country where his brother had gone, and he inquired if any one could give him any information of a boy who had many months ago travelled to that country ; but no one could give him any news. They told him that such a lad had gone as servant to a magician's house. He therefore went up to the house, knocked at the door, and the magician answered the call, who put to him the same questions that he had done to his brother, and took him at last into his service. At midnight, after having prepared everything, they started off, and on arriving at the mountain he ordered the boy to shoot at the horse's belly. The boy as he was very sharp-witted saw at once that there was some mystification in all this, and shot at the horse. The master placed the entrails of the horse into a bag and then ordered the boy to get into the horse's belly, and he began to read from the book. The horse began to ascend the mount until it reached the top, and once on the top of the mountain the magician asked the boy, " What do you see ?" " I see much wealth," replied the lad. " Very well, then," said the magician, "fill all the bags with them and send them with the horse to me, and the horse shall return for you." What did the boy do? The lad filled the bags with bones, and when the horse was descending he threw a large stone at the master and broke his legs. At this moment the giant suddenly experienced great joy and summoned the boy who was still in his palace and said to him, "Do you know that my spell is broken? some one has killed the magician." And by degrees as the magician's life was ebbing away so the giant's palace kept rising and rising. On awaking in the morning the lad looked out of his chamber window and he saw his mother's house standing near. The mother, who had also risen from her couch at the same hour as her son had done, on opening the front door saw that opposite to her house a splendid palace had risen up. She was much astonished at what she saw, and at that moment her son and his brother, the one who had killed the magician, both stood before her. The other two doves had also broken their spell and were transformed into beautiful maidens, and they married the two brothers. The giant was also disenchanted because he was a prince, and he married the beautiful maiden who in the shape of a white dove had been flying round about his palace.

IX.—The Enchanted Maiden.

There was once a man who had three daughters. In the country where he lived it was the custom to hang up a gold ball at the door when they wanted husbands for the girls who were single, as a sign to the young men. When the eldest daughter wished to get married the father hung a gold ball over the street door. Many persons passed the door, and as they saw the gold ball hanging up they did not dare enter, and would say " Oh, no, it's too rich for me, evidently it is not meant for me." One day, however, a prince passed the house, and seeing the ball, as he knew the custom of the country, he entered the house and asked the father to give him his daughter in marriage. The girl was delighted, everything was arranged, and they were married. After a time the father again hung up a gold ball outside the door to find a husband for the second daughter. Another prince passed and saw the ball and married the girl. The third daughter, seeing that both her sisters had married princes, one day told her father that she also wanted to get married. The father replied that he had no money left to order another gold ball to be made; but she said that she did not doubt him, but that at least he might have one made of silver. The father did so. A prince then passed, and seeing the silver ball, said to himself, " Oh, no, this is too poor for me; it is evidently not meant for me." After that a man passed, and looking towards the ball said, " This, in truth, is meant for me." He went into the house, asked the girl in marriage, and he espoused her; after which he went with her to a distant land. When the two girls who had married princes knew of this they were very displeased and would have nothing to do with the sister. At the end of nine months the girl gave birth to a daughter. At the moment that the father went out to get some medicine for her some fairies passed by the house and asked for shelter. The girl replied that it could not be as she was very ill; but, as they so begged and entreated to be allowed to remain, the mother at last allowed them to remain.

The fairies thanked the girl very much for her kindness, and when they were on the point of leaving they approached the child, and stroking her with the divining rod one said, " I now throw a charm over you that you may be the most beautiful woman in the world." The next fairy then said, " I endow you with all riches, that you may be the richest woman in the world." The third fairy then said, "I throw a sweet spell over you, that when you speak flowers may drop out from between your lips." They then struck the furniture with their rod and everything became of the richest form and material, and the house was also transformed into a palace; and when they had done all this the three fairies went away.

When the two sisters knew of this, and the poor sister had now become very rich, they were reconciled and became friends again with her. The enchanted maiden grew day by day more and more beautiful. There was a prince who lived quite near to them and was engaged to be married to the daughter of one of the two sisters who had espoused princes; but when he saw the enchanted little maiden he liked her better, and no longer paid any attentions to the other, who felt very jealous, but pretended she did not care. One day after this the prince became very ill and the physicians ordered him to travel. The enchanted maiden went up to the highest tower there was to take leave of him and be able to see him for a long distance as he went along. Whilst the engaged girl went behind her, and when the enchanted maiden was looking out towards the prince, the other girl went behind her with a pointed rod and pierced her eyes with it and plucked them out. After which she ran away. The enchanted maid was very much distressed to find herself blind, and began to weep. A man passed who took compassion upon her and led her to his own house. After some time the prince returned from his travels. The engaged girl presented herself to him saying that she was the enchanted maiden; but the prince said that she was not; but she persisted that she was. Meanwhile the enchanted maiden was told that the prince had arrived, but as she was blind she did not dare to go and see him; but when she knew that the prince was at last going to marry the other girl she sent to ask the girl if she would like to have a nosegay of flowers to present the prince with. She sent back to say that she would very much. The enchanted girl then replied that she should send her, her eyes, and she on her part would send her the flowers. And so it happened. The other girl who was very desirous of presenting the prince with a nosegay sent the enchanted maiden her eyes. What did she do then?—Next day just before the marriage was to take place she dressed herself in deep black and put a veil on. She knocked at the door of the palace, but they would not admit her. At last, after many entreaties, she was allowed to enter, and she went straight into the prince's room and begged him most beseechingly not to marry. The prince replied that he could not put off the marriage as the invited guests had arrived. The maiden reiterated her demand, and stretched out her hand to the prince, the hand which had on the ring that he had given her, the prince seeing which raised up her veil and at once recognized her. As the maiden had with her the divining-rod that the fairies had left her, she touched her clothes with it, and immediately she found herself richly dressed. The prince then went to meet his invited guests and said to them, "I lost something, and instead I bought another. I have now recovered that which I lost. Which ought I to make use of—that which I lost, or what I bought?" They all exclaimed with one accord, "Surely, make use of what you have recovered." The prince then went to his room to seek the enchanted maiden, who related all that had occurred to her to the guests. And it was she whom he married.

X.—The Maiden and the Beast.

There was once a man who had three daughters; he loved them all but there was one he loved more than the others. As he was going to the fair one day he inquired what they would like him to bring them. One said she would like to have a hat and some boots, the other one asked for a dress and a shawl, but the one he loved most did not ask for anything. The man, in surprise, said, "Oh! my child, do you not want anything?" "No, I want nothing; I only wish that my dear father may enjoy health." "You must ask for something, it matters not what it is, I shall bring it to you," replied the father. But, in order that the father should not continue to importune her, she said, "I wish my father to bring me a slice of roach off a green meadow." The good man set off to the fair, bought all the things that his daughters had asked him, and searched everywhere for the "slice of roach off a green meadow," but could not find it, for it was something that was not to be had. He therefore came home in great distress of mind, because she was the daughter he loved most and wished most to please. As he was walking along he happened to see a light shining on the road, and, as it was already night, he walked on and on until he reached the light. The light came from a hut in which lived a shepherd; the man went in and inquired of him, "Can you tell me what palace is that yonder, and do you think they would give me shelter there?" The shepherd replied, in great astonishment, "Oh! sir, but ..... in that palace no one resides, something is seen there which terrifies people from living in it." "What does it matter, it will not eat me up; and, as there is no one living in it, I shall go and sleep there to-night." He went up to the building, found it all lit up very splendidly, and, on entering into the palace, he found a table ready laid. As he approached the table, he heard a voice which said, " Eat and lie down on the bed which you see there, and in the morning rise and take with you what you will find on that table, which is what your daughter asked you for; but at the end of three days you must bring her here." The man was very pleased to be able to take home what his daughter had asked him for, but at the same time was distressed at what the voice had said it required him to do. He threw himself on the bed, and on the following morning he arose, went straight to the table, and found upon it the slice of roach off a green meadow. He took it up and went home; the moment he arrived his daughters surrounded him: " Father, what have you brought us? let us see what it is;" the father gave them what he had brought them. The third daughter, the one he loved most, did not ask him for anything, but simply if he was well. The father answered her, " My daughter, I come back both happy and sad! Here you have what you asked me for." " Oh! father, I asked you for this because it was a thing which did not exist; but why do you come back sad?" " Because I must take you at the end of three days to the place where this was given to me." He recounted all that had occurred to him in the place, and what the voice had told him to do. When the daughter heard all she replied, " Do not distress yourself, father, for I shall go, and whatever God wills, will happen." And so it happened that at the end of three days the father took her to the enchanted palace It was all illuminated and in a blaze of light ; the table was laid, and two beds had been prepared. As they entered they heard a voice saying, " Eat and remain with your daughter three days that she may not feel frightened." The man remained the three days in the palace, and at the end went away leaving the daughter alone! The voice spoke to her every day but no form was seen. At the end of a few days the girl heard a bird singing in the garden. The voice said to her, " Do you hear that bird sing ?" " Yes, I hear him," replied the girl, " Does it bring any news ?" "It is your eldest sister who is going to be married, would you like to be present?" asked the voice. The girl in great delight said, " Yes, I should like to go very much,—will you let me go ?" " I will allow you," rejoined the voice, " but you will not return!" " Yes, I shall come back," said the girl. The voice gave her then a ring so that she should not forget her promise, saying, " Now mind that at the end of three days a white horse will go for you; it will give three knocks,—the first is for you to dress, and get ready,—the second for you to take leave of your family,—and the third for you to mount it. If at the third knock you are not on the horse, it will go away and leave you there." The girl went home. A great feast had been prepared, and the sister was married. At the end of three days the white horse came to give the three knocks.

At the first the girl commenced to get ready, at the second knock she took leave of her family, and at the third she mounted on the horse. The voice had given the girl a box with money to take to her father and her sisters; on that account they did not wish her to return to the enchanted palace, because she was now very rich. But the girl remembered what she had promised, and the moment she found herself on the horse she darted off. After a certain time the bird returned and began to sing very contentedly in the garden. The voice said to her, " Do you hear the bird sing?" "Yes I hear it," replied the girl, " Does it bring any news?" " It is that another of your sisters is about to marry;[*] and do you wish to go?" " Yes, I wish to go; and would you allow me to go ?" " I will let you go," replied the voice; "but you will not return!" " Yes, I shall return," said the girl. The voice then said, " Remember that if at the end of

[*] There are different variations of this story, viz.: " It is that your sister has given birth to a girl; I would like you to be her godmother. And do you wish to go ?"

three days you do not come back you shall remain there, and you will be the most hapless girl there is in the world!" The girl started off. A great feast was given and the sister was married. At the end of three days the white horse came—it gave the first knock, and the girl dressed herself to go; it gave the second knock, and the girl took leave of her friends; it gave the third knock, and the girl mounted the horse and returned to the palace. After some time the bird again sang in the garden, but in melancholy tones,—very dull tones indeed. The voice said to her, "Do you hear the bird sing?" "Yes, I hear it," replied the girl: "is there any news?" "Yes, there are; it is that your father is dying, and does not wish to die without taking leave of you." "And will you allow me to go and see him?" asked the girl, indeed much distressed. "Yes, I will let you go; but I know you will not return this time." "Oh yes, I shall come back," replied the girl. The voice then said to her, "No, you will not return--you will not! for your sisters will not let you come; you and they will be the most unhappy girls in this world if you do not come back at the end of three days." The girl went home, the father was very ill, yet he could not die until he saw her, and he had hardly taken leave of his daughter when he died. The sisters gave the girl a sleeping draught as she had requested them, and left her to sleep. The girl had begged them most particularly to awaken her before the white horse should come. What did the sisters do? They did not awaken her, and they took off the ring she wore. At the end of three days the horse came—it gave the first knock; it knocked the second time; it knocked the third time, and went away and the girl remained at home. As the sisters had taken away the ring, she forgot everything of the past and lived very happily with her sisters. A few days after this fortune began to leave her and her sisters, until one day the two said to her, "Sister, do you remember the white horse?" The girl then recollected everything, and began to cry, saying, "Oh! what misfortune is mine, oh! you have made me very wretched! what has become of my ring?" The sisters gave her the ring, and the girl took her departure in great affliction. She reached the enchanted palace and found everything about it looking very dull, very dark, and the palace shut up. She went straight into the garden and she there found a huge beast lying on the ground. The beast had barely seen her when he cried out, "Go away, you tyrant, for you have broken my spell! Now you will be the most wretched girl in the world, you and your sisters." As the beast finished saying this it died. The girl returned to her sisters in great distress, weeping very bitterly, and she remained in the house without eating or drinking, and after a few days died also. The sisters became poorer by degrees for having been the cause of all this trouble.

XI.—The Tower of Ill Luck.

There was once a woman who had three sons. The eldest asked her blessing one day, and told her that if she gave him a horse and lion he would go and travel abroad. The mother replied, "Where will you go alone?" "Let me go, mother, I want to travel through different parts of the world." The mother gave him the horse and the lion, and he took his departure. He travelled on and on until he met a little old woman who was washing. The lad went up close to her, and inquired of her, "Oh! old lady, what are you doing there?" The old woman replied, "Oh! my son, I am here washing, and shall continue all my life." The lad asked her another question, "Can you tell me what tower that is yonder?" The old woman replied, "Oh! child, that tower is the Tower of Ill Luck; who ever enters never returns."* The lad replied, "Well, I shall go there and I shall return, and I shall find you here still." He proceeded on and on until he at last reached the said tower. It was an inn. He had scarcely reached the door when he saw an old woman, and he asked her if that was an inn, for he wished to take up his abode there. The old woman replied that it was an inn. "Look here," said she, "take this key, and go and open the stables. Take also this fine hair, and roll it round the neck of your horse and lion, to tie them up with." The boy did so. He opened the stable, took the horse and lion inside, and then rolled the hair round the necks of both, and left the stable. After this he went up to the old woman, and asked her for something to eat. The old woman replied, "Ah! you want to eat, yes, Sir, my little boy; but first of all let us have a wrestling match together." The lad had no other alternative, and began to wrestle with the old hag, but he found himself so overpowered, as the woman was a witch, that he began to call for his horse and lion. "Come to my help, my horse and my lion!" The old hag rejoined, "Be ye thickened, thin hair, into a strong coil, binding your horse and lion." Immediately the hair became like a thick iron chain, which secured the animals effectually, and they were not able to come to rescue the lad. The old hag continued to wrestle until at last the boy was killed. And when she saw that he was quite dead, she went and buried him in a grave where there already many other corpses buried.

After the lapse of some time the second brother, on perceiving that his brother did not return, asked his mother to bestow upon

* This tower is also called the "Tower of Somnolence" and "Tower of Babylon," in some of our popular stories. The formula varies also, "Whoever goes there, remains, and never returns," "Who goes there, never returns," &c. F. H. Coelho—*contos populares portuguescs.* "The Tower of Babylon" is not the same story as this one.

him her blessing, and give him a horse and a lion, because he also wished to travel through many countries and seek his brother. The mother replied, "Oh! my son, do you wish to go and remain away as your other brother who has never made his appearance?" He replied, "Do not fear mother;" and as he persisted in his resolve and entreaties to be allowed the mother gave him the horse and the lion, and a bag of money. The boy departed and travelled without stopping until he reached the same spot where the old woman was washing. The boy inquired, "Oh! little old lady, what are you about there?" The old woman replied, "I am washing clothes, my son, and shall be washing all my life!" The boy again inquired, "Can you inform me what tower that is yonder?" The old woman said, "Ah! child, that is the Tower of Ill Luck; who ever goes there never returns." The boy rejoined, "Very well, but I shall go there, and am certain to return, and even find you here still." "Now," said the old washerwoman, "a boy has passed this way already who said the same thing, yet he has not returned." The boy replied, "Well then, that must have been my brother; and now I am more determined than ever to go there and bring him back!" He proceeded towards the tower, arrived, and saw the same old hag, and he asked her if that was an inn as he desired to take up his abode there. The old woman replied that it was an inn. "Now listen," said she, "take this key and go and open the stable. Take also this thin hair and bind it round the neck of your horse and of your lion, to tie them up with." The boy did as he was told, opened the stables as his brother had done before him, took the horse and lion inside and fastened them to the wall with the hair the old hag had given him. After that he left the stable and went to the old woman to ask her for something to eat. She answered him, "Ah! you want some food, yes Sir, my boy; but first let us have a wrestling match." The boy called out, "My horse and my lion come to my help!" The old hag instantly rejoined, "Let the thin hair round your horse and lion be thickened into a strong coil," and immediately the thin hair became a thick iron chain which effectually fastened the animals, and they were not able to succour the boy. The old hag killed him, and when she saw that he was quite dead she buried him in the grave where his brother's corpse was laid.

After some time the youngest brother, seeing that the others did not return home, asked the mother to bestow her blessing upon him, give him a horse and a lion, and when he obtained what he wanted he travelled through the world in search of his brothers. He came up to the spot where the old woman was washing clothes, and he asked her, "Oh! old lady, what are you doing here?" to which the old woman replied, "Oh! my son, I am here washing clothes all my life, and shall be washing for ever, because I was once washing clothes on a Sunday and a poor man passing asked me if it was possible that I was employed in washing on a Sunday. I answered him that I was, because on Sundays I also required food. And he replied, 'You shall be obliged to wash clothes all your life then.'" The boy then asked her another question, "Can you inform me what tower that is yonder?" The old woman replied, "Ah! my boy, that is the Tower of Ill Luck; who goes there never returns." The boy said to this, "Well then I shall go there, I shall return and shall still find you here." "Well," said the old woman, "two boys have already passed by here who said the same as you, and have not returned." The boy then rejoined, "Well then, those must have been my brothers, I shall go there and shall yet bring them back." He directed his steps to the tower, and when he reached it the old hag was at the door. The boy inquired if that was an inn as he would wish to stay there. The old woman replied that it was, and said to him, "Look here, take this key and open the stable. Take also this thin hair, and tie it round the neck of your horse and of your lion. The boy took the horse and the lion into the stable, but instead of tying them up, he, with a pair of scissors he brought with him, cut up the hair the old woman had given him into little bits. He then left the stable and asked for his breakfast. The old woman replied to this, "You shall have your breakfast, oh yes Sir, my boy, but first of all let us have a wrestle together." The boy instantly called out to his horse and lion, "Come to my help, my horse and my lion!" The old woman said, "Let the thin hair become a very strong coil round the neck of your horse and your lion!" But the boy had cut up the hair into very small bits and had thrown them into the sea. The lion and the horse responded to the call, and came immediately. The boy then said to the hag: "You must bring my brothers to me here or else you shall die!" The old hag replied, "Oh, Sir! I know nothing of your brothers." The boy then told her that he was going to kill her; and the old woman had no other alternative left but to confess where the brothers were. She then gave an ointment and a scent for the dead brothers to smell. The boy went and anointed the bodies of his brothers, and when he put the scent to their noses they returned immediately to life. When the three brothers found themselves together again they went to the old hag, caught her, dug a grave, and buried her alive in it.

XII.—The Step-Mother.

There was once a widower who had a son and a daughter. The girl went to school, and the mistress was continually telling her to ask the father to marry her. The mistress had three daughters: one was one-eyed, the next one was lame, and the other was blind. The little girl would every day say to her father, when she came home, "Father, marry my mistress, for she gives me honey-drops." To this the father would answer, "Now she gives you honey-drops; by-and-bye she will give you gall-drops!" The father bought himself a hat, and, bringing it home, he said to his daughter, "When this hat wears out, I shall then marry your mistress." And he hung it up on a peg. The little girl went up to her mistress and recounted all that the father had said. The mistress said, "Then you must bring me the hat." When the father had gone out one day the little girl took the hat to the mistress, and she put it into an oven and tore it in several places. The girl then took it, and hung it up again. The father put it on one day, and it all came to pieces immediately. He then said to the daughter, "Now I shall marry your mistress, for my hat is completely worn out." But still he bought a pair of boots, and he said, "When these boots are worn out, I shall then marry." The girl again went up to her mistress and told her what the father had said; and she asked her to bring the boots, and she put them in the oven. The father one day went to put them on, and tore them in the act. He called his daughter to him and said, "Now I have no other remedy but to marry your mistress, for my boots are worn out." The marriage took place, but she had hardly become married when she began to ill-treat the little girl, and made her work all day, whilst the mistress's daughters did nothing whatever in the house. One day the father bought a farthing's worth of pine-nuts, and said, "My children come with me," and he took them to the wood. The son and daughter were eating their nuts, and dropping the shells as they went along on the road. They entered the wood, and as they came up to the foot of a tree the father said, "My children, remain here; and here I leave this gourd: whilst it continues to sound, it is a sign that I am in the wood; when it

THE STEP-MOTHER.

shall stop, it is then a sign that I am no longer in the wood, but am coming back for you." And he went away. The two children remained alone; and as the wind struck the gourd, it kept sounding. They kept watching and looking at the gourd; but the brother kept saying, "Oh! sister, father can no longer be in the wood!" The girl replied, "But the gourd still keeps sounding." "It sounds because the wind strikes against it," rejoined the brother. They at last resolved to leave the wood, as the sun had nearly set; and they kept following the track of the nut-shells which they had laid on the road, and as long as they could see them they went right; but after a while the shells failed to be seen, and they consequently lost their way. At night-fall they met a little old woman, who said to them, "Oh! my children, what are you doing here?" They answered her, saying, "We are here because father brought us to the wood, and then left us to remain in it alone. He told us that whilst the gourd sounded it was a sign that he was still in the wood, and that when it ceased it was a sign that he was out of the wood, but was coming back for us. But the gourd kept sounding because the wind moved it. And he went away." The old lady was a fay, and she said to them, "Now, come along with me, my little children." She placed the boy out as a servant, and the girl she took home with her. She gave her a bason and a small bouquet of flowers, saying to her, "Listen: place yourself at this window, my child, holding in your hand this posygay and bason, and say, 'Spray of Intingil, it is now time that my love should come!'" The little girl did as she was bid. Every day she sat at the window holding the posy, and the bason placed by her side, whilst she repeated "Little Spray of Intingil, it is now time that my love should come." As soon as she finished these words a bird appeared and brought her much money, after which it flew away. With this money the girl bought many things, and jewelry, and went very well dressed. The fay frequently bade her call for her whenever she should be in any trouble. Once that the girl was at the window, who should happen to pass? One of the mistress's daughters—the one-eyed one. She looked towards the window and she saw the girl, and immediately went to tell her mother how she had seen the girl so well dressed. The mistress, much surprised to hear it, asked her "How is it that, remaining in the wood as she did, wild beasts did not eat her up?" The daughter replied, "I do not know about that, but I do know that I saw her very well dressed at the window." A few days after, the lame daughter went and passed the house purposely, and saw the girl very well dressed sitting by the window with the posy of flowers and the bason standing on the window-sill, whilst she heard her repeat, "Little branch of Intingil, it is now time that my love should come." And when she had said this she saw the bird come and leave her much money. The lame girl returned home and her mother asked, "Well, did you see anything?" The girl replied, "I saw her at the window very richly clothed, but I saw nothing else." She did not, however, inform her mother that she had seen the bird come and bring her much money. The mistress then sent the blind girl. She proceeded to the house and heard the girl say, "Little Spray of Intingil, it is now time my love should come;" and she went home and said nothing. The one-eyed daughter then said, "Well, I will go once more, and I am sure I shall see something remarkable this time!" She took with her a handkerchief full of broken glass without telling any one, and on arriving at the house she hid herself, and soon heard the girl at the window repeat the words she was in the habit of saying, and also saw the bird come. The moment she saw the bird, the one-eyed daughter threw the handkerchief full of broken glass at the bird. The poor bird was much hurt and cut in many places, and bleeding very profusely fell into the bason. The girl did not see who had done the wicked deed, but in great distress of mind she summoned the fay. The fay came instantly she was called, and said, "Had you appealed to me sooner I could have saved the poor bird, but now I can do nothing, as the bird is dead!" The girl wept much for the loss of her little bird.

One day when the girl was at the window she saw a prince passing. The prince had scarcely fixed his eyes upon her than he said, "Oh! what a lovely maiden." And going into the house he asked the girl if she would marry him. The girl replied that she could not give him an answer until she should see the fay. She therefore summoned her, and told her what the prince had said to her. The fay replied that she consented to her marrying him. They were accordingly married, and ever after lived happily together.

XIII.—Saint Peter's Goddaughter.

There was a couple who had so many children that there was no man left in that part of the country to be godfather. Another child was born to them, and the father, not knowing who else he could ask to be godfather, went out to walk along the high road. He met Saint Peter disguised as a little old man, and dressed like a poor man. When Saint Peter saw the man he asked him, "What are you doing here?" The man replied, much distressed, "What can I possibly do, my good Sir; I have had so many children that I cannot find now any one to stand godfather to my youngest child." The old man rejoined, "Well, then, I shall be its godfather; call her Peter, and when the child attains the age of seven years you must bring her here to this spot." Saint Peter then gave him a purse with money and departed. The man returned home feeling most happy, and related to his wife what had occurred to him with the old man he had met on the road, and he showed her the bag of money he had given him. The girl grew to be seven years of age, and the man, who had become very rich, felt loth to take the girl to the spot arranged upon; yet as he promised to do so he took her. When he reached the place he found the godfather waiting for them. Saint Peter then said to the man, " Go away and leave her here with me, as I shall take charge of her." And the man returned home without his daughter. Saint Peter took the girl by a road where there was a pear-tree loaded with fruit. Saint Peter asked the girl, " Do you see those pears?" " I do," replied the girl. " And do you like them?" asked Saint Peter. "I like them very much, godfather," replied the girl. They went on further, and they saw some very fat sheep in a place of very poor pasture. After this they met other sheep which were very lean, notwithstanding there was plenty of pasture. They proceeded on further, and at a great distance they descried a great blaze, and by it a dark column rising up. Saint Peter said to the girl, " Do you see that blaze?" The girl replied, " I can see it, godfather; what is it?" Saint Peter replied, " What you see there is purgatory, where people go who are proud and wicked. Did you not see those sheep that were lean with so much food before them? Those are persons who are proud and are sent there for their purgatory. And did you not see those fat sheep with very little to feed upon? Those are the good people who did much good in this world and who go to heaven. And did you perceive that pear-tree loaded with fruit? The pears are the angels, who being good also go to heaven. And now you are going into service. and will have to put up with many, many untoward things, because those that suffer and are patient go to heaven." After this Saint Peter gave her much good advice, and told her to call upon him whenever she should find herself in any very great trouble; moreover that she should never dress as a woman. The girl went to the king's palace and offered herself as a servant. One of the chamberlains went to inform the king of her request, and the king sent him to say that she might enter his service. They asked her at the palace what her name was, and she said that it was Peter. She entered the king's palace, and her duty was to tend the ducks. At night when Peter retired to bed, the queen went into Peter's room. But Peter ran away, and the queen felt vexed; and when she rose up next morning she threw a ring into the sea, and then went to the king and said, " Do you know what has happened to me! I let fall a ring into the sea, and Peter says he is sure he can dive to the bottom and find it." The king sent for Peter and said to him, " Oh! Peter, the queen has informed me that you say you are able to dive to the bottom of the sea and search for the ring which she let fall this morning into the water. Are you really able to do so?" The poor girl replied, "I suppose that if the queen says so, it is because I am able." She then went to her room and began to cry very bitterly, because she had not said such a thing, and she did not feel equal to attempting such a deed. However, she remembered to call for her godfather, and she said, " Come to my help, oh! my godfather." Saint Peter appeared to her at once, and asked her, " Why are you in tears? have patience, for it is thus we should bear all things." The girl recounted to Saint Peter all that had happened to her with the queen, and what her majesty had told the king out of revenge to try and disgrace her. Saint Peter then said to her, " Very well, now listen to me. To-morrow they will buy some fish, and you must go and ask the servant whose duty it is to prepare and open the fish, to allow you to do it." The girl did as she was instructed to do. Next day some fish was brought into the palace, and she asked the servant to allow her to prepare the fish for the cook. She opened the fish's belly and there she found the ring, and she took it to the queen and gave it to her. The queen felt very much annoyed at this, but made no remark, and kept her displeasure to herself. Next day she again went into Peter's chamber, but Peter again ran out of the room. The queen feeling piqued and annoyed at the repetition of Peter's provoking conduct, again went to the king to make mischief, saying, "Do you know that Peter says that he is capable of grinding three quarters of wheat this evening?" The king sent for Peter and said to him, "Oh! Peter, the queen has told me that you say that you are able to grind three quarters of wheat this night; is it so?" Peter replied, "If the queen says so, it must be because I can do it." Peter went to her room to give vent to her grief, and said, "Oh! my godfather, do come to my help." St. Peter once more appeared to her and asked her, "What ails you, that you weep so?" The girl replied, telling him of her trouble, and all that had taken place. Saint Peter then said to her, "I will tell you what to do. Ask for the necessary machine for grinding the wheat, take it to your room, and lay yourself down to sleep. In the morning rise up and look for the flour." The girl did as she was bidden. She asked for the necessary things to grind the wheat. She put everything in the room, and she laid down to sleep. When she arose next morning she found the flour already ground, and went with it to the king. This increased the queen's annoyance and anger against Peter, but she remained silent and betrayed no displeasure. At night she again went into Peter's chamber, and, as before, Peter ran away. The king had a daughter who was spell-bound in Moirama. The queen, remembering this, went to the king and said to him, "Do you know that Peter says that he feels confident of being able to disenchant our daughter who is in Moirama?" On hearing this the king summoned him to his presence and asked him, "Oh! Peter, the queen informs me that you say you feel confident of being able to disenchant our beloved daughter who is in Moirama,—can you really do so?" To this Peter replied, "I suppose that if the queen says so it is because I can." Peter returned to her room to have a good cry, for she thought that this would be impossible for her to accomplish. But in the midst of her doubts and affliction she turned and said, "Come to my assistance, oh! godfather." Saint Peter instantly stood before her and asked her, "What is the matter now, and why are you grieving so?" The girl told him all the impossible things the queen had told the king she vaunted she could accomplish, all out of spite. To this Saint Peter replied, "Take these three tubes. Ask to have two horses saddled for your journey, and travel on and on, and where your horses shall stop there you will find the princess waiting for your arrival. On your return to the palace, look back, and you will find that the Moors are chasing you; then it is that you must throw the first tube; and if they continue to pursue you throw the second, and after that the third tube." The girl did as she was instructed to do. She asked the king to let her have two saddle-horses and started off, travelling until she arrived at a certain spot where the horses of their own accord suddenly stopped and refused to go any further; and there she found the princess waiting for her. As she was returning to the palace with the princess she looked behind her, and she saw the Moors in pursuit, and she had hardly seen them than she threw at them the first tube; and immediately a great fog came on. The girl and the princess could see their way, but the Moors could barely see the road and follow them. When they had quitted the land of Moirama the princess, who had been dumb, gave utterance to a short exclamation, saying, "ah!" When they had proceeded further on the girl again looked back and she saw the Moors still in pursuit. She threw to them the second tubing, and a thick almost impassable bush grew up. The girl and the princess were able to pass this easily and quickly, but the Moors found it difficult to effect a path through it. When they had reached half way on their road home the dumb princess a second time exclaimed "ah!" Further on the girl again looked behind her, and saw the Moors were still behind. She threw out the third tube and a sea was formed. They crossed with ease the water, and this time the Moors found it impossible to follow the fugitives. When the girl and the princess arrived at the palace the princess a third time uttered an exclamation, and said, "ah!" When the queen saw her daughter she was very angry and went to the king to say that Peter vaunted that he could give speech to the princess, who was dumb. The king called up Peter and asked her if she was capable of executing what she said she could do. The girl replied as before, that if the queen had said so it was because she could do so. But she went to her room to weep, and she called out saying, "Oh! my godfather, come to my help," who instantly appeared and asked her, "Why are you weeping?" The girl told him everything, and St. Peter instructed her what she was to do. From there the girl went up to the king and told him that he could put her to death if he chose, but that she could not possibly give the princess speach. The queen was delighted to hear her say this; and it was decided that Peter should be hung. When the rope was already round her neck she asked leave in the presence of all the court assembled in front of the scaffold to publish three things to the world. The king gave the desired permission and she then asked:

"Oh! Anna Deladana, why didst thou exclaim ah! as we left Moirama?"

The princess replied: "Because my mother went to seek for you in your bed."

The girl again asked: "Oh! Anna Deladana, why didst thou exclaim a second time ah! when half way home?"

The princess replied: "Because Saint Peter is your godfather!"

The girl again asked: "Oh! Anna Deladana, why didst thou utter an ah! at the entrance of the palace?"

The princess replied: "Because you are a woman and they believed you were a man!"

The king then saw that the girl was innocent, and ordered her to be taken down from the scaffold, married her, and had the queen put to death.

XIV.—The Two Children and the Witch.

There was once a woman who had a son and a daughter. The mother one day sent her son to buy five reis' worth of beans, and then said to both: "My children, go as far out on the road as you shall find shells of beans strewed on the path, and when you reach the wood you will find me there collecting fire-wood." The children did as they were bid; and after the mother had gone out they went following the track of the beans which she went strewing along the road, but they did not find her in the wood or anywhere else. As night had come on they perceived in the darkness a light shining at a distance, easy of access. They walked on towards it, and they soon came up to an old woman who was frying cakes. The old woman was blind of one eye, and the boy went on the blind side and stole a cake, because he felt so hungry. Believing that it was her cat which had stolen the cake, she said, "You thief of a cat! leave my cakes alone; they are not meant for you!" The little boy now said to his sister, "You go now and take a cake." But the little girl replied, "I cannot do so, as I am sure to laugh." Still, as the boy persisted upon it and urged her to try, she had no other alternative but to do so. She went on the side of the old woman's blind eye and stole another of her cakes. The old woman, again thinking that it was her cat, said, "Be off! shoo you old pussy; these cakes are not meant for you!" The little girl now burst out into a fit of laughter, and the old hag turning round then, noticed the two children, and addressed them thus: "Ah! is it you, my dear grandchildren? Eat, eat away, and get fat!" She then took hold of them and thrust them into a large box full of chestnuts, and shut them up. Next day she came close to the box and spoke to them thus: "Show me your little fingers, my pets, that I may be able to judge whether you have grown fat and sleek." The children put out their little fingers as desired. But next day the old hag again asked them: "Show your little fingers, my little dears, that I may see if you have grown fat and plump!" The children, instead of their little fingers, showed her the tail of a cat they had found inside the box. The old hag then said: "My pets, you can come out now, for you have grown nice and plump." She took them out of the box, and told them they must go with her and gather sticks. The children went into the wood searching one way while the old hag took another direction. When they had arrived at a certain spot they met a fay. This fay said to them: "You are gathering sticks, my children, to heat the oven, but you do not know that the old hag wants to bake you in it." She further told them that the old witch meant to order them to stand on the baker's peel, saying: "Stand on this peel, my little pets, that I may see you dance in the oven; but that they were to ask her to sit upon it herself first, that so they might learn the way to do it. The fay then went away. Shortly after they had met this good lady they found the old witch in the wood. They gathered together in bundles all the fire-sticks they had collected, and carried them home to heat the oven. When they had finished heating the oven, the old hag swept it carefully out, and then said to the little ones, "Sit here, my little darlings, on this peel, that

THE TWO CHILDREN AND THE WITCH. 61

I may see how prettily you dance in the oven!" The children replied to the witch as the good fay had instructed them: " Sit you here, little granny, that we may first see you dance in the oven." As the hag's intention was to bake the children, she sat on the peel first, so as to coax them to do the same after her; but the very moment the children saw her on the peel they thrust the peel into the oven with the witch upon it. The old hag gave a great start, and was burnt to a cinder immediately after. The children took possession of the shed and all it contained.

Another version:—There was once three brothers who went along a certain road. When night overtook them they saw a light at a distance, and so they walked on towards it until they came to it. The light proceeded from a spot where an old woman was frying some cakes. The brothers said one to another, " Let us get upon the roof." They made a very long hook-stick, and got upon the roof. As the old hag fried her cakes she placed them upon a dish by her. Her cat, meanwhile, sat by her side. The boys with their long hook, from the top of the roof, fished up the warm cakes one after the other, as the old hag placed them on the dish. As the cat was by her side, and every time she placed a cake on the dish she found the other gone, she kept repeating and exclaiming:—" Shoo, you naughty thief of a pussy, how can you manage to eat so many cakes?" These brothers were consecrated to St. Peter, and when they heard what the old hag said, they began to laugh, unable to suppress their merriment. The old hag, looking up towards the roof, startled, saw the boys, and told them to come down. The boys feared to do so, and refused to descend; but the old witch so managed to threaten, and then to cajole them, that she at last induced them to come down from the roof. When she saw them down she addressed them:—" Look here, my children, stand on this baker's peel for an instant." The boys replied, " No, no, old lady, you get upon it first, and one can then easily learn how it is to be done." The old witch, believing them to be innocent and artless, stood upon the peel! "Saint Peter, come to our help!" cried out the brothers, the moment they saw her upon the peel. Saint Peter came, pushed the old hag into the oven, stirred the fire, and shut the oven door. After this the boys continued to partake of the remaining cakes very comfortably.

XV.—The Maiden with the Rose on her Forehead.

There was once a prince and a princess who were brother and sister, and were very great friends. The prince had a garden which no one was allowed to cultivate but himself. As it happened he had to go to the war; and he was sorry to go, because he did not like to trust any one with the care of his own garden. His sister, however, said to him:—" Dear brother, have no anxiety about your garden, leave it to me, and I promise you that no one but myself shall look after it." The prince then departed, well pleased with his sister's arrangement. The princess not wishing to leave the garden for one minute, as her brother was there constantly when at home, had her couch brought to the garden and placed under a large rose tree. After a time she gave birth to a child, a girl, with a rose on her forehead. The princess was much distressed at this, as it had come upon her without her knowledge, and she was always in the garden day and night. The child began to grow, and the mother sent her to school, enjoined her very particularly never to make herself known to any one, because, if she did, she would kill her. The child went to school; and the prince was expected to arrive home very shortly, and it was thought probable that as soon as he should reach the capital, he would go and visit all the schools and colleges, as well as the school where the little princess went to. The princess, who knew this, told her little daughter that the prince would visit her school, but that she was on no account to make herself known to him, as otherwise she would put her to death.

When the prince at last visited the said school he immediately noticed a new face and said: "Ah! there is one girl more since I last was here, I see!" The other children talked and made a noise, but this little one never once raised her head, that the rose on her forehead should not be noticed; nor did she laugh and be merry like the others. The prince, addressing the children, asked which of them would make him a shirt. The girls all answered at once: "I will, I will, I will," but the girl with the rose on her forehead remained silent. The prince noticed this and said, "Then the girl who has remained silent and has not said whether she would or not is the one who shall have the honour given her of making me a shirt! You will, will you not?" The girl signified by a movement of the head that she would. She went home and told her mother what the prince had asked her to do for him. The prince never once suspected any thing, and though the girl lived in the palace he did not know it. The princess told her daughter to make the shirt, but on no account to make herself known to the prince else she would have her put to death. The maiden went to school, set to work, and finished the shirt in one day, and when the prince came into the school she gave him the shirt ready finished. He thanked her very graciously, and he found it very well stitched and finished, but he never once noticed that she had a rose on her forehead, as she always went about with her head covered. When the prince came into the palace he told the princess that he had found a girl in the school who was very clever and handy at her needle, for she had made him a shirt in one day which was beautifully finished. As the prince finished saying this a man passed by the palace selling and crying out cherries—he called the man and bought of him the basketful of cherries; he then took them to the school and gave the girls the cherries to eat. They all began eating the fruit, much pleased, and it was only the maid with the rose on her forehead that did not attempt to partake of them. The prince perceiving it asked her, "Well then will you not taste some?" She made a sign that she would not have any. The prince, surprised at not ever having heard her speak, inquired of the mistress, "Is that little girl dumb?" The mistress replied, "She is very shy, and if any one endeavours to make her speak or take any notice of her she immediately begins to cry." The girl's all began to play with the cherries and throw them about in their fun, but where should one of them fall but on the little girls head who had a rose on her forehead! Next day, when her mother combed her hair to go to school, finding a cherry entangled in it said to her, "Ah! tyrant, I see you have made yourself known," She stuck the comb into her head violently and killed her. She then had the corpse put into an iron chest together with all her jewels, and locked the chest in a chamber of the palace; but after a while from remorse and grief at what she had done to her poor daughter she pined away and died. Before she died she gave the prince the key of the room, telling him never to touch anything in it. The brother, in order to comply with the princess's injunction, took special care to keep those keys separate. The princess died after she had said this.

The prince, feeling lonely, now decided to marry, and gave his wife all the keys, at the same time telling her that she could open every door she liked except the one leading to the room which his sister the princess had asked him before she died never to examine. As the prince went one day to hunt, his mother-in-law, who lived with them in the palace, had a great wish to open this room, but her daughter told her not to do so because the prince had enjoined her not. The mother then said that if the prince objected to having that room opened it was because it contained something which he wished to conceal from her. At last she insisted so much upon it that she obtained the key of the room and opened it. They both went in, and the first thing that they saw was a large iron chest. The mother then said, "Ah! I shall see what we can find in that large chest." She opened it and found inside a most beautiful maiden with a star on her forehead, who was sitting down engaged in embroidering. When the mother saw her she said to her daughter, "Did not I tell you that there was some hidden secret here?" The wife now, jealous of the maiden's beauty, heated an iron, took the maiden out of the chest, and burnt her skin with the heated iron, so that she remained all over scorched. When the prince returned from the hunt his wife said to him, "Do you know that I have bought a mulatta girl to serve us to run errands?" The prince, who was going to the fair, asked his wife what she would like him to bring her; but she told him to ask the mulatta girl what she also would like. So the prince asked the maid what she wished from the fair. The girl replied that she did not wish anything, but as he persisted in asking her to tell him something she would like to have, she asked him to bring her a talisman. When the prince returned from the fair he gave the girl the talisman. She took it to her room and lay on her bed. As the prince was curious to know what she would do with it, he hid himself under the bed. The mulatta girl began to tell her history to the stone, saying, "Oh! talisman, I am the daughter of a princess, sister to the prince my uncle, who lives in this palace and is married. But he does not know that I am his niece, for I was kept spell-bound in an iron chest; and his wife and her mother burnt my skin all over with a hot iron, and I remained scorched and browned; and when the prince returned home from the hunt they told him that I was a mulatta girl,

Now my talisman I have told you all my history, and you know all my life." The prince who was listening attentively under the bed, quickly came out, embraced the maiden, and asked her what she desired him to do to his wife, as he no longer would allow her to remain in the palace. The maiden replied, "Do to her the same she did to me." The prince then ordered that the same piece of iron should be heated and his wife to have her skin well scorched with it, and that her mother should also undergo the same punishment, after which he inclosed them alive in a wall. He lived in the palace with his niece and never more entertained the idea of marrying.

XVI.—The Princess who would not marry her Father.

There was once a king and a queen. But a few years after their marriage the queen died. At her death she placed a ring on a table, and bade the king marry whomsoever that ring should fit. It happened that their daughter, the princess, approached the table by chance, saw the ring, and tried it on. She then ran to the king her father, and said:—"Sire, do you know that a ring which I found on the table fits me as though it had been made expressly for me! . . ." The king, on hearing this, replied:—"Oh! my daughter, you will have to marry me, because your mother, before she died, expressed a wish that I should marry whoever this ring would fit." The princess, greatly distressed, shut herself up in a room which had the window looking into the garden, and gave vent to her grief. Soon, however, a little old woman appeared to her, and asked her: "Why do you weep, royal lady?" To which the princess replied: "Well, what else can I do? My father says that I must marry him." The little old woman then said to her: "Listen to me, royal lady, go and tell your father that you will only marry him on condition that he buys you a dress of the colour of the stars in the heavens." And after saying this she departed. The princess then went up to the king, who asked her: "Well, my daughter, are we to be married?" To which she replied: "Well, father, I shall marry you when you bring me a dress of the colour of the stars in the heavens." The father, on hearing this, went out and bought her the dress, and gave it to her ready made. The princess again went to her room to cry. The little old woman again appeared to her, and asked her, "What ails you, royal lady?" She replied: "What can ail me! my father has bought me the dress I asked him for, and he wishes to marry me." The old lady rejoined: "Never mind, you must now ask him to bring you a dress of the colour of the flowers that grow in the fields." The princess again went to her father and told him that she could only marry him on condition of his bringing her a robe of the colour of wild flowers. The king bought the dress and gave it to her made up, and quite ready to be put on. The princess, again in trouble, retired to her chamber to weep. The old lady again appeared and demanded: "What ails you, royal lady?" To which the princess replied: "What can ail me, indeed! my father has bought me the second robe, and is determined to marry me." The good old lady rejoined: "Ask your father now for a robe of various colours." The princess did so, and asked for a robe of various colours, and the king bought her the dress and brought it to her ready to be put on. The princess returned to her chamber to weep over her new trouble, but the little old woman came to her and asked her what troubled her. The princess replied that the king had bought her the third robe she required of him, and was now determined that the marriage should take place. "And now what shall I do to prevent it?" inquired the princess. The little old woman replied: "Royal lady, you must now send for a carpenter and order him to make you a dress of wood; get inside it and go to the palace of the king who lives yonder, who requires a servant to tend the ducks." The princess did as she was told, had a dress made of wood, put all her jewels, and everything else she would require, inside, and getting inside it herself; and one fine day she ran away. She walked on and on until she arrived at the said palace. She knocked at the door, and told the servants to ask his majesty the king if he required a maid to mind the ducks. He replied that he did; and he asked her what her name was, and she rejoined that her name was Maria do Pau; and after this the king sent her to tend the ducks, which were in a field next to the palace gardens. The moment the princess reached it she took off everything she had on, and the wooden dress also; she washed herself, as she was travel-stained, and then put on the richest robe she had, which was the one the colour of the stars. The king was taking a walk in the garden, and noticed a lovely maiden who was in the field driving the ducks, and heard her repeat—

> "Ducks here, ducks there,
> The daughter of a king tends the ducks,
> A thing never seen before!"

When she had finished saying this she killed one of the ducks; then took off her robes, and again got into her wooden dress. At night she went indoors, saying: "Oh! king, I have killed one of the ducks." The king asked her: "Maria do Pau, who was that beautiful maiden so splendidly robed that minded the ducks?" To this she said: "Indeed there was no one else there but myself in disguise." Next day the king again sent Maria do Pau to tend the ducks. And when she was in the field she did the same thing as the day before. She took off her wooden dress, washed and combed herself carefully, put on the

THE PRINCESS WHO WOULD NOT MARRY HER FATHER. 69

robe the colour of wild flowers, and went about driving the ducks, saying as before:—

"Ducks here, ducks there,
The daughter of a king tends the ducks,
A thing never seen before."

After which she killed another duck. Next day she did as the day before, put on the robe of many colours, and killed another duck. In the evening when she went indoors, the king said to her: "I do not wish you to take care of the ducks any longer, for every day we find a duck has been killed! Now you shall remain locked up in the house. We are to have a feast which will last three days, but I promise you that you shall not enjoy it, for I shall not allow you to go to it." To this she said to the king: "Oh! my liege, do let me go." But the king replied, "No, indeed, you shall not go." On the first day of the feast she again begged of the king to allow her to repair to it, and his majesty replied: "God, preserve me! What would be the consequences of taking Maria do Pau to the feast!" The king put on his gala robes and then sent for her to his chamber, asked her what dress she would like to put on, and the princess replied by asking him to give her a pair of boots, which the king threw at her and took his departure for the feast. She then repaired to her chamber and removed from inside the dress made of wool a wand she had, which the little old woman, who was a fairy, had given her, and holding it up she said: "Oh! divining rod, by the virtue that God gave you, send me here the best royal carriage, which is the very one that took the king to the feast." The carriage was instantly in sight, and entering it she made her appearance at the feast, in the robe of the colour of the stars. The king, who had his eyes continually fixed upon her, went out to the guards and told them not to allow the maiden to pass. But when she wished to get out she threw them a bag of money, and the guards allowed her to pass, but they asked her to what country she belonged, to which she replied that she came from the land of the boot. The king went home, and on arriving found the princess was already in the palace. The king, who wished to find out whether the lovely maiden which he had seen at the feast could possibly be Maria do Pau, went to see if she was safe in her chamber, and afterwards sent for her and and said to her: " Oh! Maria do Pau, do you happen to know where the land of the boot is situated?" "Oh! my liege, do not come troubling me with your questions. Is it possible that your majesty does not know where the land of the boot is situated?" The king replied: "I do not. A maiden was at the feast. I asked her where she came from, and she said that she came from the land of the boot, but I do not know where that is." Next day the king again attended the feast, but before leaving he said to Maria do Pau: " You shall not be allowed to go there" "Do allow me for once," replied she. The king then asked her to give him the towel, and as she presented him with it he threw it at her, and departed for the feast. The princess repaired to her room, struck the divining rod, and put on the robe, which was the colour of the wild flowers. The king who had been charmed with her on the first day of the feast, now admired her all the more, because she appeared more beautiful than ever. He went out to the guards and told them to ask the beautiful maiden when she passed to what country she belonged; and when she went out she informed them that she was from the land of the towel. As soon as the king was told of this he returned to the palace to think over, and try to guess, if possible, where the land of the towel could be situated. And when he arrived at the palace the first thing he did was to ask his maid if she knew where the land of the towel could be found. To his inquiries she replied: "Well, well! here comes a king who does not know, and cannot tell, where the land of the towel is situated! Neither do I know." The king now said: "Oh! Maria do Pau, every time that I have been at the feast I have seen such a pretty maiden. If the one I saw yesterday was beautiful, the one of to-day is perfectly lovely, and much more charming than the first." Next day as the king was on the point of going out the princess said to his majesty: "Oh! my liege, let me go to the feast, that I may see the maiden that is so beautiful!" The king replied: "God, preserve me! What would be the result if I were to present you before that maiden?" After which he asked her to give him his walking-stick, and as he was going out he struck her with it. He went to the feast, and when there the princess presented herself before him in the robe of many colours. If on the previous days she appeared most beautiful, on this day of the feast she looked perfectly ravishing, and more interesting than ever. The king fixed his eyes upon her so as not to lose sight of her, as he wished to see her go out, and follow her to where she lived, as it was the last day of the feast. But the king missed seeing her depart after all, and he could find her nowhere. He went to the guards and asked them what she had said, but the guards replied that she had come from the land of the walking-stick. The king returned to the palace and inquired of his maid where the land of the walking-stick could be found; but she replied: "Oh! my liege, that I should know where the land of the walking-stick is situated. Does not my liege know?—neither do I." The king again asked her: "Do you really not know? To-day I again saw the same girl who is so beautiful; but I begin to think it cannot be the same one every time, because at one time she says that she comes from the land of the boot, next time that she is from the land of the towel, and lastly she says she is from the land of the walking-stick.

The princess repaired to her room, washed and combed herself, and dressed herself in the robe she had on on the first day of the feast. The king went to look through the key-hole to find out why she was so long away and remained in her chamber so quiet, and also to see what she was at. He saw a lovely maiden, the same one who had appeared at the feast dressed in the robe the colour of the stars in the heavens, sitting down busy with some embroidery. When the princess left her chamber to repair to the dinner-table again disguised the king said to her: "Oh! Maria do Pau, you must embroider a pair of shoes for me." She replied: "Do I know how to embroider shoes?" and she left the parlour to go back to her chamber. Every day she put on one of the dresses she had worn at the feast, and on the last day she robed herself with the one of many colours. The king begged her every day to embroider him a pair of shoes, and she always returned the same answer. He had a key made to open the princess's room, and one day when he saw through the key-hole that she was robed in her best, he suddenly opened the door without her perceiving it and entered the chamber. The princess startled, and very much frightened, tried to run away, but the king said to her: "Do not be troubled for you shall marry me! But I wish you first to tell me your history, and why it is that you wear a wooden dress." The princess recounted all the events of her life and the king married her. The king next sent for the little old woman who had given her the wand, to come and live in the palace, but she refused to live there because she was a fairy.

XVII.—The Baker's Idle Son.

There was a woman baker who had a very indolent son. When the other boys went to gather firewood and he was told to go also he never would go. The mother was very unhappy to have such a lazy son, and really did not know what she should do with him. As she one day insisted upon his joining the other

THE BAKER'S IDLE SON. 73

boys he went along with them, but the moment they reached the wood whilst the other boys were collecting the sticks and small branches of trees for firewood he went to lie down by the side of a brook and began to eat what he had brought with him. While he was doing so a fish came close to him and began to eat up all the crumbs he let fall, until at last he caught it. The fish entreated him not to kill him, that he would do for him all he could wish for. The lazy boy, who did not trust the fish, said to it, "In the name of my God, and of my fish, I wish that this very moment a faggot of wood larger than any of the ones held by the other boys, shall appear before me, and that the bundle shall proceed without my being seen under it." All at once a faggot made its appearance ready tied; and he then allowed the fish to go back into the sea. He turned to go home, and as he passed the palace, the king, who was at the window with the princess, was very much astonished to see the faggot move along by itself; and the princess was so very much amused at it that she laughed. The lazy boy then said: "In the name of God, and of my fish, let the princess have a son without its being known whose son he is." The princess then began to feel that she was with child, and the king became very displeased with her, and ordered her to be imprisoned in a tower with her maids of honour. After a time she gave birth to a male child. The lazy boy returned to the wood, and the fish again appeared and told him that the princess had given birth to a son. The lazy boy, being instructed by the fish, ordered a palace to be erected which should be more splendid than the one belonging to the king. There was a garden in this palace replete with flowers of every colour and shade, and, wonderful to relate, there was an orchard full of fruit trees in which grew an orange tree with twelve golden oranges. All this was brought about by the fish and the fairies. The lazy boy went to this palace transformed into a prince, and no one knew him to be anything else. The king sent a message asking to see the palace, and he replied that he would be most happy to show him over it, and sent his majesty an invitation to breakfast and to all his court. The king and his chamberlains were much surprised on their arrival to see so much luxury and splendour. After they had inspected the whole palace they went into the garden. They were charmed with the variety of flowers in it, but were much more astonished to see an orange tree bearing golden oranges. The lazy boy informed the king and his courtiers that they could take of everything in the garden which they might desire, except gathering any of the oranges. They all returned to the palace and sat down to the breakfast. When the breakfast was over, and the king was taking his departure to return to his own palace, the lazy boy told the king that he was much surprised to find that after he had treated them so luxuriously they should have gathered one of the golden oranges. The courtiers all commenced to deny that any of them had taken the orange, and took off their coats that he might see for himself that they had not been guilty of the accusation. The king, who felt very much abashed, was now the only one who had not been examined. He took off his coat and nothing was found on examination in its pockets; but the lazy boy asked him to look carefully again when he had put his coat on, because since his courtiers had not taken the orange it must be himself who had. The king then put his hands again in his pocket and drew out the orange, very much confused and ashamed, for he could not imagine how it could have come there as he had not touched the oranges. The lazy boy then said to him that the very same thing had happened to the princess who had borne a son without knowing by whom. The spell under which the fish was bound was then broken, and it was transformed into a prince and married the princess. The lazy boy returned home a rich man.

XVIII.—The Hearth-Cat.

There was once a schoolmistress who was a widow, and had a daughter who was very plain. This mistress had a pupil who was very pretty, and the daughter of a traveller. The mistress was very attached to her father, and every day would beg the girl to ask him to marry her, promising to give her porridge made with honey. The girl went home to ask her father to marry her schoolmistress, as she would then give her porridge made with honey. To this request the father replied that he would not marry her, for he well knew that though she said now that she would give her porridge made with honey, later on she would give her porridge with gall. Yet, as the child began to cry, begging her father to consent, the father, who loved his child very much, in order to comfort her, replied that he would order a pair of boots to be made of iron, and hang them up until the boots would rust to pieces with age, when he would marry the mistress. The little girl, very pleased to hear this, went immediately to tell the mistress, who then instructed her pupil to wet the boots every day. The little girl did so, and after a while the boots fell to pieces, and she went and told her father of it. He then said that he would marry the mistress, and on the following day married her. So long as the father was at home the child was treated with kindness and affection, but the moment he went out the mistress was very unkind to her, and treated her badly. She one day sent her to graze a cow, and gave her a loaf, which she desired her to bring back whole, and an earthen pot with water, out of which she expected her to drink, and yet was to bring back full. One day the mistress told the girl that she wished her to employ herself in winding some skeins of thread until the evening. The little girl went away crying and bewailing her lot;

but the cow comforted her, and told her not to be distressed,—to fix the skein on her horns and unravel the thread. The good cow after that took out all the crumb from the loaf by making a small hole with one of her horns, and then stopped the aperture, and gave the girl the loaf back again entire. In the evening the girl returned home. When her stepmother saw that she had finished her task, and brought all the thread ready wound, she was very vexed and wanted to beat her, saying that she was sure the cow had had something to do with it, and next day ordered the animal to be killed. At this the girl began to cry very bitterly, but the step-mother told her that she would have to clean and wash the cow's entrails in a tank they had, however grieved she might feel for the loss of the animal. The cow, however, again told the girl not to be troubled, but to go and wash her entrails, but was to be careful to save whatever she saw come out of them. The girl did so, and when she was cleaning them she saw a ball of gold come out and fall into the water. The girl went into the tank to search for it, and there she saw a house with everything in it in disorder, and she began to arrange and make the house look tidy. She suddenly heard footsteps, and in her hurry she hid herself behind the door. The fairies entered and began to look about, and a dog came in also with them, and went up to where she was and began to bark, saying: " Bow, bow, bow, behind the door hides somebody who did us good, and will yet render us more services. Bow, bow, bow, behind the door hides somebody who has done us good, and will yet render us more services." The fairies, as they searched about, hearing the dog bark, discovered where the girl was hiding, and began to say to her, " We endow you by the power we possess with the gift of beauty, making you the most lovely maiden ever seen." The next fairy then said, " I cast a sweet spell over you, so that when you open your mouth to speak, pearls and gold shall drop from your lips." The third fairy coming forward said, " I endow you with every blessing, making you the happiest maiden in the world. Take this wand, it will grant you whatever you may ask." The girl then left the enchanted region, and returned home, and as soon as the mistress's daughter saw her approach she commenced to cry out to her mother to come quickly and see the hearth-cat, who had come back at last. The mistress ran to greet her, and asked her where and what she had been doing all that time. The girl related the contrary of what she had seen, as the fairies had instructed her to do—that she had found a tidy house, and that she had disarranged everything in it, to make it look untidy. The mistress sent her own daughter there, and she had hardly arrived at the house when she began at once to do as her half-sister had told her; she disarranged everything, to make the house look untidy and uncared for. And when she heard the fairies coming in she hid behind the door. The little dog saw her, and barking at her said, " Behind the door stands one who has done us much harm, and will still continue to molest us. Bow, bow, bow, behind the door stands one who has done us much harm, and will continue to molest us on the first opportunity." The fairies hearing this approached her, and one began to say, " I throw a spell over you which will render you the ugliest maid that can be found." The next one took up the word and said, " I bewitch you, so that when you attempt to speak all manner of filth shall fall out of your mouth." And the third fairy said, " I also bewitch you, and you shall become the poorest and most wretched maid in existence." The mistress's daughter returned home, thinking she was looking quite a beauty; but when she came up close to her mother, and began to speak, the mother burst out crying on seeing her own daughter so disfigured and wretched. Full of rage, she sent her step-daughter to the kitchen, saying, that she was the hearth-cat, and that she should take care that she kept there, as the only place which was fit for her. On a certain day the mistress and her daughter repaired to some races which were then taking place, but when the girl saw that they had left the house, she asked her divining rod to give her a very handsome dress, boots, a hat, and everything complete. She dressed and adorned herself with all she had, and went to the races, and stood in front of the royal stand. The mistress's daughter instantly saw her, and began to exclaim and cry out at the top of her voice, in the midst of all the people present, saying, "Oh! mother, mother, that beautiful maiden over there is our very hearth-cat." The mother, to quiet her, told her to be calm; that the maiden was not her step-sister, as she had remained at home under lock and key. The races were hardly over when the girl departed home; but the king, who had seen her, was in love with her. The moment the mother reached home she asked the hearth-cat whether she had been out. She replied, that she had not; and showed her face besmeared with smut. Next day the girl asked the wand to strike and give her another dress which would be more splendid than the previous one. She put on her things and repaired to the races. The moment the king perceived her he felt very pleased indeed; but the races were hardly concluded than she retired in haste, and went into her carriage and drove home, leaving the king more in love than ever with her. The third day the girl asked the divining rod to give her a garment which should surpass the other two in richness and beauty, and other shoes; and she went and attended the races. When the king saw her, he was delighted, but was again disappointed to see her depart before the races were concluded. In her hurry to enter her carriage quickly, she let fall one of her slippers. The king picked it up and returned to the palace, and fell lovesick. The slipper had some letters upon it which said, "This shoe will only fit its owner." The whole kingdom was searched to find the lady whose foot would be found to fit the slipper exactly, yet no one was found. The schoolmistress went to the palace to try the slipper on, but all her efforts were in vain. After her, her daughter followed, and endeavoured her best to fit the slipper on, but with no better success. There only remained the hearth-cat. The king inquired who was the next to try on the slipper, and asked the mistress if there was any other lady left in her house who could fit on the slipper. The schoolmistress then said that there only remained a hearth-cat in her house, but that she had never worn such a slipper. The king ordered the girl to be brought to the palace, and the mistress had no alternative but to do so. The king himself insisted on trying the slipper on the girl's foot, and the moment she put her little foot into the slipper and drew it on, it fitted exactly. The king then arranged that she should remain in the palace and married her. And he ordered the mistress and her daughter to be put to death.

XIX.—The Aunts.

There was an old woman who had a granddaughter; and whilst one day the girl was looking out of the window, the king, happening to pass by the house at the time, was immediately struck with her beauty. He knocked at the door, and the old woman came to open the door, and asked his majesty what might be his pleasure. The king replied that he wished to see the maiden. The old woman then told him that the maiden he had seen at the window would make him a shirt that could be drawn through the eye of a needle. The king hearing this, said that he would marry the maiden if she succeeded in doing such a wonderful thing; but that in the event of her not succeeding, he would have her put to death. When the king departed, the girl who had not said or thought of doing such a thing began to weep: an old woman however appeared to her, and told her not to be troubled, for she would make the shirt for her, but she must promise her to call her "aunt" before every one present at the wedding banquet on her marriage day. The maiden readily promised her to do so; after which the shirt appeared all at once ready made, and it was given to the king. On receiving the shirt the king said that he was not yet satisfied, and that the girl must prove herself more clever still. Upon which the grandmother told him that her granddaughter could hear anything that was said three leagues off. When the maiden knew of this she commenced to cry again, but the woman returned and informed her that if she promised to call her "aunt" on the day of the marriage, before every one, she would tell her what the king would say at the hunt he had gone to three leagues off. The girl promised to comply; and the woman shortly after came and informed her of what the king had said at the hunt. The grandmother then went to the king to tell him. But, as his majesty required yet more proofs of the maiden's extraordinary cleverness, the granny told him that her daughter was so quick at her work, that she could wind in half-an-hour a whole skein of thread. When the girl heard of this she began to weep, because she knew she was not able to do so. The woman, however, who always came to her help, returned once more and offered to do it for her if she complied with the usual promise; which the maiden readily agreed to, and immediately the skein appeared ready wound. The day of the marriage was at last fixed upon, and the king married the maiden. Whilst they were sitting at the banquet which was given on the occasion, a knock was suddenly heard at the door of the hall, and a woman entered who was exceedingly ugly and had very large prominent eyes. The maiden, now a queen, rose at once from the table, and addressed her in this way: "Good afternoon, aunt, give me your blessing!" Every one present was much surprised at what they saw and heard; but the ugly woman, turning towards the king, explained to him that the reason of her having such very large eyes came from straining them to make a shirt that could pass through the eye of a needle. After a while another knock was heard at the door, and in came another woman with exceeding large ears. The queen rose and saluted her thus, " Good afternoon, aunt, bestow me your blessing!" Every one present was much surprised, but the woman went up to the king and explained that her ears had become so exceedingly large from her constantly listening to what was said at the distance of three leagues. Not long after this a third knock was heard, and another woman entered who was very, very ugly, and had very long arms. The queen rose from the table and said to her, saluting her, " Good afternoon, aunt. bestow your blessing upon me." All the people were much astonished, but the woman told the king that she had such long arms because she had been obliged to wind a whole skein in half-an-hour. The king then rose and said to the queen that he did not require her to make the shirt, nor to hear what was said at the distance of three leagues, nor did he expect her to wind a whole skein of thread in half-an-hour. And thus it was that the maiden was saved from having to accomplish what her grandmother had told the king she was capable of doing.

XX.—The Cabbage Stalk.

There lived once a little maid who was the daughter of poor people. This girl had a cabbage which grew in her kitchen garden, and she was in the habit of watering it. The little maid was always watching the cabbage sprout to see when it would come to seed. One day she noticed that on the cabbage stalk there was formed a ladder by which one could descend into the ground. She went down these steps and quickly found herself in a splendid palace in which there was a table very well laid out, and a beautiful bed. The maid sat down at the table and partook of the good things laid upon it with avidity, and went up again along the cabbage stalk and returned home. Whenever she felt hungry she would secretly go down the steps on the cabbage stalk and feast upon the delicacies she found in the palace. The little maid was growing fat, much to the surprise of her father and mother, who never saw her eat anything. At night when her parents were gone to sleep she would very quietly descend the cabbage stalk, and lie down to sleep on a beautiful couch which she found prepared in the palace. The mother, who began to suspect her daughter, one night arose from her bed to follow her down the ladder. She watched and saw her daughter get upon her couch, in which there was a beast. The mother then lit a candle, went to the couch, and uncovered the bedclothes. Three drops of candle-grease fell upon the sleeping beast and immediately it became transformed into a prince. The prince then said to the mother: "You little know the harm you have done me! You have broken my spell, and now I cannot marry your daughter!" He then told the little maid to leave the palace, and gave her a rock of gold, a pair of iron shoes, and a staff, and said when the shoes were worn out to come again to see him in the palace. The little maid departed, and walked and walked on until at last the shoes began to wear out and she went about begging for alms. She met an old woman and she asked her to give her some things whilst she related her history to her. The old woman told her that she was no longer in time to marry the prince because there was a princess already in the palace who was destined for him. The old woman then gave her a rock of gold, a spinning-wheel, and a reel, and took leave of her, wishing her good luck. The maid arrived at the palace gate with her shoes and garments all torn, and begged for alms, and when the princess saw her standing on a rock of gold she sent to ask her for it. The maid replied that if she gave her the rock of gold she must allow her to go into the prince's chamber and sleep there one night, The princess would not consent, but the prince's mother told her to allow her to sleep at the prince's feet, for there was no fear that he would be aware of it, as she would take care to give him a sleeping-draught. And so it happened the maid went into the chamber to sleep without the prince knowing it, and during the night as she awoke she began to say—

"Prince of love
I have come many leagues,
To see thee, oh, my Lord!
My shoes are torn ··
My staff is travel-worn,
Yet here I am come back to thee!"

The prince made no reply to this, and as soon as the day dawned they sent her away; but the prince remained quite ignorant of her stay there. The maid, however, continued before the palace gate at her wheel spinning, and the princess seeing her sent to ask her for her spinning-wheel of gold. The maid replied that she would only give it to her on condition of her allowing her to remain and sleep in the prince's apartment another night. The princess consented, but made her promise to leave the chamber early in the morning. The maid entered and again settled herself to sleep at the prince's feet, and on awakening repeated her former appeal—

"Prince of love
I have come many leagues,
To see thee, oh, my Lord!
My shoes are torn—
My staff travel worn,
Yet here I am come back to thee.

To this the prince, as before, made no reply, for he was fast asleep. The maid again left the chamber very early; but a valet who appeared to occupy an apartment next to the prince told him what he had heard repeated during the night. The prince was much astonished to hear it, and swore he would not take the usual draught next evening as he retired to rest. Next day the princess saw the maid again at her work before the palace, and as she remarked she had a golden reel she went to ask her for it. The maid replied that she would on condition that the favour she had begged for on the previous evening should be granted her once more. To this the princess said she consented, and sent the prince the usual draught to take that night. But the prince made only a pretence to drink it, and threw it away, and then ordered his valet to leave the chamber. During the night the little maid repeated—

> " Prince of love
> I have come many leagues,
> To see thee, oh, my Lord !
> My shoes are torn—
> My staff travel worn,
> Yet here I am come back to thee !"

The moment the prince heard her he felt very pleased, but the next moment he was much distressed in his mind because he remembered that he was already engaged to be married to the princess. He told the little maid to remain and not to leave his chamber. And when the marriage day arrived he asked the princess's father to settle a question for him, which was this: that his apartment had two keys; the first had been mislaid and lost, but he ever had hopes of finding it: now that he had a new key which he had ordered to be made, the old one had appeared—which ought he, he therefore asked his majesty to advise him, to keep ? The king replied that in this case he advised him to retain the old one. The prince then recounted to his majesty the whole history of the little maid, and reminded him at the same time that *he* it was who had given the sentence. He married the little maid, and the princess went to another kingdom.

XXI.—The Seven Iron Slippers.

There lived once together a king and a queen, and a princess who was their daughter. The princess had worn out every evening seven pairs of slippers made of iron; and the king could not make out how that could be, though he was always trying to find out. The king at last issued a decree, that whosoever should be able to find out how the princess managed to wear out seven slippers made of iron in the short space of time between morning and evening, he would give the princess in marriage if he were a man, and if a woman he would marry her to a prince.

It happened that a soldier was walking along an open country road carrying on his back a sack of oranges, and he saw two men fighting and giving each other great blows. The soldier went up to them and asked them, " Oh, men, why are you giving each other such blows?" " Why indeed should it be!" they replied, "because our father is dead, and he has left us this cap, and we both wish to possess it." " Is it possible that for the sake of a cap you should be fighting?" inquired the soldier. The men then said, " The reason is that this cap has a charm, and if any one puts it on and says, " Cap, cover me so that no one shall see me! no one can see us." The soldier upon hearing this said to them, " I'll tell you what I can do for you; you let me remain here with the cap whilst I throw this orange to a great distance, and you run after it, and the one that shall pick it up first shall be the possessor of the cap." The men agreed to this, and the soldier threw the orange to a great distance, as far as he possibly could, whilst the men both ran to pick it up. Here the soldier without loss of time put on the cap saying, "Cap, make me invisible." When the men returned with the orange they could see nothing and nobody. The soldier went away with the cap, and further on he met on his road two other men fighting, and he said to them, "Oh, foolish men, why do you give each other such blows?" The men replied, "Indeed, you may well ask why, if it were not that father died and left us this pair of boots, and we, each of us, wish to be the sole possessor of them." The soldier replied, "Is it possible that for the matter of a pair of boots you should be fighting thus?" And they replying said, "It is because these boots are charmed, and when one wishes to go any distance he has only to say: 'Boots take me here or there,' wherever one should wish to go, and instantly they convey one to any place." The soldier said to them, "I will tell you what to do; I will throw an orange to a great distance, and you give me the boots to keep; you run for the orange, and the first who shall pick it up shall have the pair of boots." He threw the orange to a great distance and both men ran to catch it. Upon this the soldier said, "Cap, make me invisible, boots take me to the city!" and when the men returned they missed the boots, and the soldier, for he had gone away. He arrived at the capital and heard the decree read which the king had promulgated, and he began to consider what he had better do in this case. "With this cap, and with these boots I can surely find out what the princess does to wear out seven pairs of slippers made of iron in one night." He went and presented himself at the palace. When the king saw him he said, "Do you really know a way of finding out how the princess, my daughter, can wear out seven slippers in one night?" The soldier replied, "I only ask you to let me try..." "But you must remember," said the king, "that if at the end of three days you have not found out the mystery, I shall order you to be put to death." The soldier to this replied that he was prepared to take the consequences. The king ordered him to remain in the palace. Every attention was paid to all his wants and wishes, he had his meals with the king at the same table, and slept in the princess's room. But what did the princess do? She took him a beverage to his bedside and gave it to him to drink. This beverage was a sleeping draught which she gave him to make him sleep all night. Next morning the soldier had not seen the princess do anything, for he had slept very soundly the whole night. When he appeared at breakfast the king asked him, "Well, did you see anything?" " Your majesty must know that I have seen nothing whatever." The king said, " Look well what you are at, for now there only remains two days more for you, or else you die!" The soldier replied, " I have not the least misgivings." Night came on and the princess acted as before. Next morning the king asked him again at breakfast, " Well, have you seen anything last night?" The soldier replied, " Your majesty must know that I have seen nothing whatever." " Be careful, then, what you do, only one day more and you die!" The soldier replied, " I have no misgivings." He then began to think it over. " It is very curious that I should sleep all night—it cannot be from anything else but from drinking the beverage which the princess gives me. . . Leave me alone, I know what I shall do; when the princess brings me the cup I shall pretend to drink, but shall throw away the beverage." The night came and the princess did not fail to bring him the beverage to drink to his bedside. The soldier made a pretence to drink it, but instead threw it away, and feigned sleep though he was awake. In the middle of the night he saw the princess rise up, prepare to go out, and advance towards the door to leave. What did he do then? He put on the cap, drew on the boots, and said, " Cap make me invisible, boots take me wherever the princess goes."

The princess entered a carriage, and the soldier followed her into the carriage and accompanied her. He saw the carriage stop at the seashore. The princess then embarked on board a vessel decked with flags. The soldier on seeing this said, " Cap, cover me, that I may be invisible," and embarked with the princess. She reached the land of giants, and when on passing the first sentinel, he challenged her with " Who's there?" " The Princess of Harmony," she replied. The sentinel rejoined, " Pass with your suite." The princess looked behind her, and not seeing any one following her she said to herself, " The sentinel cannot be in his sound mind; he said 'pass with your suite;' I do not see any one." She reached the second sentinel, who cried out at the top of his voice, " Who's there?" " The Princess of Harmony," replied the princess. " Pass with your suite," said the sentinel. The princess was each time more and more astonished. She came to the third sentinel, who challenged her as the others had done, " Who's there?" " The Princess of Harmony " " Pass on with your suite," rejoined the sentinel. The princess as before wondered what the man could mean. After journeying for a long time the soldier who followed her closely saw the princess arrive at a beautiful palace, enter in, and go into a hall for dancing, where he saw many giants. The princess sat upon a seat by the side of her lover who was a giant. The soldier hid himself under their seat. The band struck up, and she rose to dance with the giant, and when she finished the dance she had her iron slippers all in pieces. She took them off and pushed them under her seat. The soldier immediately took possession of them and put them inside his sack. The princess again sat down to converse with her lover. The band again struck up some dance music and the princess rose to dance.

When she finished this dance another of her slippers had worn out. She took them off and left them under her seat. The soldier put these also into his sack. Finally, she danced seven times, and each time she danced she tore a pair of slippers made of iron. The soldier kept them all in his sack. After the ball the princess sat down to converse with her lover; and what did the soldier do? He turned their chairs over and threw them both on the middle of the floor. They were very much surprised and they searched everywhere and through all the houses and could find no one. The giants then looked out for a book of fates they had, wherein could be seen the course of the winds and other auguries peculiar to their race. They called in a black servant to read in the book and find out what was the matter. The soldier rose up from where he was and said, " Cap, make me invisible." He then gave the negro a slap on the face, the negro fell to the ground, while he took possession of the book and kept it. The time was approaching when the princess must depart and return home, and not being able to stay longer she went away. The soldier followed her and she returned by the same way she came. She went on board and when she reached the city the carriage was already waiting for her. The soldier then said, " Boots take me to the palace," and he arrived there, took off his clothes, and went to bed. When the princess arrived she found everything in her chamber just as she left it, and even found the soldier fast asleep. In the morning the king said, " Well, soldier, did you see anything remarkable last night?" " Be it known to your majesty that I saw nothing whatever last night," replied the soldier. The king then said, " According to what you say, I do not know if you are aware that you must die to-day." The soldier replied, " If it is so I must have patience, what else can I do?" When the princess heard this she rejoiced much. The king then ordered that everything for the execution should be prepared before the palace windows. When the soldier was proceeding to execution he asked the king to grant him a favour for the last time and to send for the princess so that she should be present. The king gave the desired permission, and the princess was present, when he said to her, "Is it true to say that the princess went out at midnight?" "It is not true," replied the princess. "Is it true to say," again asked the soldier, "that the princess entered a carriage, and afterwards went on board a vessel and proceeded to a ball given in the kingdom of the giants?" The princess replied, "It is not true." The soldier yet asked her another question, "Is it true that the princess tore seven pair of slippers during the seven times she danced?" and then he showed her the slippers. "There is no truth in all this," replied the princess. The soldier at last said to her, "Is it true to say that the princess at the end of the ball fell on the floor from her seat, and the giants had a book brought to them to see what bewitchery and magic pervaded and had taken possession of the house, and which book is here?" The princess now said, "It is so." The king was delighted at the discovery and happy ending of this affair, and the soldier came to live in the palace and married the princess.

XXII.—The Maiden from whose Head Pearls fell on combing herself.

There lived once a woman who had a son and a daughter. The son was a sailor. One day the mother, feeling very ill, and at death's door, called her daughter to her and said, "There, I give you this towel and comb; never use another towel but this

THE MAIDEN FROM WHOSE HEAD PEARLS FELL, ETC.

one to wipe yourself with, or other comb to smooth your hair with." After saying this she died. After her mother's death, the girl always complied with the injunction of her mother. Whenever she used the comb many seed pearls and large-sized ones fell from her head; and when she wiped herself with the towel the same thing happened always. The maiden related this to her brother, and he advised her to keep all the pearls that fell and string them up in bunches. The maiden then formed six bunches with the pearls she had, and the brother told her he would take and sell them to some king next voyage he should make. And so it happened that after a time he embarked, and on reaching a certain country he went to the palace to offer the six bunches of pearls for sale to the king. A servant appeared and offered to take them and show them to his majesty, but the sailor refused to allow him to do so, saying that he must himself present them to the king in person, in order to settle about the price. He entered the king's apartment, and his majesty found the pearls to be very precious and rare, and paid him a large sum for them, asking him where he had been to discover such a valuable article. The young man told his majesty everything, relating how his mother, when she was dying, gave his sister a towel and a comb, and that every time she combed herself or used the towel, many large pearls and a number of seed pearls fell from her head. The king said that he must bring his sister and present her to him, together with the towel and comb; and that if what he said was true, he would marry his sister; if it was all false, he should die.

The young sailor returned home happy and delighted, and gave his sister an account of what had occurred. The sister, very pleased at the result of his interwiew with the king, resolved to take the towel and the comb with her, and accompany her brother to the said country to marry the king. Before her departure she informed a neighbour of hers that she was going to be a queen. The neighbour asked her to do her a good turn, seeing that she was now going to be so rich and noble, and to allow her and daughter to go in her company.

The day arrived for the departure, and they all embarked; the maiden and brother, the neighbour and the daughter. When they were sailing far at sea the neighbour gave the maiden a drink to poison her. As the maiden became very ill, the brother, anxious for her safety, every day came to inquire how she was getting on. One day the neighbour gave her such a quantity of poison in the beverage that the maiden remained like one dead. The brother, believing that she was dead, had her corpse, with much grief, thrown into the sea, as was the custom. After that he began to lament, saying that he was very wretched and unfortunate now, as in his sister were centred his only hopes of advancing in life. The wily neighbour, hearing this, advised him to pass off her daughter as his sister to the king, and take her to the palace to present her. The brother replied, that the difficulty did not consist in that, but that he feared the towel and comb would not act with her as with his sister. They tested the girl, but no pearls or anything else ever fell when she made use of them. The neighbour then said that it was not to be expected that they would work there, but the moment they were in presence of the king the towel and comb would without a doubt work the miracle. They reached the said land, and they all three directed their steps to the palace. The young sailor presented his neighbour's daughter, the towel, and the comb to the king, saying she was his sister. The king ordered her at once to use the towel, but nothing fell. She combed herself with the comb, but instead of pearls, scurf fell from her head. The king being very angry, said to the sailor, " Then, you have deceived me. Now you must go to prison, and afterwards you shall be put to death." Just at this interval, a servant who had gone to the beach with his net to catch a fish for his majesty's service, on reaching the sea, saw a large whale which had been thrown on the beach and was dead. But inside the fish he saw something move, and heard a voice that said, " Take me out of this, take me out of this." The servant fetched a knife, and very carefully cut the skin of the whale, and he then saw the head of a maiden, and he continued to rip up the fish, greatly astonished at what he saw, and at last extricated alive the maiden from the belly of the great fish. He took her with him, but told her she must for the present remain shut up in a room of the palace, and let no one know that she was there. The maiden told him her history, and all that had happened to her during the voyage, and how she had been in the depth of the sea, and a whale had saved her. The servant, on his part, related to her what her neighbour had been at in the palace, presenting her daughter under false colours to the king, and all that followed; and he informed her that her brother was on her account imprisoned and sentenced to die. On reaching the palace the maiden was locked up in an apartment. She looked out of her window every day towards the prison door where her brother was detained, and on one occasion as she did so she saw a little bitch belonging to herself and her brother, and calling out to her pet she spoke to it thus: " Cylindra, tell me how my brother is to-day?" The bitch replied: " He is daily expecting to be sent to execution; and to-day is the first day the town crier publishes it." The next day the maiden again looked out of the window, and again asked her bitch: " Cylindra, tell me how my brother is to-day?" The bitch replied: " To-day the crier publishes his sentence of death for the second time!" But the servant who had delivered the maiden, on hearing this, went up to the king and revealed the whole plot against the maiden. The king, on hearing it, said: " If what you say be true, call me to-morrow when the maiden speaks to the dog, for I wish to listen to what she says." Next day, at the right time, the king stood close to the window of his chamber to observe and listen to the maiden. He heard her say: "Cylindra, how is my brother to-day?" The bitch replied: "To-day the execution is published for the last time!" When the king heard this, he ordered that the brother and sister should be brought before him into his presence; and on seeing the maiden he told her to wipe her face with the towel, and instantly that she did so showers of seed pearls began to fall from her head. He ordered her to comb herself with the wonderful comb, and immediately large and rare pearls fell in profusion of the same class as the ones in the bunches. The king then commanded the wily neighbour and daughter to be put to death, and he married the maiden. And the brother had the great honour to be brother-in-law to the king.

XXIII.—The Three Princes and the Maiden.

There was once three princes who were great friends. One day, as they walked out together, they saw a beautiful maiden looking out of a window, and they were all three, unknown to each other, struck and charmed with her loveliness; and one of them sought an occasion when he could go alone to ask her to name the hour when he should come to speak to her. The maiden told him to come at ten in the evening. The second prince came and begged of her the same favour, and she appointed him to come at eleven in the evening. The third prince also came and asked the same question and favour, and the maiden said that she would expect him at midnight.

At ten o'clock in the evening the first prince came to see her; at eleven the second prince arrived; and at midnight also came the third prince, and there he found the other two. " You are willing to speak to all three because you do not care for any." The maiden replied to him that she liked all three much. One of the princes then said that she could only marry one, and, therefore, that she should say which she would choose. The maiden again assured them that she did not make an exception, and that all three pleased her much. As the three princes were on the eve of undertaking a long journey, she at last decided that on their return they should all three bring her a keepsake, and that the one who should bring her the present she liked best, that one would she marry. They all three took leave of her, promising to bring the presents agreed upon. And when they had travelled for some distance came to a cross road, where they decided to part company, and at the end of their journey to meet again at the same spot. After this they each went their way. One of them arrived at a country where he saw many people going into a joiner's shop. He was much surprised at it, and he also went to see what was going on. He found that the excitement was created by no less a thing than a most marvellous looking-glass; that the moment it was told, " Looking-glass, I wish to see this or that person," they would immediately appear reflected upon it. The prince bought it at once, and, delighted at the discovery, said: " Now I have found, indeed, an excellent present to take to my sweetheart!" The second prince reached another country where he saw many persons meet to buy a candle. He asked why they were all so anxious to purchase such an indifferent article as a candle, and of so little value; but they informed him that the candle had a particular mysterious property, so that if any person was dead, and the candle was put in the dead person's hands, he would immediately come to life again. The moment the prince heard this he lost no time in buying it, and, much pleased, he said: " I have now found a valuable present for my lady-love." The third prince saw in another country a man who was selling wool rugs. This man asked a great sum for one in particular. The prince inquired the reason why he asked so much more money for one rug than he did for the others. The man replied that the particular rug had a distinct peculiarity from the others, which was, that if any one wished to undertake a journey he had only to open it out on the ground, stand upon it, and say to it: "Oh! rug, take me to such a country in an instant." The moment the prince knew of this, he bought it, and, in great glee at finding such a treasure, said, "Now, indeed, I have a present worthy to present to my sweetheart."

When the three princes met at the appointed road, they showed each other the presents which they had bought. The one of the looking-glass said to the other two friends: "I order the looking-glass to show me my lady-love." And as he said so they looked into the glass, and there saw the dead form of the maiden. The prince who had bought the candle said: "Oh! that we could place this candle in her dead hands, that so she may come to life!" The prince with the rug then added, laying open the rug on the ground: "Rug, take us all three in an instant to where she is!" In a moment the three princes found themselves by the side of the dead maiden. They placed the candle in her hands, and she instantly rose once more to life. They were all exceedingly delighted at the result, yet now each put forth his claims for the maiden. The prince to whom the candle belonged said, that if it not been for it she would never have risen again. The one who held the looking-glass urged that had he not seen her in the looking-glass they would never have known that she was dead. Whilst the prince who had the rug said, that had it not been for his rug they would not have found themselves there so quickly; and, compared to his rug, the other presents were useless. The maiden now came forward and said: "As you all three have a right to marry me, and as I cannot have three husbands at one time, I shall not marry any of you!" The maiden shut herself up in a tower; and the three princes, much disappointed and grieved, also retired into a dismal tower.

XXIV.—The Maiden and the Fish.

Once there was a widower who had three daughters. The two eldest thought of nothing but dress and finery, and going to amusements, or sitting at the window doing nothing; whilst the youngest occupied herself with the household management, and was fond of assisting the servant in the kitchen, and for which reason her sisters called her the "Hearth-Cat." One day the father caught a fish and brought it home alive, and as the youngest daughter was the one who occupied herself in cooking, and was besides his favourite child, he gave her the fish to prepare for their supper. As the fish was alive, and she took a great liking to it on account of its pretty yellow colour, she placed it in a large pan with water, and begged her father to allow her to keep it for herself, and not kill it. As soon as the father consented to her keeping it, she at once took it to her own room and gave it plenty of water to swim in; and when the sisters saw what had been done with the fish they began to cry out and complain that, for the sake of pleasing the "Hearth-Cat," they were to be deprived of eating that excellent fish.

At night, when the little maiden had already laid herself down to sleep, the fish began to say to her, "Oh! maiden, throw me into the well! Oh! maiden, throw me into the well!" The fish repeated this so often and so imploringly that at length she rose and threw the fish into the well. The following day she took a walk in the garden to try and see the fish, as she quite yearned to have a look at it once more; and as she drew close to

H

the well she heard a voice inside which said: "Oh! maiden, come into the well! Oh! maiden, come into the well!" She ran away with fear; but on the following day, when the sisters were gone to the festival, the maiden again approached the border of the well, and she heard once more the same voice calling for her, and, impelled by it, she went into the well; and she had hardly reached the bottom when the fish appeared to her, and, laying hold of her hand, he conducted her to a palace of gold and precious stones, and said to her: "Go into that chamber and attire yourself in the best and most elegant robe you find there, and put on a pair of gold slippers which are ready for you, as you will see, for I mean you to go to the same festival as your sisters are gone to. You will proceed to it in a splendid state carriage which you will find ready for you at the door when you leave this palace. At the conclusion of the festival be careful to take your departure before your sisters do, and return here to take off your robes, for I promise you that a time is in store for you when you will be very happy indeed." When the maiden had put on garments worked in gold and precious stones of very great value, she came out of the well, and on reaching the palace door she found a splendid carriage ready for her. She stepped in and proceeded to the festival. When she entered the edifice every one there was in admiration, and wondered from whence had come such a lovely, comely maiden with such rich robes. She left the edifice without loss of time the very moment that the festival was concluded; but in her hurry to get out she lost one of her slippers, and the king, who was following close behind her, picked it up, and ordered an edict to be issued that he would marry the maiden to whom that slipper belonged. When she reached home she went into the well at once to take off her rich garments, and when she left the enchanted palace the fish told her to return in the evening, for he wished to ask her something. The maiden promised to comply with his wish, and departed.

When her sisters returned home she was seen busy in the kitchen, and they gave her a glowing account of the beautiful lady they had seen at the feast, who had on such rich robes full of gold ornaments and precious stones such as they had never seen before in their lives, and how this fair and lovely maiden had dropped one of her dainty slippers in her hurry to leave the edifice, which the king had picked up, and now signified his intention of marrying the maiden to whom it belonged. They told her that such being the state of affairs, they would go to the palace to try the slipper, and were certain that it would fit one of them, who would then be made a queen! and then would she give the "Hearth-Cat" a new dress. The moment the sisters left for the palace the maiden went to the well to see the fish, who said to her the moment he saw her, " Oh, maiden! will you marry me?" The maiden replied, " I cannot possibly marry a fish!" but he so entreated her, and urged his suit so ardently, that she at last consented. That very instant the fish was transformed into a man, who said to her, " Know, then, that I am a prince who was enchanted here, and am the son of the sovereign who governs these realms. I know that my father has published an edict, ordering all the maidens of his kingdom to repair to the palace and try on the slipper which you dropped to-day on coming away from the feast; go, therefore, there yourself, and when the king tells you that you must marry him, inform him that you are already engaged to the prince, his son, who was enchanted, for his majesty will then send for me on hearing this." The maiden left the well, and shortly after her sisters returned from the palace looking very downcast and disappointed because the slipper after all did not fit them. The maiden then hinted to them that she also thought of repairing to the palace, to try on the slipper in case it should fit her. The sisters indignantly said: " Just see what airs the 'Hearth-Cat' is putting on, and is not ashamed of herself. Go, and show your tiny, dainty foot! go." The maiden went to the palace, nevertheless; and the sentinels, seeing her so shabbily dressed, would not let her pass; but the king, who just happened to be at the window, ordered them to let her enter. He had hardly given her the tiny slipper to try on when his majesty remained struck with wonder to see how soon she drew it on, and how beautifully the slipper fitted her, and he that moment told her that he would make her his queen. The maiden, however, very respectfully signified to him that it could not be as she was already engaged to be the bride of his majesty's son, the prince who had been spell-bound so long. The king, on hearing her, could scarcely contain his delight to think that he would soon see his son again, disenchanted as he was now. He immediately sent a retinue of the grandees of the realm to bring his son out of the well, and he married him to the beautiful maiden. There were great rejoicings and much feasting in honour of the occasion; and the sisters of the "Hearth-Cat," filled with jealousy and bitterness at the sudden turn of affairs, were punished, and commenced to throw all manner of filth out of their mouths. The "Hearth-Cat" remained in the palace the bride of the prince, who afterwards succeeded to the throne, and became king.

XXV.—The Slices of Fish.

There lived a man in a certain country who was a fisherman, and as he went fishing on one occasion he caught a beautiful fish. The poor fish finding itself caught and on dry land begged the fisherman to throw it back again into the sea, promising the man if he did so he would have a great catch of fish next time he went fishing. The fish added, however, that should the man succeed in securing it once more, he was then at liberty to keep it. The fisherman did so that day, and he took such a large haul of fish that he did not know what he should do with all the fish he had caught in his net. Several days after this the fisherman again let down his nets at the same place, and again caught the beautiful fish. The fish then said to the man: "Take me to your house and cut me into twelve slices, and three slices you will give your wife, three to your mare, three to your bitch, and the remaining three you must bury in your garden." The fisherman did as he was told, and when another year had passed his wife gave birth to three boys, the mare had three colts, the bitch three lions; and in the garden three lances had risen up. When these boys grew up to manhood they asked their father to give them each a horse, a lion, and a lance, for they wished to go travelling. The father and mother, much against their inclination, gave them leave to go, and the boys left home and proceeded all three along a road until they came to a part of the highway where three roads met. They separated, each taking a different road; the eldest brother went to the left, the second to the right, and the youngest took the middle road. But before parting they agreed to meet in that same spot in a year's time, and then each went his own way. The eldest brother after journeying for many days without arriving at any country, at last came to one where there was a very high tower. He remained at a house, where at the end of a week he married the owner of it; and when he was already married he asked his wife what tower that might be, and she informed him that it was the "Tower of Death," for whosoever went into it never returned alive. But the young man said: "Well, I shall go there, and I shall return." At night when he lay down to sleep he placed his lance between himself and his wife on the bed, and on the following day he went straight to the tower with his lion. He knocked at the gate and an old woman appeared, who asked him what he wanted, and he replied that he wished to see the tower. The old woman said that if he wished to inspect it he must first have a wrestling match with her, to which the young man agreed, and the woman asked him to fasten the lion with one of her hairs, as she was very much frightened of those animals. The young man said he would, and the old hag gave him one of her hairs, with which he secured the lion, after which he commenced to wrestle, until the youth finding that he was nearly overcome by the hag cried out to his lion: " Advance, my lion, to my assistance.! " And the old hag quickly said: "Be thickened, oh, my hair!" And as she repeated these words, the hair which kept the lion secure became a thick heavy chain. The old hag overcame the youth, and when she had him on the ground cut his head off and threw it into a subterranean cave and then entered the tower again.

After a year the two brothers met again at the spot agreed upon, and as the eldest brother had not arrived they waited for him some days, until finding that he did not come they went home, believing that he would meet them there; but as they did not find him with their parents, the second brother asked to be allowed to go in search of him. The father gave him the desired permission, and he started, following the same road as his eldest brother had taken. After travelling a few days he arrived in the same country and city, and he went to live in the same house, and married his brother's widow. And after the marriage he asked her if she could tell him positively if a man like him, having the same kind of horse and lion, and carrying a lance, had passed that way. The woman replied that a man had arrived about a year ago who had married her, and that next day he had gone to the "Tower of Death," that whoever went in it never returned, and that having gone he had never come back, as had already happened to many men like him. The young man then said, as others before him, " Well, I shall go, and I mean to return." At night he also placed the lance between himself and wife on lying down, and next day, early in the morning, he departed with his lion to the " Tower of Death." When he had knocked at the gate the same old woman appeared who had killed his brother, and she also wrestled with him, after making him first secure the lion with one of her hairs. When he found himself hard pressed he called out for his lion, saying, " Come to my help quickly, my lion!" but the old hag rejoined instantly, " Thicken, oh, my hair!" and knocking the boy down to the ground she cut his head off and threw it in the same cave underground where his eldest brother's body had been cast, and she went into the tower again.

A whole year had passed, and the youngest brother, finding that his elder brothers did not return, asked his father leave to go in search of them. The father replied, " Then you wish, my son, to leave me and remain away, dead or alive, as your brothers have done before you!" but the boy replied, " Let me go, father, and I promise you that I shall come back to you in a year's time with my two brothers, and bring much wealth with me!" The father consented, and he took the same road as the other two brothers; and he arrived at the said tower. He married the same woman that his brothers had, and he asked her if she would give him any information respecting the two men who must have passed that same way—one two years ago, and the other one year since. She replied that they had passed that way, and both had married her, and that on the following day each had in turn proceeded to the " Tower of Death," that who goes into it never returns alive, and thus had they remained there! When the youth heard this, he said resolutely, " Well, I also shall go, and I know that I shall surely return!" And having gone to rest that night with his lance lying on his bed ready by his side, he early next morning went on his way to the " Tower of Death," accompanied and protected by his lion. On arriving he knocked at the gate of the tower, and the old hag opened it for him. He said that he wished to see the tower, and she replied that he might enter, but he must first of all have a wrestling match with her. The youth consented to it, and the hag then asked him to secure the lion with one of her hairs first of all, as she had great fear of that race of beasts. The youth promised to do so, but instead of fastening the lion he threw the hair away over a wall, and when he found himself nearly overcome by the old hag, he called out for his lion saying, "Advance and come to my aid, oh lion!" while she instantly replied: "Be thickened, oh, my hair!" But as the lion was not tied up it sprang upon the old hag and laid her flat and helpless on the ground. The boy, perceiving that she lay powerless on the ground, was about to cut her head off, when she entreated him to spare her, for she would give up to him his two brothers, and would besides allow him to inspect the tower. The boy desisted from killing her, but left her pinned down by the lion whilst he went over the tower; and there he found three princesses who were enchanted in it. He brought them down, and, having done that, he commanded the hag to show him where his brothers were detained. The old woman lifted up the trapdoor and told him to go down the cave till he reached the bottom, and he would there find them. But the boy would not go alone and made her descend before him. When they reached the bottom he saw many dead bodies in heaps, the trunks on one side and the heads on another. When he saw that ghastly spectacle he said to the old hag, "How can you possibly give me back my brothers alive if their heads are cut off?" She answered him: "Go to the cupboard and bring a bowl you will find there full of ointment, rub their necks with it, and join the heads to the necks and they will be immediately cured; but I must make it a condition that you only anoint your dead brothers." The youth, however, insisted upon including all the bodies which were there; but as the old silly hag would not consent to it the boy killed her. He then went for the ointment and anointed the bodies and necks of all, and they rose up, and they went each to their respective countries. The youth and his brothers married the princesses they had found there, and proceeded each to their realms, not forgetting to take to their father and mother much wealth.

XXVI.—The Prince who had the head of a Horse.

There once lived a king and a queen who had been married many years, but had not any children. This was a great source of sorrow to them. The queen, however, took it to heart more than the king did, and one day, when she felt more sad and unhappy than usual, she prayed God to give her a son, even if he were born with the head of a horse. The first time that she went to the garden after this she met an exceedingly old woman, who said to her, "I know that you are sad and in trouble because you are childless, but I foretell you that you will in nine months' time bear a son; but how much better it would have been for you not to have such a son! because, instead of having a man's head, he will be born with the head of a horse." The queen was very sorry to hear this, but at the same time could not help rejoicing at the prospect of having a son born to her. Accordingly before long the queen felt she was with child, and in due time gave birth to a prince with the head of a horse. As the prince grew up those around him after a time became quite accustomed to the unusual appearance of his head, and even forgot that it was that of a horse. Having arrived at an age when his father thought it time to look out for a wife for him, he sent his portrait to all the cities in hopes that some princess might desire to marry him. But there was not one single princess who would entertain the idea, and all of them, when they saw his portrait, used to exclaim, " What, I marry a prince who has the head of a horse? After a time we should have children who would be altogether horses!" The prince was very unhappy, seeing that he could not succeed in getting a wife, but those near him told him, to console him, not to despair for he would be certain to find one. The king after a time resolved to make a proclamation with sound of trumpet that any maiden, rich or poor, who should be willing to marry the prince would receive a good dowry, a handsome trousseau, and the jewels appertaining to a princess. Still no maiden came forward to offer herself; until at last, after much trouble, and when they had almost lost all hopes of finding one, a very poor girl, with very shabby clothes on, offered herself, who on account of her extreme poverty was willing to marry the prince. This maiden had three sisters who, the moment they knew their sister's intention, began to abuse her, and even to beat her, saying to her, " You have no shame in you. We are older than you are and are very poor, but we would not deign to marry a prince who had the head of a horse!" The maiden, however, paid no attention to their abuse and allowed them to say all they liked, and insisted upon marrying the prince. The maiden had hardly made up her mind to marry the prince when there appeared to her robes and everything necessary for a princess to wear; and at the same time a proclamation was issued in the capital declaring the approaching marriage of the prince in three days' time, that great rejoicings would take place and many festivities before the day, among which there would be held some races. The prince went each day to visit the maiden, and on the last day, when the cavalcade was passing the house, behind them all there came a very handsome knight, who rode most magnificently. When the whole suite had passed by, while the maiden's sisters were looking out, one said to the other, "If our sister were at least to marry that handsome knight, who does nothing but look towards us!" And they commenced to abuse and beat her, saying, "You are going to marry a prince with the head of a horse merely to become a princess." The girl at last, being afraid of worse treatment at their hands, said to them, "Do not abuse me or beat me any more, for that knight who was going behind that retinue, and looked towards us, is the prince who I shall marry." At that instant a crow came in at the window and began to flap and beat the girl with its wings, saying, "You ungrateful girl! most ungrateful! You have broken my spell! and if you wish to find me again you will have to wear a pair of iron shoes on your way to the Crows' Tower; you will have to enter and wait a long time for an opportunity to lay hold of my wings, for only then shall I again be yours and you mine; and should you not have sufficient courage to undertake this task, and sufficient perseverance and patience to wait for your opportunity to catch me, you will never see me again!" Having said these words the crow flew out of the window, taking the same direction as when it came. The girl remained very much grieved and began to cry, saying, "I am now wretched and unhappy on account of my sisters!" She then ordered a pair of iron boots to be made, and when she received them she put them on at once and begun her journey without taking leave of any one. She walked and walked and walked all day, and at nightfall she saw a hut and approached it. The door was closed and she could see no one, but taking courage she knocked at the door. She heard the voice of an old woman reply, "Who is there?" The girl answered, "A poor helpless creature who begs for shelter to-night!" The old woman opened the door to her and listened to what the girl had to say in explanation to her, that she had lost her way and entreated her to afford her shelter for the night. The good old woman then said to her, "My son lives here with me who is the south wind, but I do not know what my son will do to you if he sees you." The girl to this replied: "Never mind, I must have patience, and if he kills me why there will be an end of me and that is all!" The old woman felt pity for the girl and said, "Get inside this wooden chest." The girl went inside and the woman fastened down the cover after the girl had told her the whole history of her life, and who begged the woman to ask her son the way to the "Crows' Tower;" and the old woman promised to find out for her where the tower was. The wooden chest was hardly closed upon her when a great noise of wind was heard, and the door moved as though great force was used to break it open. The woman opened the door and the south wind came in whistling softly vunuu .... vuuu .... vuuuu .... saying, "I smell human flesh!" The old woman rejoined: "My son be calm, there is no such thing here." As soon as the wind became lulled and quieted she informed him of what had occurred, and asked him whether he knew where the "Crows' Tower" was situated. The son replied: "I do not know where it is, but the north wind is sure to know," and he showed the girl where it was to be found, and said that since she had iron boots the only way to destroy them was by wetting them over, as otherwise she might walk for years and years and yet would never succeed in tearing them. After this the wind went to lie down, and at day dawn rose up and left the hut. He had hardly gone out when the old woman opened the chest and told the girl of all her son had said, and the information he had given for her guidance, and then she dismissed her. The girl thanked the old lady very much for her kindness to her, and set out on her expedition, remembering to wet the boots occasionally. She walked and walked and walked, and at nightfall she again saw another hut, and she resolved to knock at the door. She saw an old woman come to open to her, who told her that her son was the north wind. The girl asked to be allowed to remain there for the night, and begged she would ask her son where the "Crows' Tower" was situated, because she had been told that the north wind would know where it was. Shortly after this the north wind came in by the door, blowing strongly as it whistled vuuuu .... vuuuu .... and crying out with a shrill voice, "Mother I smell human blood." The mother replied, "Be calm, my son, it is nothing whatever." And she then told him of all that had passed since he had left home, and she asked him to inform the girl she had there where the "Crows' Tower" was situated as she wished to go to it. He replied, and told his mother that she must tell the girl that the north-east wind was sure to know, and that he himself was ignorant of its whereabouts. The wind departed, and the woman, uncovering the wooden chest, gave the girl all the information she had received from her son, and the injunction that she was not to forget to wet her boots over continually. She set out on her expedition at once, was mindful to wet her boots, and continually examined them to see if they were getting worn out; and at first she was much distressed because the boots did not seem to wear out, but after a while she was happier, for she saw them getting rusty. She walked all day, and only as night approached did she find another hut. She also knocked at the door of this hut, and an old woman appeared, who made the girl the same speech as the other had done. The girl entreated her to allow her to go in for the night, as she had nowhere to go, and begged the old woman kindly to ask her son, where the "Crows' Tower" was situated, and the way to reach it, as she had been informed that the north-east wind was the only wind that could tell her. The woman shut her up in the chest, and very soon after the north-east wind came in whistling; hoom . hoom ...... hoom .. "Oh! mother, I smell human flesh." "Oh no, my son, you make a mistake," was the mother's reply; and she told him to be quieted, for it was only a poor girl who wished to know the way to the " Crows' Tower." The north-east wind said he knew where it was, but that it lay very far indeed, and that the girl would have to walk for three nights and three days without resting to get there. He further told his mother that she must explain to the girl that when she reached the tower she would not be able to enter as there were a number of crows who would prevent her, because inside the tower there lived a prince who was spell-bound, and knew that the girl was seeking for him. That if she wished to find him she was to wait until the crows were all inside the tower, so that they should not peck at her and hurt her—that the largest crow among them was the prince himself; to get as close as possible to him and put her hands on his wings suddenly and not to leave go on any account; for if she lost him this time she would never find him again. After saying all this the north-east wind blew himself out of the hut. The girl began her journey, and for three days and three nights she walked without ever resting. The boots were already torn in several parts, and on the third day she could scarcely walk with them, as the sharp points pierced her feet. She at last reached the "Crows' Tower," and waited for an opportunity to enter. She gradually approached, keeping as close as she could to the largest crow, and at a moment when he was engaged in singing, and his mind was diverted from her, she suddenly and dexterously put both her hands upon the bird, holding its wings down, saying, "You are caught; you are now mine." The crow did its best to fly away, but remarking before long that it was his own maiden that held him, and had caught him, he transformed himself into a prince, without further resistance, the crows into noblemen and courtiers, and the tower into the court. The prince married the maiden, and the sisters, as a punishment, were imprisoned.

XXVII.—The Spider.

There lived once a boy whose father and mother were desirous that he should learn some trade. He had no wish to do so, but, as his parents insisted upon it, he undertook to learn the trade of a shoemaker. But as soon as the father died he desisted from work and gave up making shoes. The mother was very angry with him for this and turned him out of doors. The boy told his mother that he would be sure to return home a rich man some day, and that he meant to marry the first female he met on his way. He took a basket with all his shoemaker's tools and went away. He journeyed many leagues through some forest and overgrown places, and meeting with a large square stone on his way he sat upon it, took out a loaf from his basket, and began to eat. From under the stone a large spider came out, and the boy had hardly seen her when he said to her, " You shall be my wife." The spider upon hearing this crawled inside the basket, but the boy made a hole in the loaf he carried and put her in it. He walked and he walked, and he sighted at a great distance an old house. He entered it, placed the basket on the floor, and the spider came out of it and went crawling up the walls until she reached the ceiling, and commenced to make a web. The boy turned towards her and looking up said, " That is the way I like to see women, fond of work." The spider made no answer. The boy then went seeking for work at a neighbouring village. As it happened that in that village there were no shoemakers he was welcomed among them, and they gave him plenty of work to do. As the youth found that he was making a fortune he engaged a servant-maid to attend upon his wife, and brought her to the old house where the spider had remained. He furnished the house and bought a little clay stove and some plates and dishes for the dinner. He then went out and left the servant with the spider. The maid remained much astonished, and wondered still more when the spider told her to open a certain door which led to the fowl-house and kill a chicken, and afterwards to open a cupboard where she would find everything necessary for cooking and for the general use of the house. When the youth returned home he found the house swept and a dinner prepared of the best and most delicious viands. Being very pleased, he turned round to the spider and said, "See what a good choice I have made in my wife!" The spider from the ceiling threw down all manner of embroidered stuffs which she had worked for beautifying her house: and after they had lived in this way a whole year, and the youth had already become very rich, and no longer required to work at his trade, for everything he required in the way of clothing and food and everything else necessary for life always made its appearance without his knowing how, he resolved to return to his mother's house as he had promised her he would do at the end of a year. He ordered two horses to be saddled and got ready, and said to his servant, "You shall now act as my wife, because I am going to tell my mother that I am married." The maid was delighted at this and mounted the horse prepared for her and went with the youth. The spider came down from the ceiling and went to the fowl-house where she only found a cock left. She got inside it, and thus went walking behind the two on horseback. On reaching the forest they entered it, and both sat on the same stone, from under which the spider had come out before. They were looking on the ground when they saw the cock and heard it crow·

"Ki kiri ki,
Ki kiri kioh!
Here is the king,
And I am the queen oh!"

At that moment the stone broke open in two parts, and became transformed into a splendid palace. The spider was turned into a beautiful princess and married the youth, who became king and she a queen. They then sent for the mother; while the servant-maid continued with them as lady in waiting.

XXVIII.—The Little Tick.

There were once two brothers and a sister who lived together, and, being poor people, the brothers one day apprised their sister that they intended going to travel to try and seek fortune. The sister requested them to return in a year's time to see her. They journeyed on through a straight and long road, and they came to a spot where there were two narrow paths. They took leave of one another and separated, saying that in a year's time they would meet in that same place, and they took each a different turning. The eldest went to a farm where he engaged himself as labourer. The youngest brother travelled until he sighted a very old palace, and, as he had nowhere to go to for the night, he entered it and found that it was a most beautiful place inside although it was deserted. He wished to sup and instantly a table on which was laid an excellent supper made its appearance. After supper a good bed appeared for him to take his rest. When he fell asleep he was suddenly awakened by feeling something coming in contact with him on the bed, which felt very cold and clammy. The first night he was much frightened by this, but he soon became accustomed to the sensation, and lost all fear; and every night that same object came into his bed and held a long conversation with him. When a year had passed, he told the unknown object that he must go to meet his brother, for them both to return to their own country as agreed upon. The object told him that he might, and on the following night presented him with a complete suit of clothes, some money, and a horse. The young man departed and journeyed on until he reached the place agreed upon to meet his brother. He found that his brother had his hands rough and horny from hard work, whilst his own hands were smooth and white because he had done no work during the whole of that year. They went home and their sister was delighted to see them back again. When they were again leaving home she gave each of them a pound weight of flax, telling them that in a year's time they must return bringing it spun. The brothers took leave of one another and each went his way. When the youngest arrived at the palace, he told the unknown object that always came into his bed every night, and which proved to be nothing else but a tick, that his sister had given him so much flax which she had ordered him to take spun to her in a year's time. The tick made very light of the work, and merely remarked that it was a very easy task indeed and he need not be troubled about doing it so soon. When the year had nearly expired he asked her for it so as to spin it in time to take it home; and that instant the tick produced the flax beautifully spun and ready packed to take with him: and she gave him also another suit of clothes, money, and a horse, and the youth left the palace to go and meet his brother. The brother was carrying the flax in his hand very badly spun and carelessly folded, and it was of a very ugly yellow colour. He asked his brother—" Where is your flax for I do not see it?" And great was his surprise when he saw that he carried it in a little dainty basket. When the two brothers arrived at the sister's house she was very much surprised to find that one of her brothers brought his pound of flax very badly and loosely spun, whilst the other brought it so well spun and so neatly packed. On the brothers' departure she gave them each a puppy to take with them and to bring up. They took leave of each other for a year, and separated. When the youngest brother arrived at the palace the tick was much surprised that he should have brought her a puppy to bring up. She took it out of sight and he never saw it again until at the end of the appointed time, when she brought it to him in a little basket very comfortably packed ready to carry home. The brothers met at the usual rendezvous, and the eldest brother made his appearance with a very large powerful dog, which followed him. When they reached home the sister was delighted that they brought back the dogs; and she told them that next time on their return in a year's time they must each bring a wife, as she wished to see her sisters-in-law. The eldest brother told her that he was engaged to be married to his master's daughter; but the youngest did not know what to say about it, as he only knew the tick. They took leave of each other, and each went his way. The youngest brother reached the palace, and told the tick what the sister expected him to do. The tick then asked him if he would like to marry her; but he replied, "You are so very small." The tick rejoined that he need not be troubled about that. At the end of a year the youth felt much ashamed to have to take to wife this little tick. On the marriage-day the palace appeared in great splendour, with a number of pages, ladies in waiting, and the tick transformed into a most beautiful princess dressed as a bride. The carriages were ready for them, and they proceeded to their sister's country; and a state carriage and horses also went in the procession for his brother and his bride. When the procession reached the place of meeting the brother was there with a countrywoman of the Lisbon suburbs, who wore short petticoats. They entered the carriage, and they all arrived at the sister's house in much pomp. The two brothers were then married, and they afterwards returned to the palace of the tick, who was an enchanted princess; and they all lived very happily together.

XXIX.—The Three Little Blue Stones.

There was once a king who was married, but had taken a great dislike to his queen because they had no family. The queen for this reason was always in great distress of mind, and often prayed to God to give her at least a son. Soon after she found herself with child, and when her hour had arrived and she was on the point of being delivered a poor man came to the palace gate begging for alms. The lady in waiting refused to give him anything, and the beggar said that he knew she refused him then because the queen was in labour and about to give birth to a girl; but he would foretell her that at the age of fifteen a large bird would come and take the girl away in his beak. The lady in waiting went in, but told no one what she had heard. All the inmates of the palace were rejoicing, and fondled and caressed the little princess, and kissed her often, but this lady was the only one who wept when she did so, which surprised every one, and they asked her why she wept. The lady in waiting at first did not wish to state her reason, but in the end she related what had passed between her and the beggar, and how he had said that, when the little princess should arrive at the age of fifteen, a bird would come and carry her away in his beak. On hearing this every one in the palace felt much distressed and grieved. As the princess grew up her chief amusement was to play with a table placed in the centre of a garden. A certain prince having arrived at the palace one day to pay his respects to the king, saw the little princess, and was charmed with her pretty ways, and he gave her as he was going away three little blue stones as a keepsake and remembrance. In the course of time the princess attained her fifteenth year, and the period had arrived for the accomplishment of the prophesy respecting her fate. The child never went out anywhere and did nothing but play with the little blue stones on the table.

One day the king and queen left the palace to travel, and the child remained alone under the care of the lady in waiting. She was amusing herself playing in the garden when a large bird flew close to her and asked her when would she prefer to go through and accomplish her destiny, in youth or in old age. The lady in waiting advised her to say that she would prefer it in her youth rather than in her old age. The bird then instantly laid hold of the little princess with his beak and flew away with her. The bird took her through the air and left her alone in a great and dense forest. When she had been there one night and a day she began to weep because she felt very hungry and cold. There was a city near this forest to which a certain prince was in the habit of going once a month to hunt in the neighbourhood. It so happened that on this same day the prince came to hunt in the forest, and as he was traversing it he heard what appeared to him suppressed sobbing. He asked his chamberlain to accompany him, and went searching until he came upon the princess. He was delighted to find her, and he put her upon his horse and took her to the palace, and then locked her up in a room without any one knowing it. But the queen, suspecting the prince because he was always in that room, waited until one day when the prince had gone out, and opened the door to see what was there, and found the princess in the chamber. She scolded the prince very much for his conduct when she saw him, but he begged her not to illtreat the princess. Neither the queen his mother nor his sister liked the princess in the least, but she continued to live in the palace. One day she found herself with child, and gave birth to a boy, just at the time when the prince had been obliged to take a journey. The queen took up the child and cut off one of his little fingers, rubbed the princess's lips with the blood from it, and putting the child in a basket ordered it to be thrown into the sea. When the prince returned the queen told him that the princess had eaten up the child. The prince went up close to her and asked thus: " Then you ungrateful girl, you have had a boy, and you have eaten it up?" The answer she gave was to tell him that she prayed God to discover the truth. The prince then said to her, that, if such a thing should happen to her a second time, he would kill her. After the lapse of some time the princess again found herself with child, and when her hour had come the prince as before was obliged to go on a journey, and the poor princess gave birth to another boy. The child was hardly born when the queen laid hold of it and cut its little finger off and smeared the princess's lips with the blood from it, and placing the child in a basket consigned it to the waves. When the prince came home she told him the same story concerning her child. The prince went to the princess and said as before, " So you have again eaten up your child, as I have been told; you are an ungrateful creature!" But she gave him no other answer but that she prayed God to discover the truth. The prince said then that he would forgive her only once more, but if that happened to her again he would certainly kill her. Some time elapsed and the princess again found herself with child, and when her hour had arrived the prince had to take another journey, and the princess gave birth to another boy. The queen that moment took up the child and cut its little finger off and placed it in a basket and ordered the child to be thrown into the sea. The prince returned home, and the queen, who had smeared the princess's lips with the child's blood, told her son that she had demolished her child. The prince, being exasperated and growing very angry, went up to the princess, scolded her, and ordered her to he buried up to her waist in a small courtyard leading to the principal staircase; and every one that passed her was to beat her.

The princess had already been sometime undergoing her punishment when she heard it said that the prince was starting for the fair which was to take place at some distance where he would have to pass her father's house, so she entreated him to bring her from the fair a knife, and, as he had to pass by her father's palace, to go in and ask his majesty to allow her to have the three blue stones she had left in the drawer of the table she had in the garden, and to bring them to her. She begged him not to forget to do this as it was the last thing she would ask him to do for her. The prince went to the fair and complied with her request. He arrived at the palace and asked to see the king, and he began by making up a story saying that he had heard a voice on the way, and that voice had told him to come to the palace and take away with him three blue stones that were in a drawer of a table in the garden. The king on hearing this recollected that it could only be his daughter that knew of their existence, and the king, being very pleased to come across any one who knew of her, asked him how she was, and told him that since the bird had carried the princess in his beak the garden had been converted into a wilderness, full of serpents and wild beasts, and was dangerous for any one to attempt to enter it. A servant then came up and offered to go into it and look for the blue stones, provided the king allowed him to have a large pair of boots, a sword, and a weeding-hook. And having had permission given to him the servant went in, cutting down and felling trees and weeding the brambles in his path; and as he proceeded serpents came in his way which he killed with his sword; and he was thus able to reach the table, and brought away the three little blue stones, which were the three boys the princess had given birth to. The king then gave up the stones to the prince, and told him that if in a month's time he did not bring back his daughter he would put him to death. The king wanted to accompany the prince, for he had a great desire to see his daughter once more, but the prince pretended that he had to take a journey to a distant part before returning home, and this he said because he did not wish the king to know the disgrace he had put her to. The prince took leave of the king and made haste to reach his palace, and the moment he arrived he gave the princess the knife and the three little blue stones. He then hid himself to see what she would do. The princess placed the three stones before her, and asked the first stone, "Do you remember, little blue stone, that when I gave birth to a child the queen cut his little finger off, rubbed my lips with the blood that came from it, and then told the prince that I had eaten it up, and how she afterward placed it in a basket and had it thrown into the sea?" And the stones then commenced to beat against each other making a noise: *Tlin tin tin*, and said that what the princess stated was quite true. The princess then asked the second little stone if it remembered what the queen had done to her second child born to her, relating all that had passed; and the little stones again commenced to beat one against the other, *Tlin tin tin*, and said that what the princess related was the truth. The princess then once more asked the third blue stone if it recollected the treatment inflicted on her third child, and how the queen had drowned it and said that she had eaten it up; and the little blue stones recommenced to beat against each other, *Tlin tin tin*, and saying that it was perfectly true all that the princess had stated. When she had finished asking the three questions she took hold of the knife, saying, "Now I shall put an end to my sufferings and cut my head off." When the prince heard her say this he ran to prevent her killing herself. He instantly lifted her out of the pit she was in, and took her to his chamber. He then called up the servant who had thrown the three children into the sea, and asked him if it was true what the princess said, and the servant owned to the truth of it; and the prince immediately had him put in prison, and he placed the queen and his sister in a tower; and when the princess had quite recovered from the effects of the illtreatment she had undergone the prince and the princess each mounted a horse and rode to her father's house. On arriving at the palace the king and queen could not contain their delight, and seemed perfectly mad with joy to see their long-lost darling daughter again. There were great rejoicings, and at the end of a fortnight the prince married the princess. And as the king had no other child he asked them to remain in the palace, where they lived very happily.

XXX.—The Hind of the Golden Apple.

There once lived a woman who had a son, and they were so poor that the boy went every day for wood to burn in the pine forest. One day when he was in the forest he saw a hind, which was very small and most beautiful, come towards him with a golden apple hanging from its neck. The pretty hind commenced to speak to the boy to know what he was doing there, and after a while she asked him: " Would you like to come with me to see my lair? If you do I will give you so much money!" The youth then heard a voice say: " Do not accept anything from her!" And he therefore replied to the hind that he did not want anything. The hind again said to him: " Come to my lair, oh youth, and I will give you much money, and I can make you very happy indeed!" The voice again said: " Do not on any account accept anything, but tell her you would like to have the golden apple that hangs from her neck." The youth followed the advice given, and said to the hind, " The only thing I wish to have is the golden apple you possess; I desire nothing else." The hind gave it to him as she said, " Here, take it then !" The boy took it and divided it in two, and instantly four giants came out, who said to him, " What is it you want?" " Well, I should very much wish to have all this wood taken to my mother's house until she had more than she wanted or knew where to store it." The youth again opened the apple and the giants appeared as before and asked him, " What can we do for you?" " I want a palace with a princess in it, and everything requisite." The giants at once set to, forming a magnificent palace, and a most comely princess was waiting for him inside; and the youth took possession of it and went to live in it.

There was a man who, seeing the youth's wealth and good fortune, was envious of him, and one day spoke to a witch he knew to ask her to devise some means by which she could take away the apple from the youth. The witch so managed it that she succeeded in taking it away from him; and instantly everything disappeared, and the palace was changed into a beach; and the princess and the youth were seen without a rag of clothes upon them in the midst of the beach. They began to cry and bewail their unfortunate existence. The boy, however, after a while looking about him, said to the princess: " You had better go to your father's house and I will remain here." The princess returned home, and the youth then began to saunter about the beech in an aimless manner, and he met a little old lady, who was the Virgin; but he did not know her. Our Lady asked him, " Where are you going to?" " I'm only loitering because I do not know what to do." She then said, " Well, listen to me; before many minutes have elapsed you will find a number of cats, who are very fat and sleek, but do not lay hold of any except the one that is covered with sores, and in a dreadful state, and that one you must take with you." The youth walked along and soon saw a quantity of fine-looking cats, but he left them alone; but after a while he saw one very thin and in a wretched condition. He took it up by the neck and went away with it. He walked on further along the beach and he saw a ship and went on board. The man who had stolen the apple, seeing the youth in the ship, had him apprehended and shut up in a tower. The youth took the cat with him to the tower. The man who provided him with food only gave him a bean each day, and the boy eat half and gave the other half to the cat; whilst the cat hunted for mice and rats, of which it caught many, laid them down before the youth, eat half of them up, and gave him the other half. One day, as the cat was peeping slyly through a chink watching for game, she saw a piece of paper folded. She commenced to mew desperately, calling the youth. He went to see what ailed her, and found a letter there from the king of the rats, asking him what he could do for him, so that the cat in recompense for his services should leave the rats in peace, and not catch any more. The youth sent to say that the only way that the king could serve him would be by trying to get the apple for him which had been stolen from him. The king of the rats formed his subjects into an army, and went to the place where the golden apple was to be found. The man had the apple hanging from his neck. The rats set to work with much prudence and caution, and waited until the man was asleep, and arranged themselves each side of the sleeping man, ready to act. One of the rats then began to tickle the man's nose, and to stop his breath with its tail; and the man awoke, feeling stifled, and he then raised his head. The rats, who were ready to take advantage of the first occasion, on seeing the man raise his head, took off the chain with the apple from his neck, and carried it off in triumph to their king, who himself took it to the youth in the tower. The moment the cat saw the apple coming she began to mew out, loudly calling the youth to come. He came and took possession of it once more in great delight. He opened it, and forthwith the giants came out of it, who said, "What do you want us to do?" And the youth replied, "I want a palace, and my princess back in it." Instantly everything came back as before. The youth went to the king, and asked his majesty to order the man who had robbed him of his golden apple to be put to death; and he ever after lived happily with the princess.

RESEARCHES
RESPECTING THE BOOK OF SINDIBÀD.

RESEARCHES

RESPECTING THE

BOOK OF SINDIBÂD.

BY

DOMENICO COMPARETTI.

London
PUBLISHED FOR THE FOLK-LORE SOCIETY
BY
ELLIOT STOCK, 62, PATERNOSTER ROW, E.C.
1882.

CONTENTS.

	PAGE
PREFACE	vii
INTRODUCTION	v
CHAP. I.—FORM AND CONTENTS OF THE STORY IN THE BOOK OF SINDIBAD	10
,, II.—OF THE TALES CONTAINED IN THE VARIOUS VERSIONS	24
,, III.—CONCERNING THE EIGHTH NIGHT OF THE TUTI-NAMEH OF NACHSCHEBI, AND THE SECOND TALES OF THE VIZIERS IN THE BOOK OF SINDIBAD	37
,, IV.—UPON THE AGE OF THE SYNTIPAS AND OF THE HEBREW VERSION	53
LIBRO DE LOS ENGANNOS	71
BOOK OF THE DECEITS AND TRICKS OF WOMEN	115
INDEX	165

PREFACE.

IT is well known what a prominent place belongs to the *Book of Sindibâd* (or, in its European name, *Book of the Seven Sages*) in the history of popular literature. During a certain time the best authority on this book was Loiseleur Deslongchamps's *Essai sur les Fables Indiennes*, published in 1838. Our knowledge of mediæval and Oriental literature and folklore is now so much increased and improved that Loiseleur's work has become almost useless, especially after Benfey's work on the *Pancatantra* and Comparetti's *Ricerche intorno al Libro di Sindibâd*, whose conclusions are commonly approved and accepted. Professor Comparetti's work having been published in the *Transactions* of the Istituto Lombardo for 1869, and only a few separate copies given to the trade, a wish was expressed by several scholars in France and Germany as well as in England that it should be rendered more accessible to the general body of folk-lore students; and the Folk-Lore Society willingly accepted Mr. Coote's proposal to publish an English translation of it. This labour was undertaken by Mr. Coote himself with the help of the author, who revised it, and wrote a few additional notes to his text. The early Spanish language not being known to all folk-lore students, it was thought useful to give a translation of the important old Spanish text published by Professor Comparetti for the first time.

The absence of such a translation in the Italian edition had been already deplored. Mr. Coote did his best to overcome the difficulties which this task presented, due to the corrupt state of the Spanish text, and to this being itself a translation, very imperfect in some passages, from the Arabic.

The sad illness which overtook Mr. Coote before he had revised his translation caused some considerable delay in the publication, but through the unwearied labours and prompt and valuable assistance of Professor Comparetti, who has kindly read all the sheets, the Council has been able to complete the task of publication. Since Mr. Coote has once more been able to resume his interest in the work of our Society—and it is a deep and abiding interest—he has been constant in the expression of his desire to see this translation worthy of the learned and instructive original; and as no labour or trouble has been spared in endeavouring to obtain this object, it is hoped that it may be considered in some degree to merit its position. I am sure the members of the Society will appreciate the labours, as they have already done the kindness and learning, of Mr. Coote, who has been one of the mainstays of the Society from the commencement, and from whom I still continue to receive every assistance within his power.

G. LAURENCE GOMME.

2, Park Villas, Lonsdale Road, Barnes, S.W.
June, 1882.

RESEARCHES

RESPECTING THE

BOOK OF SINDIBÂD.

INTRODUCTION.

THAT family of popular books which has for its common basis the tale of the Seven Sages divides itself into two principal groups, the Eastern and the Western. To the first belong all the texts in Eastern languages, and also some in European languages; the latter, however, springing from Oriental texts, which they represent as more or less free translations. To the other belong the *Dolopathos*, the *Historia Septem Sapientum*, the *Erasto*, and other numerous texts of the various European literatures of the Middle Ages, all resembling one or other of those already cited. These two groups represent two profoundly different phases in the history of that ancient Indian book from which the one and the other proceed. In the midst of their many divergences, the Oriental texts have so many common elements, that, comparing them one with the other, there may be recognized in them collectively the form and sometimes the words of a *book* which is the common basis of all. So soon, however, as the Western texts are placed side by side with the former, a distinction is at once seen, and all those more special and minute points of contact that unite the various Oriental texts with each other disappear almost completely. The relationship between the two groups, and even more precisely the actual derivation of the Western from the Eastern, are easily recognizable; but it is impossible, as in the Eastern versions, to trace out and identify any one particular book as the original. There is no Eastern version which differs so much from the others as the whole Western group differs from the Eastern group, whether it be in the form of the fundamental story or in the tales inserted in it, of which scarcely four are common to both groups. It is all very well to attempt to assimilate these Western texts with one or another of the Eastern texts, as Loiseleur and others have done. The profound differences in question will never be explained by the supposition of intermediate links having been lost, so long as the remark is applied to written versions. Only oral tradition transmutes the contents of a popular book in that manner, and it is that certainly which stands between the Eastern and the Western groups. It should be remarked that the Western texts have given rise also to oral traditions, and from these certainly proceeds the tradition which has been found still existing in the mouth of the people in Hungary.* However evident be the derivation of the latter from the Western texts, yet the variation is such that if we were still in the Middle Ages, and a monk or a minstrel got hold of it, and, completing it out of his own head, should make a book of examples or tales out of it, this book would differ as much from all the Western texts as they do from the Eastern.

The Western versions are, therefore, secondary offshoots of the ancient Indian book. They belong, in fact, to this family, and have a place in its history; but of it they

* Stier, *Ungarische Volksmärchen*, p. 113, *et seq.*

represent a more distant and separate, and almost posthumous, phase. To this species of isolation it is attributable that the numerous writings which have been published in various countries upon the subject of these Western versions, and the numerous texts brought to light, all belonging to this group, have so little illustrated the other group, which bears within itself the most important part of the history of the *Sindibâd*. To this Eastern group no one has devoted any special study since the few remarks which Loiseleur made upon it in 1838. Besides all that could be observed upon Loiseleur's book, the age itself in which it was published is indeed a mark of its insufficiency. Since that epoch more than one Oriental text of the *Sindibâd* that had remained unknown has been brought to light; several Eastern collections of tales have been published and illustrated; and, in general, researches upon the relations between the popular stories of Europe and the East have made notable progress, of which Benfey's beautiful work upon the *Pancatantra*, which for these stories may be said to be fundamental, is a bright example, and, indeed, Benfey is the only one to whom we are indebted for any serious research upon the *Sindibâd*. Besides the light which his introduction to the *Pancatantra* diffuses upon a great number of tales contained in the Eastern and in the Western versions, Benfey has contributed to disperse somewhat the mist that envelopes the origin of the *Sindibâd*, and to elucidate its Indian and Buddhistic origin, in a separate work of much interest, which I shall more than once have occasion to cite.* But the more essential

---

* *Einige Bemerkungen über das Indische Original der zum Kreise der Sieben Weisen Meister gehörigen schriften*, in *Mélanges Asiatiques tirés du Bulletin Hist. Philog. de l'Acad. Imp. des Sciences de St. Pétersbourg*, vol. iii. (1858), p. 188, *et seq.* See also *Orient und Occident*, iii. p. 177.

investigation which shall serve as a foundation for the others has not yet been made. The various Oriental texts which we possess belong to different epochs and literatures; evidently they all spring, though not immediately, from a common text, of which, however, none of them can be said to be an entirely faithful translation. From a comparison of them it clearly appears that in all, in different ways and in different degrees, there have been suppressions, additions, and changes, as well in the principal story as in the number, in the order, and in the nature of the inserted tales. The first thing to be done, therefore, is to inquire what are the original elements in the Eastern versions at present known, what those which are due to the caprice of each author; to put together all that, from a comparison of the various versions, can be judged to belong to that more ancient text which is the common basis of all; to discover what in this was the form of the principal story, what and how arranged were the tales inserted in it. When this has been done it will be necessary to see to what age this ancient text goes back.

It is known, indeed, that the most ancient mention of a *Book of Sindibâd* is found in Arabian writers of the tenth century. Everybody will see that for the history of the *Sindibâd* it is most important to know what were the form and the contents of the book at that epoch. It would be a result of no small importance if from a chronological inquiry respecting the age, still unknown, of some version evidently more ancient, it should come to be known that this particular text from which all are derived, and of which it has been settled what are the contents, is of an age at any rate not posterior to the tenth century. Such is the scope of these my researches, the results of which I propose to lay before the reader.

THE BOOK OF SINDIBAD. 5

From what I have said the reader will understand what I mean by the *Book of Sindibâd*. In speaking of this, or designating it as the *ancient*, the *original* text, &c., my meaning is not to allude to the ancient Indian prototype, to which I do not extend my researches, but only to that particular redaction which can be shown to be more immediately the common basis of all the Eastern versions at present known. These versions are as follows :—

1. The *Syntipas*, a Greek text translated from the Syriac by Michael Andreopulos, during the last years of the eleventh century, as I shall show in its place. The Syriac version, as is said in the prologue of the Syrian translator, mentioned by the Greek, was made from a text (very probably Arabic) of which the Persian Musa was the author. The Greek text exists in several manuscripts, two of which are in the Imperial Library of Paris. Upon these is founded the edition of Boissonade. A Syriac text has been found recently by Rödiger ; it is, however, still inedited, with the exception of a tale published in the second edition of the *Chrestomathia Syriaca* of Rödiger (Halle, 1868), p. 100, *et seq.**

2. The Hebrew version, entitled *Parables of Sandabar* (Mischlè Sandabar), translated from the Arabic: of unknown age, but, as we shall see, probably of the first half of the

---

[* The Syriac text has been since published with a German translation by Dr. Baethgen : *Sindban, oder die Sieben Weisen Meister, Syrisch und Deutsch,* von Fried. Baethgen, Leipzig, 1879. See upon this publication the learned and important paper, written by Th. Nöldeke, in the *Zeitschrift der Deutsch. Morgenl. Gesellsch.*, vol. xxxiii. pp. 513-536. Since the publication of my own work a good critical edition also of the *Syntipas* has seen the light, through the labours of Dr. A. Eberhard, in the first volume of the collection *Fabulæ Romanenses Græce conscriptæ ex recensione et cum adnotationibus Alfred. Eberhardi*, Lipsiæ (Teubner), 1872.]

thirteenth century. Translated into German by Sengelman,* into French by Carmoly.†

3. The *Sindibâd-nâmeh*, an inedited Persian poem, written in 1375. The author had before him a Persian text in prose, translated from the Arabic. The only manuscript known, existing in the Library of the East India Company in London, is injured and imperfect. The contents of this version are known from an abstract given of it by Forbes Falconer in 1841,‡ reproduced somewhat inexactly in French in the *Revue Britannique* of 1842 (May, June).

I possess only this French reproduction, not having been able, in spite of every endeavour, to procure the work of Mr. Falconer. Professor Benfey has kindly afforded me valuable assistance in some doubtful passages. The abstract of Falconer leaves much to be desired, being in some respects contradictory, and in many cases insufficient, as it gives only the titles of the stories. Two of the latter have been courteously communicated to me by Dr. Sachau, who at the request of Professor Max Müller searched for the manuscript, and after finding it read the stories, and sent them translated to me.

4. The eighth night of the *Tûtî-nâmeh* of Nachschebî. This Persian poet died in 1329. His *Tûtî-nâmeh* is not yet published, but the whole is well known through the careful abstract of it published by Pertsch.§ The eighth night was, however, well known before, viz.,

* *Das Buch von den Sieben Weisen Meistern aus dem Hebräischen und Griechischen, zum ersten Male übersetzt*, Halle, 1842.

† *Paraboles de Sandabar traduites de l'Hébreu*, Paris, 1849.

‡ *Asiatic Journal*, vol. xxxv. p. 169, *et seq.;* vol. xxxvi. p. 4, *et seq.;* p. 99, *et seq*. Cf. Défréméry in *Journal Asiatique*, 1842, p. 105, *et seq.*

§ In *Zeitschrift der Deutschen Morgenländischen Gesellschaft*, 1867, vol. xxi. pp. 505-551.

from 1845, through a work of Professor Brockhaus.* This work is unobtainable, twelve copies only having been printed. I have used the Italian translation of Professor Teza.†

5. The *Seven Viziers*, an Arabic text, which forms part of some redactions of the *Thousand and One Nights*: of uncertain age, but certainly of little antiquity. I have been enabled to avail myself of three different redactions, viz., 1. Habicht's text (a Tunis manuscript);‡ 2. Scott's text (a Bengalee manuscript);§ 3. The text which is in the Arabic manuscript of the *Thousand and One Nights* printed at Boolak in 1863 (vol. iii. pp. 75-124), examined for me by my learned and very dear friend Professor Fausto Lasinio. Of these texts the most complete, as regards the number of the tales which it contains, is that of Boolak, which, however, is of no value at all as regards the fundamental story, which is so corrupted as to be entirely useless. The text which has best preserved the fundamental story is that of Habicht.

6. Besides these texts already known I have made use

* *Nachschebi's Sieben Weisen Meister, Persisch und Deutsch*, von H. Brockhaus, Leipzig, 1845.

† In Professor D'Ancona's publication, *Il Libro dei Sette Savî di Roma*, Pisa, 1864, pp. 49-64.

‡ *Tausend und Eine Nacht*, Breslau, 1840, vol. xv. pp. 102-172. The Tunis MS. of the *Thousand and One Nights* that contains the *Seven Viziers* is of the year 1731.

§ *Tales, Anecdotes, and Letters, translated from the Arabic and Persian*, by F. Scott, Shrewsbury, 1800, pp. 38-198. This book is very rare. A very extended analysis of the version of the *Seven Viziers* contained in it, made by Loiseleur, accompanies the French translation of the *Thousand and One Days* in the *Panthéon Littéraire*, Paris, 1840, pp. 285-300. The notices that Loiseleur had already given of it in his *Essai sur les Fables Indiennes*, pp. 131-141, are insufficient.

of another text, still inedited, of great authority and interest for these researches. This is brought to light for the first time, and is appended to this memoir. It is an ancient Spanish translation of an Arabic text, the existence of which Professor Amador de los Rios was the first to reveal in his *Historia Critica de la Literatura Española*, vol. iii. pp. 536-541. The codex, which is the property of Count de Puñonrostro, is of the fifteenth century. The translation was made, as the prologue says, by order of the Infante Don Fadrique in 1291 of the Spanish era, or in 1253 of the common era. It is known that King Alfonso, brother of Don Fadrique, two years before, in 1251, while he was still Infante, had had the *Calila and Dimna* translated from the Arabic.* This *Libro de los Engannos et Asayamientos de las Mugeres* is of all the texts that which most agrees with the *Syntipas*, often even verbally. Sometimes, however, it is excessively abridged. The text in the only copy known is very corrupt.

All these versions constitute a well-connected and distinct group, to which two other Eastern texts, *The Ten Viziers* and *The Forty Viziers*, can in no way be considered to belong. These two books do belong to the family of the *Sindibâd*, but constitute the sporadic part of it. They are books that stand each by itself, and preserve too little of the *Sindibâd* to be of any utility in the researches that we are upon.

The investigation of the contents of the original text might perhaps be carried on with still greater minuteness; above all, the form of each of the stories contained in that text should be inquired into. This research I have made for my own use. Here, however, I have thought it right

---

* See Benfey in *Orient und Occident*, i. pp. 498-502; Amador de los Rios, *Hist. Crit. de la Lit. Españ.*, iii. p. 525.

to confine myself to pointing out only what is the essential characteristic of the book, considering that when once this basis has been laid down, and the relative authority of the various versions has been thus also fixed, the rest would be easily found when it is wanted by continuing the comparison in the same manner. The examination of each single story would have taken up greater space than is allowed me.

CHAPTER I.

FORM AND CONTENTS OF THE STORY IN THE 'BOOK OF SINDIBAD.'*

THERE was in India a king named Kûrush.

In India, S. N., M. S., N.; in China, S. V. H.; L. E. has, by a mistake of the copyist, *Judea;* S. and S V. S. do not name the country. The name of the king is Kῦρος in S., *Kûrush* in Masudi (cf. Benfey in *Mélanges Asiat.*, &c., iii. p. 191, *et seq.*); M. S. has *Baibor* (or *Bibor*), which Benfey (*l.c.*, p. 192) believes may be a corruption of *Kai Kur*, the latter itself a corruption of *Kai Kûrush;* L. E. has *Alcos*. The other texts do not give the king's name.

He was powerful, wise, just, and loved by his people.

M. S.; S. N.; S. V.; L. E.; N.; not all, however, *all* these qualities. Cf. Benfey, *l.c.*, p. 193.

Being already advanced in years, he had had no children by his wives, and the thought of leaving no heir saddened him.

M. S. was eighty years old; S. V. was old; N. had passed the springtime of life; the others do not speak of his age. S. seven wives; M. S. eighty; L. E. ninety; S. N. a hundred. In S. V. the king's sorrow is such

---

* I employ the following abbreviations:—

S., *Syntipas.*
L. E., *Libro de los Engannos.*
M. S., Hebrew version (*Mischlè Sandabar*).
S. N., *Sindibâd-nâmeh.*
N., *Nachschebî.*
S. V. H., *Seven Viziers* of Habicht's text.
S. V. S., *Seven Viziers* of Scott's text.
S. V., *Seven Viziers* of both texts.

that he shuts himself up in his palace, and his subjects not seeing him believe he is dead.

One night one of his wives, seeing him sorrowful, asked him the reason; he told her it, and she advised prayer. He followed the advice, and had a son.

> S. suppresses the scene between the king and the favourite. It preserves, however, the fact of the prayer (παρεκάλει τὸ θεῖον). N. suppresses that episode entirely. In the dialogue between the favourite and the king, which was certainly in the original, L. E., M. S., S. N., agree in general very well. In M. S. the woman is called *Beria*. There is in S. V. also a colloquy between the king and the queen, but different from that of the other texts; nor is there in that any mention of prayer. Besides prayer, M. S. and S. N. add fasting. There are variants of little importance respecting the manner and the time in which the prayer is performed.

The child being born, the king assembles the astrologers, in order that they may draw his horoscope.

> In S. and in S. V. S. all this part of the horoscope has been suppressed. It is found in all the other texts. In M. S. the king assembles all the sages, and by his order they select a thousand out of themselves, these select a hundred, and the hundred select seven. These seven (all named) draw the horoscope. This manner of election is found in S. V. H. for the preceptor. The other versions have no trace of it.

They find that the prince is threatened by a misfortune at twenty years of age.

> M. S. and L. E. at twenty years; N. at thirteen years; S. V. H. in youth; S. N. does not say when. In S. V. H., N., and S. N. it is added that he will escape the threatened danger.

At seven years the prince is entrusted to masters; at

thirteen he had not learnt anything. The king assembles the sages for advice. These find that the best master is Sindibâd. The prince studies another six years and a half under Sindibâd, but uselessly. At nineteen and a half he had learnt nothing.

The education commences at seven years in M. S. and S. V. H., at ten in S. N., at three in S. V. S., "at the close of boyhood" in S.; in N. it is not said when. S. N. intercalates two tales in the discussion amongst the wise men, both told by Sindibâd. N. has no name of a person; consequently the name of Sindibâd is not there, but simply "one of the sages." In S. and S. V. S. Sindibâd is not proposed by the sages; but the king, who has heard his wisdom spoken of, sends for him. In S. N. a tale of Sindibâd to the king after the bad success of his teaching is intercalated.

All the versions, except S. N., suppress one of the two unsuccessful attempts, either the first or the second. M. S. and S. V. H., in which, consequently, the prince is immediately entrusted to Sindibâd, suppress the first. S., L. E., N., and S. V. S. suppress the second. The suppression is seen in S. V., in which, accordingly, the prince is tempted by the woman when he is little more than ten years old. It is seen, however, better in L. E. In this, perhaps to make the prince a little more mature and capable of exciting the woman's love, two years have been added, and his education has been made to commence at seven, and go on to fifteen. In the meanwhile, however, some gross contradictions have been left. While the astrologers predict, as in M. S., the misfortune for twenty years, the prediction is verified at fifteen and a half. In addition, when the king, at the prince's attaining his fifteenth year, assembles the sages, there appears for the first time a sage, "who was named Sindibâd." But afterwards, in the colloquy amongst the sages, one says to Sindibâd (as in

M. S. and in S. N.), "Why have you not instructed the prince in these years that he has been with you?" Now, as the first attempt had been made by several masters (*quel mostrasen escrivir*), as in N. and S. V. S. (S. N. has *a preceptor;* S., however, ἐν τῷ διδασκαλείῳ), and not by Sindibâd, it follows, consequently, that these words allude to a second unfortunate attempt, which, as in S. N., was made by Sindibâd, and which in L. E. has been suppressed. N. has been much more consequential, and having suppressed the second unfortunate attempt has made the danger predicted by the astrologer to be not for twenty but for thirteen years of age, an epoch at which, as it seems to me, the first attempt was made to end in the original text. More exact, the author of M. S. has taken account also of the six months of successful teaching, and suppressing the change of master at thirteen, and reducing the two unfortunate attempts to one only, has preserved the number of years of both, and has made the unsuccessful teaching last continuously twelve years and a half, from seven to nineteen and a half, which, together with the six months of successful teaching, lead up exactly to the epoch of twenty years in which the danger occurs, in accordance with the prediction of the astrologers.

The duration of the second unfortunate attempt in S. N. is six years. The education begins at ten, but in this version the astrologers do not determine with precision the epoch of the danger.

I have thought it necessary to disentangle the confusion which the various redactions present on this point; the more so that between this part of the *Sindibâd* and the introduction to the *Pancatantra* there is more than one interesting, and certainly not fortuitous, coincidence, which Professor Benfey has already opportunely noted, *Pantsch.*, i. p. 39, *et seqq.*

The king again assembles the wise men to advise him. Sindibâd offers to teach the prince in six months, on pain of losing his life and property if he fails; he only asks the king to promise " not to do to another what he would not wish should be done to himself." After a dispute between Sindibâd and the wise men, who do not believe his promise can possibly be performed, the offer is accepted and the agreement put into writing, with the day and the hour of the prince's return.*

> L. E.; M. S. (the king's promise, however, is not in this, being transferred to the end of the book); S. V. H. (in seven weeks; the king's promise is augmented by two others, the dispute of the wise men is suppressed); S. V. S. (in two years; there is no promise of the king, nor dispute, nor written agreement); S. N. (there is no promise of the king nor written agreement); N. (the dispute, the king's promise, the written agreement suppressed); S. (there is no assembling of wise men; the king summons Sindibâd, of whom he has heard much; except this, and consequently the dispute, the rest is all there).

Sindibâd takes the prince with him, has a palace constructed, inscribes the *omne scibile* on the walls, and shuts himself up with the prince, separating him from all other society.

All the texts agree in general, except that in some

---

* The promise of teaching in *six months*, the anger of the other sages, and the engagement made in the written agreement are all found in the introduction to the *Pancatantra*. See what Benfey remarks as to this, vol. i. p. 39, *et seqq*. Let me be permitted here to remark by the way that the maxim with which one of the sages expresses his doubt regarding Sindibâd's promise—a maxim which, with some variation, is found in two of the texts that have preserved the dispute of the sages, L. E. and M. S. (a gap in the manuscript prevents us from knowing whether it was in S. N.)—recurs in Indian collections. See (besides the well-known book of Böhtlingk) Weber's *Indische Streifen*, p. 263, 37.

nothing is said about the separation (N., S. N., S. V. S.). In S. V. there is some detail in regard to the instruction given to the prince which is not found in the others.

Before the term which has been fixed expires the prince has learnt everything. The king asks for information; Sindibâd replies that the prince is ready, and that to-morrow he will bring him back.

In L. E. the king sends for Sindibâd for information, and the latter replies that he will bring back the prince "to-morrow at two o'clock." In S. the king sends to Sindibâd for information, and Sindibâd replies that he will bring back the prince "to-morrow at three o'clock" (but later on he says *at two o'clock*); there is in this text an interpolation of some words interchanged between the king and the prince which can in no way belong to the text. In M. S. and S. V. the hour is not mentioned. In S. V. Sindibâd, without being requested, informs the king that the prince is ready. All this is wanting in S. N. and N.

Before bringing him back Sindibâd consults the stars, and sees that the prince incurs danger of death if he shall speak before seven days.

L. E., M. S., S. V. S. In S. the text is evidently corrupted, but from the words of the prince to Sindibâd the original agreement with the other versions is clearly seen. In S. V. H., S. N., N., Sindibâd finds that the prince is threatened by a misfortune, and in order to avoid it he advises absolute silence for seven days.

Sindibâd hides himself away, the prince goes to court, there is a grand reception, the prince remains dumb; they seek for Sindibâd, and do not find him.

All the texts agree, except that in N. the master does not hide himself, but brings the prince back to court in person.

Some attribute the prince's silence to the effect of a beverage given to him by Sindibâd in order that he might learn quickly; others to timidity.

> L. E.; S.; M. S. (there is not a word, however, about timidity); S. V. H. (there is not a word about the beverage, and it is proposed to conduct the prince to the rooms of the harem); N. (the same). In S. N. the manuscript has a gap in this place. S. V. S. has nothing of this.

One of the king's women says that the prince was accustomed from a boy to confide in her; she proposes to take him into her own room and induce him to speak.

> L. E., M. S., S., N., S. V. S.; S. N. (in this, however, the woman does not speak of the former familiarity; she is already in love with the prince, and avails herself of this opportunity to have him alone with her). In S. V. S. the prince is, according to the prevailing opinion, taken at once to the harem.

The woman does not succeed in making the prince speak. Then she tells him that his father is old and that it is his turn to reign. She proposes to him that they shall kill his father and afterwards marry.

> All the versions agree, only in N. and S. V. S. there is no proposal to kill the father, but simply a declaration of love.

The prince is angry at this proposal; he forgets his resolution not to speak, and says: "In seven days I shall be able to give thee the answer that thou deservest."

> S., M. S., S. V., L. E. In S. N. the prince breaks silence by asking what the woman will do in order to kill his father, and having learnt it, after gravely reproving her he flies from the room. In N. the prince does not speak, but after looking at the woman with angry eyes he flees away. However much of a contradiction this may be, the answer of

the prince was certainly in the original text. In fact, the woman learns from this that the prince will not speak for seven days, and for that reason she endeavours to get him killed before he shall be able to speak. In S. V. S. the prince says this answer *to himself*.

The woman, seeing herself compromised, desires to procure the prince's death before the seven days are over. She tears her clothes and cries, accusing the pretended dumb man of having attempted violence against her.

Nearly all the texts agree; in S. N. the woman accuses the prince not only of having declared his love to her, but also of having asked her assistance in his project of killing his father and taking possession of the throne. S. V. S. also is nearly like this.

The king condemns his son to death. Hearing this, his seven viziers assemble, and resolve to intercede.

Nearly all the texts agree, only N. has suppressed entirely the meeting of the viziers, the first of whom intercedes at once, then the second, &c. It must be observed that these viziers should not be confounded with the wise men, one of whom is Sindibâd. S. N. amplifies the discussion of the viziers, and intercalates a tale by the oldest of them in favour of interceding; it does not say how many they were; those, however, who intercede are only six. In S. V. S. they have been already informed by Sindibâd.

A vizier presents himself to the king, and by two tales obtains the suspension of the execution for that day. The next day the woman goes to the king, and by a tale obtains the confirmation of the condemnation, but a second vizier procures the suspension of it again by two tales; and so on to the seventh day, on which the woman, seeing her calumny now on the point of being found out, has a funeral pile erected, and mounts it in order to be burnt. But the king on learning this saves her, and orders his son to be killed. Again, however, the seventh wise man by two tales procures the suspension of the execution, and thus the eighth day arrives, on which the prince speaks. On one of the days preceding the seventh the woman, besides telling her tale, threatens to pierce herself with a dagger unless justice is done to her; on another she threatens to poison herself. The seven viziers, therefore, have each two tales, the woman one tale a day from the second to the sixth, and only the threat of killing herself on the seventh.

S., M. S., L. E. agree in this, except that in L. E. the third vizier has only one tale instead of two, and in M. S. the woman on the seventh day, instead of throwing herself on to the funeral pile, throws herself into the river. The woman's threat to pierce herself with the dagger occurs in L. E. on the third day; in S. on the fourth; in S. V. on the fifth. I do not know if it is found in S. N.; it is wanting in M. S. The threat of poisoning herself occurs in S., L. E., S. N., on the fifth day; in S. V. on the sixth. It is wanting in M. S.; in S. V. on the last day the woman, besides threatening to burn herself, has a tale.

The tales thus told by the viziers and the woman are in the following order:—

First day	First Vizier	The Lion's Track.
"	"	The Woman and the Parrot.
Second day	The Woman	The Calenderer and his Son.
"	Second Vizier	The Loaves.
"	"	The Double Infidelity.
Third day	The Woman	The Lamia.
"	Third Vizier	The Drop of Honey.
"	"	The Druggist.
Fourth day	The Woman	The Changed Sex.
"	Fourth Vizier	The Bath-keeper.
"	"	The Go-between and the Dog.
Fifth day	The Woman	The Ape and the Wild Boar.

THE BOOK OF SINDIBAD.

Fifth day	Fifth Vizier	The Dog and the Snake.
"	"	The Burnt Loaf.
Sixth day	The Woman	The Thief and the Lion.
"	Sixth Vizier	The Two Pigeons.
"	"	The Elephant of Honey.
Seventh day	The Woman	Has no tale.
"	Seventh Vizier	The Three Wishes.
	"	The Man who understood Female Wiles.

Of all the versions S. is the only one that has preserved *all* these tales. After this comes L. E., in which is wanting only the tale of *The Druggist*. But of all that concerns the tales in the various versions I shall speak in a separate chapter.

On the eighth day, at an early hour, the prince sends a woman to call the first of the viziers. He tells him all, thanks him and his companions, promises reward, and begs him to go to his father and announce to him that he speaks. Having learnt this the king sends for the prince.

S., L. E., S. N. (the seventh day); S. V. H. (the prince sends for the viziers); S. V. S. (sends for the viziers and Sindibâd, for he knew where the latter was hidden). All this is suppressed in M. S. and in N.

The king sits on his throne at a full court; the prince presents himself, does homage, and, being questioned by the king, tells of the threatening of the stars and the plot of the woman. He asks that all the sages may be sent for; with them comes also Sindibâd.

S., L. E. The latter abridges the prince's answer, which we find more complete in S.; in that there is no mention of the project against the king's life. In S. V. the prince presents himself accompanied by Sindibâd; in S. V. H. the latter is questioned upon the cause of the prince's silence. In S. N. Sindibâd arrives before the prince and sits down; then comes the prince and speaks. All this is suppressed in M. S. and in N.

C 2

The king asks Sindibâd the reason of his absence; the latter explains it. "Meanwhile," the king says, "suppose I had had my son killed, whose fault would it have been—mine, my son's, the woman's, or Sindibâd's?" Each of these cases finds a supporter. Sindibâd observes that no one has hit the mark. The king puts the question to the prince, who answers by the tale *The Poisoned Guests*, and asks who was in fault—the maidservant, the snakes, the bird, or the master of the house. These four opinions having been supported by four sages, Sindibâd finds that no one has hit the mark; the prince resolves the problem, saying that in these cases the fault is that of destiny.

S., L. E., S. N., in which, however, the interrogations of the king do not occur, neither does Sindibâd speak. But the prince in his discourse says that life and death are in the hands of God, and tells *The Poisoned Guests*, as in the two texts already cited. In S. V. H., which abbreviates, the sages get out of the trouble of answering the king's question by saying, "We do not know," and the prince rises and tells *The Poisoned Guests*, proposing only two cases, whether the fault was of the company or of the maidservant. In S. V. S. the king's question is answered differently by various persons. As to the prince's tale, the blame is by one attributed to the master of the house. All this is suppressed in M. S. and N.

All admire the prince's wisdom; Sindibâd says that he has nothing else to teach him, and that nobody is wiser than he. The prince, however, observes that he knows three persons who know more than he does, and he tells three tales:—

    1. The Boy of Three Years.
    2. The Boy of Five Years.
    3. The Blind Old Man.

S., L. E., S. N. (in the last, however, is one tale more, *The Mother who in order to look at a Young Man lets her Son 'fall into the Well*, and, further, the tales are united to what in the two more ancient texts comes after). In S. V. H. the prince tells only *The Child of Five Years* and *The Blind Old Man*, and nothing is said of Sindibâd. In M. S. the prince on the eighth day tells his father why he has not spoken, and then recounts *The Blind Old Man* as an "example of female wiles." All this part is suppressed in N. and S. V. S. As far as here L. E. accompanies us; that little which follows in it is foreign to the original. All is suppressed in N.

The king asks how it was the prince did not learn at first what he succeeded in learning afterwards. The prince's answer.

The only texts that have not suppressed this part are S. and S. N., in which the last portion of the book has been less sacrificed to the desire of abridging. S. N. inserts in the prince's answer the tales above mentioned. In S. V. H. the king asks the prince the truth about the woman, and the prince tells what in the other texts he has told before. All suppressed in N.

The king orders the woman to come. She confesses everything. The king asks of the court what ought to be done with her. Some propose various mutilations, others death. Then the woman tells *The Fox*.

In the abstract we have of the S. N. (such at least as I read it in the *Revue Britannique*), after the prince's last day of silence the woman is entirely lost sight of, and it is not said what was her end. This cannot be attributed to the Persian poet, but either to the Frenchman or to Falconer, or to a *lacuna* of the manuscript. The woman's confession is found only in S., and perhaps was in the original, and has been omitted for brevity's sake in M. S. and S. V. H., which otherwise agree very well with S. The proposed punishments are: in S., either to cut off her hands and feet, or to tear out her tongue or her heart; in M. S., to cut off her hands, or blind her or kill her; in S. V. H., to cut out her tongue, or cut out her tongue and afterwards burn it. All suppressed in N.

The king leaves the decision to the prince. The latter excludes death, and substitutes a less grave punishment.

Such, I believe, was the original form, to which it seems S., S. V. H., and M. S. more or less adhere. In the last the woman is pardoned altogether. In S. death is excluded, but the woman is condemned to wander through the city upon an ass, with her head shaved and her face dirtied, accompanied by two criers who proclaim her crimes. N., L. E., and S. V. S. get rid of the woman in a few words, the first saying that she was hanged, the second that she was burnt in a dry caldron, the last that she was thrown into the sea with a stone tied to her foot.

A dialogue follows between the king, Sindibâd, and the prince, in which many principles of morality are set forth. In this dialogue is intercalated a tale of Sindibâd, by which he answers the king, who asks to whom the wisdom of his son has been due.

All this very long portion has been suppressed in all the texts, with the exception of S. and S. N. It is difficult to say which of the two versions is the more faithful to the original. Clearly every presumption is in favour of S., not only because it is more ancient, but also because it is much less free than S. N. Sindibâd's tale is quite different in the Greek and the Persian; the occasion, however, in respect of which it is told is identical. Of the two, that of S. would seem to be the original. The abstract of S. N. is made by Falconer with so much carelessness that the tale is attributed first to the prince and afterwards to Sindibâd, but certainly should belong to the latter. In S. the king inquires of the prince what Sindibâd has done to teach him so much wisdom; in the answer the moral principles that Feridun wrote upon the walls of his palace are mentioned. In S. follow twenty maxims in the form of question (by the king) and answer (by the prince). Also in S. N. the dialogue concludes in this manner. In both the texts we find so much in common as to be able to conclude that even this portion, suppressed (for obvious reasons) in the other versions, was in the original; which of them, however, has reproduced it faithfully, and up to what point, it is difficult to decide. The subject being treated on the philosophical rather than on the narrative side, Andreopulos as a Christian, and the author of S. N. as a poet, are both open to suspicion.

The king crowns his son publicly, giving up the throne to him, and retires into solitude to serve God.

This conclusion is suppressed entirely in S., which closes with the dialogue between the king and the prince; it is, however, in S. N., S. V. H., and N. In S. N. the king, thinking of abdicating in favour of his son, retires to pray for a week, and has a dream, in pursuance of which he carries out his project. In S. V. he gives up his power to his son directly after having judged the woman. N. ends thus : " The girl is hung, and the king gives the crown to his son." Also M. S., like S. and L. E., has omitted this final portion; some one has wished to supply this want by adding the passage which is found in some manuscripts and of which Carmoly has given a translation. According to this, Sindibâd died (at one hundred and thirty years of age) contemporaneously with King Bibor, and then the son mounted the throne.

CHAPTER II.

OF THE TALES CONTAINED IN THE VARIOUS VERSIONS.

IN order to facilitate the comparison, I lay before the reader on the opposite page a comparative table of the tales in the various versions. By the aid of this table it will be easy to recognize which are the original tales in each of them, and which are not. A glance is sufficient to show that each version has tales common to the others, each has some exclusively its own; that the tales common to most versions are all found in *Syntipas*—as we shall see, the most ancient of all; and, finally, that the *Libro de los Engannos*, which represents an Arabic text anterior to A.D. 1253, accords with *Syntipas* more than every other version. After making these preliminary observations let us speak of each separately.

Syntipas.—This version contains two tales which are not found in others; one of these is the last, which may be entitled *Destiny*. It belongs to a portion of the book which has been suppressed entirely in the other versions, except S. N., in which, in the place of this tale, is found another quite different. I will not repeat here what I have said in the previous chapter upon the subject of this portion of the *Book of Sindibâd*. The other tale does not appear in the comparative table because it is interwoven with the second tale of the seventh vizier, *The Man who understood Female Wiles*. In this (which recurs only in S., L. E., S. N., and N.) the S. has *two* female

THE BOOK OF SINDIBAD. 25

SYNTIPAS.	LIBRO DE LOS ENGANNOS.	PARABLES OF SANDABAR.	SINDIBAD-NAMEH.	SEVEN VIZIERS. B(ulaq), H(abicht), S(cott).	NACHSCHEBI.
1st Vizier	Lion	Id.	Id.		Id.
,,	Parrot	Id.	Id.	1st Vizier 1	Id.
Woman	Calenderer	Id.	Id.	Id.	Id.
2nd Vizier	Loaves	Id.	4th Vizier 1		Id. (B. H.)	...
,,	Infidelity	Id.	5th Vizier 2	1st Vizier 2	Id.	1st Vizier.
Woman	Lamia	Id.	Id.	Id.	Id.	...
3rd Vizier	Honey	Id.	...		Id.	...
,,	Druggist	...	4th Vizier 2	2nd Vizier 2	Id. (B. H.)	6th Vizier.
Woman	Sex	Id.	Woman 2	Woman 5	Id.	...
4th Vizier	Bathman	Id.	5th Vizier 1	Id.	Id. (B. S.)	...
,,	Dog	Id.	2nd Vizier 2	3rd Vizier 2 4th Vizier 2	Id.	2nd Vizier.
Woman	Wild Boar	Id.	Id.		Woman 3	
5th Vizier	Snake	Id.	3rd Vizier 1	3rd Vizier 1	...	
,,	Cloth	Id.	3rd Vizier 2		7th Vizier	
Woman	Thief	Id.	Woman 3	Woman 4	...	
6th Vizier	Pigeons	Id.	2nd Vizier 1	2nd Vizier 1	Woman 6 (B.)	...
,,	Young Elephant	Id.	...	...	...	3rd Vizier.
7th Vizier	Wishes	Id.	6th Vizier 2	6th Vizier	6th Vizier	...
,,	Connoisseur	Id.		5th Vizier		4th Vizier.
Prince	Guests	Id.		Id.	Id.	
,,	Boy 3 years old	Id.		Id.	Id. (B.)	
,,	Boy 5 years old	Id.		Id.	Id. (B. H.)	
,,	Blind Old Man	Id.	Id.	Id.	Id. (B. H.)	
Woman	Fox	Id.	Id.		Id. (B H.)	
Syntipas	Destiny	...				
		Prince, The Abbot				
			Woman 5, Rev. of Absal.			
			6th Viz. 1, Death of Absal.			
			7th Vizier 1, Disguise			
			7th Viz. 2, Three Hunchbacks			
				Introd. Ape		
				,, Camel		
				,, Elephant		
				,, King of the Apes		
				Prince, Careless Mother		
				Sind. 4 Liberators		
		...			Woman 1, Blackguard (B. H.)	
		...			Woman 4, Jeweller	
					3rd Viz., Curiosity	
					Woman 5, Chest	
					6th Vizier, Four Lovers (B. S.)	
		...	...	...	Woman 6, Magpie	...
		...	...	...	,, Amazon	...
		...	...	...	1st Viz., Ahmed (S.)	...
					7th Vizier, The Ring (B.)	
						5th Viz., The Father-in-law.

wiles, the first of which is simply *told* by the woman to the man, who pretends to understand their cunning; the other instead is a trick which the woman plays on him. Now that wile *told* by the woman is altogether wanting in L. E. and in N. Whether it be found in S. N. Falconer does not say, but through the kindness of Dr. Sachau, who has communicated to me the tale such as it is in the manuscript, I am enabled to say that in S. N. that wile is not to be found. N. also has two wiles, but that which is *told* in S. is not there. There are two jokes, both played off upon the pretended connoisseur of female wiles. The first is in L. E. and in S.; the second, evidently added by Nachschebî, is attributed to the woman's sister, and is a tale which we find again in *The Forty Viziers*.* It is to be remarked that the *Çukasaptati* has the story such as it is in L. E., and has neither the wile which is first in S., nor that which is the second in N. In the form we now know it —a very compendious abstract—the *Çukasaptati* puts principally in evidence the cunning behaviour of the woman towards the young man, suppressing almost entirely all that has reference to his studies of female wiles; not, however, so much so that no trace remains of them, as, for example, where it is said that he was acquainted with "all the amorous signs and gestures shown by women." And in *Çukasaptati* and in N. the man who is duped has a sacred character, being in the first a Brahmin, in the other a Dervish. What is the importance of the *Çukasaptati* as regards these *second* tales of the viziers we shall see in the sequel. Meanwhile from all this we are enabled to conclude that the first wile, which is in the second tale according to the version of S., appears as an interpolation whether due to the Greek or the Syrian we know not.

Libro de los Engannos.—Twenty-two of the tales that,

* P. 241 (Behrnauer).

besides being found in S., recur in several other versions, are found again in L. E., and all precisely in the same place as they occupy in S. One is wanting altogether, and is the second tale of the third vizier, *The Woman and the Druggist.* It was certainly not wanting in the Arabic original, and perhaps not even in the Spanish translation. It is probable that the very wretched and careless copyist to whom we owe this very bad copy has, through inadvertence, skipped over the chapter which contained it. Besides, S., M. S., S. V. H., S. N., and N. contain that tale; there is no doubt, therefore, that it should be found in the Arabic text.

There is, moreover, wanting in L. E. the tale of *The Fox*, told by the woman when her condemnation is under consideration, which tale is in S., M. S., and S. V. H. But, as we have seen, all the last part of the book, to which that tale belongs, has been suppressed in this text. Instead of it is substituted a fifth tale of the prince, due perhaps to the Spanish translator, or to some one else who has meddled with the translation, which has certainly not come to us untampered with. Though the text is very corrupt and certainly mutilated in some parts, we recognize in this tale a novel of Bandello (iv. 8) which has an equivalent in the nineteenth night of the *Çukasaptati* (Galanos).

Parables of Sandabar.—After S. and L. E., the version which is the least removed from the original is M. S., though in that the tales have undergone more than one mutation. They are as follows, in the order in which they exist in the text:—

First Vizier	The Footstep of the Lion.
,,	The Woman and the Parrot.
The Woman	The Calenderer and his Son.
Second Vizier	The Two Pigeons.
,,	The Go-between and the Dog.
The Woman	The Lamia and the Changed Sex.

Third Vizier	The Dog and the Snake.
„	The Burnt Cloth.
The Woman	The Thief and the Lion.
Fourth Vizier	The Loaves.
„	The Druggist.
The Woman	The Man and the Wild Boar.
Fifth Vizier	The Bathman.
„	The Double Infidelity.
The Woman	*The Revolt of Absalom.*
Sixth Vizier	*The Death of Absalom.*
„	The Three Wishes.
Seventh Vizier	*The Disguise.*
„	*The Three Hunchbacks.*
The Prince	The Blind Old Man.
The Woman	The Fox.

The last tale of Sindibâd is wanting altogether, the portion of the book to which it belongs being, as in other versions, here suppressed. There are wanting also three of the four tales of the prince, and they are the first three, which were entirely suppressed. We have further four quite new tales, that have nothing like them in any other version, and are wholly foreign to the original. Two of these, being of Jewish argument, are evidently due to the Jewish translator. These two tales, being intended to serve contrary purposes, could not be both told by viziers. The translator has given the first, *The Revolt of Absalom*, as a fifth tale to the woman, instead of *The Thief and the Lion*. The latter, therefore, should have been suppressed, but he has preferred preserving it; and in order to do this he has transferred it, making it the fourth; the fourth he has made the third; and, lastly, the third having some affinity with the second, he has fused the two together, making only one tale of them. The tale of *The Revolt of Absalom* should have been immediately followed by that of *The Death of Absalom*, which serves as an answer to it. Consequently the latter has been given as a first tale to the sixth vizier, instead of *The Two Pigeons*. This (*The Two Pigeons*) has been given as a first tale to the second vizier, instead of *The Loaves*. This last has been given as a first tale to the fourth vizier, instead of *The Bathman;* this as a first tale to the fifth vizier, instead of *The Dog and the Snake;* and, finally, the latter as a first tale to the third vizier, instead of *The Drop of Honey*, which has been suppressed. To the seventh vizier have been given two new tales, instead of his own two stories, which were *The Three Wishes* and *The Man who understood Female Wiles*. This latter has been suppressed, and the other has been given as a second story to the sixth vizier, instead of *The Young Elephant*, also entirely suppressed.

These three versions, S., L. E., and M. S., agree also in not giving any tale to the woman on the last day, substituting therefor the threat which she makes of killing herself, either by mounting the funeral pile, as in S. and L. E. (and this must be the primitive form), or by throwing herself into the river, as in M. S.

Sindibâd-nâmeh.—We know from the author of this poem himself that he had before him a Persian prose text, translated from the Arabic. The collations which we have instituted in regard to the principal tale already completely prove that that Arabic original was no other than the same which served as a basis to other versions, or one derived from it. Certainly, as the result of comparing with the *Syntipas* the latter portion of the book, suppressed in the other versions, this was very complete. But, however each principal portion of the book may have been preserved in this version, it is evident that each one has been handled by the author with some freedom, according as his own character of poet required or permitted. This can not only be recognized in the amplifications of single parts and in the free use of all Persian poetical rhetoric, such as was in fashion in the times of the author, but also in his having driven amplification and freedom so far as to introduce tales into some parts of the book in which no other version has any. These are:—1. *The Fox and the Ape*; 2. *The Fox, the Wolf, and the Camel* (both told by Sindibâd to the other wise men when it is under consideration to find a good preceptor for the prince); 3. *The Tame Elephant* (told by Sindibâd to the king in order to excuse himself for the bad success of his teaching); 4. *The King of the Apes and the Burnt Elephant* (told by the oldest vizier to the others for the purpose of proving that they should intercede with the king in order to dissuade him from killing his son). Not one of these tales is found in any of the other versions; they are certainly foreign to the *Sindibâd*, and have been introduced into this version from other collections. The latter three are again found in the *Avadânas*,* and the last of them also in Nachschebî.†

The other tales are in the following order:—

First Vizier	The Husband and the Parrot.
” . . .	The Double Infidelity.
The Woman	The Calenderer and his Son.

* N. 17, 27, 33. As is well known, this is an argument for the Buddhistic origin of such tales. It being very probable, as Benfey has maintained, and with good reason, that the *Sindibâd* itself is of Buddhistic origin, Gödeke (*Or. u. Occ.*, iii. 393) has wished to deduce from it that these tales were original in the *Sindibâd*, and that the S. N. is the most faithful representative of this book. But the community of Buddhistic origin proves nothing. A hundred tales that may be found or not in the *Avadânas*, and even several collections of tales, are of certain or probable Buddhistic origin. There may very well have been tales introduced at an epoch even very recent into the *Sindibâd*, and they may be nevertheless of Buddhistic origin. So, for example, the two tales of *Curiosity* and *The Magpie*, which are found in *The Seven Viziers*, may very well, as Benfey (*Pantsch.*, i. §§ 52–58) thinks, have that origin; yet (though Benfey has not seen this) there is no doubt that they are altogether foreign to the original *Sindibâd*.

† Fifth night. Cf. Rosen, *Tûtî-nâmeh*, i. 130; Pertsch, art. cit., p. 519; Benfey, *Pantsch.*, i. pp. 358, 583, *et seq.*

Second Vizier .	The Two Partridges.
,, .	The Druggist.
The Woman	The Lamia.
Third Vizier	The Dog and the Snake.
,,	The Libertine Husband (second part of the tale).
,,	The Go-between and the Dog.
The Woman	The Ape and the Wild Boar.
Fourth Vizier	The Bathman.
,,	The Go-between and the Dog (the first part only).
The Woman	(A *lacuna* in the MS.)
Fifth Vizier	The Man who understood Female Wiles.
The Woman .	The Thief and the Lion.
Sixth Vizier	The Three Wishes (*lacuna* in the MS.).
The Woman	The Changed Sex.
The Prince	The Poisoned Milk.
,,	The Careless Mother.
	The Child in the Cradle.
,,	The Boy of Five Years.
,,	The Blind Old Man.
Sindibâd (?)	The Four Liberators.

Here we find again in great part the usual tales, including the second ones of the viziers, which, as we shall see, are a characteristic of that text whence all the versions proceed. The change of order is another proof of the freedom used in this version. The fifth vizier has only one tale, and the sixth also.

The seventh vizier is out altogether. Before the surviving tale of the fifth vizier there is a *lacuna*; and a *lacuna* deprives us also of the tale of the sixth vizier, of which the title only remains. It does not seem that the absence of the seventh vizier should be attributed to the latter *lacuna*; at least, according to Falconer's abstract, as it is given in the *Revue Britannique*, the prince in this version begins to speak again on the seventh day, as in N., and not on the eighth. From this it seems that the seventh vizier, as in N., has been deliberately suppressed by the author.

Did the last two viziers (fifth and sixth) have each one tale only, or did they have two like the others? Perhaps a more accurate examination of the codex and of the presumable extent of the *lacunæ* may give the answer. I will only observe that there is no need for supposing the existence of these tales to explain the *lacunæ*, since other parts of the narrative besides the tales are wanting there.* It is to be observed that the missing tales (including those of the seventh vizier) are precisely four—in other words, as many as have been added in the introduction; so that this version, such as we now know it, contains twenty-four tales, just as many as *Syntipas* contains, and as many as the *Book of Sindibâd* contained. Gödeke has thought that the missing tales have been suppressed on account of their obscenity. He would not have said this if he had observed what the tales are that are missing, what those are that exist. The tales of *The Loaves* and *The Drop of Honey*, which are amongst the missing ones, have nothing obscene, nor even of gallantry; the others wanting are very far from reaching the obscenity of *The Three Wishes* or of *The Bathman*, neither of which, nevertheless, has been suppressed.

The woman has all her tales as in the original, except that the order is somewhat changed. Where the *lacuna* is after the fourth vizier the woman does not appear to have any tale. If she had one, it must have been a new tale, foreign to the *Sindibâd*, given to her by the poet; since she has already, without exception, all the five tales

* The observations of Falconer respecting the *lacunæ* and the displacement of sheets in the MS. do not appear to be accurate. Dr. Sachau informs me that in each page the word with which the following page commences is marked by the same hand, and this indication always corresponds, except once only (No. 86, 87). From this it would appear that if anything is really wanting, or is not in order in some places, it is not through deficiency of the MS.

that she should have, according to the original, during the silence of the prince. Perhaps the threat of burning herself that the woman makes, without any tale, on the eighth day in the original has been transferred to that place. In point of fact the woman on the preceding day has, as in S. and in S. V. H., besides the tale, the threat of poisoning herself.

The tale of *The Fox* is wanting. As a compensation, however, the prince, besides the four usual ones, has one new (*The Careless Mother*). Of the final tale—according to Falconer's abstract, one does not know if it is the prince's or Sindibad's—I have already spoken elsewhere, remarking that the S. in this part of the book, only preserved in these two versions, has indeed a tale, but quite different from that which the S. N. has. This tale of the S. N. is found again in Nachschebî (No. 35), in the *Thousand and One Nights*, and in other collections. That other collections of tales besides the *Sindibâd* have been used for this version is evident. Not only from these have the entirely new tales been taken, but also versions of some tales of the *Sindibâd*, entirely different from that to which this book belonged. Thus for the tale of *The Two Pigeons*, which indeed is found again, just as it is in the *Sindibâd*, in the *Anvâr-i-Suhaili* (written, as is well known, not long after the S. N., about the beginning of the fifteenth century), has been substituted the tale of *The Two Partridges*, which is very different. (See Benfey, i. § 227, and p. 594, but mark that the tale of *The Two Pigeons* is one of those that, without any doubt whatever, belong originally to the *Sindibâd*.) The same may be said, though the difference is less great, of the tale of *The Ape and the Wild Boar*. (See Benfey, i. § 173, and observe, in answer to the query which he makes at p. 424, that now we know this tale is *not* found in Nachschebî.) The form which this tale has in S. N. approaches much nearer to that which it has in the *Pancatantra*. In the *Anvâr-i-Suhaili* it is found again such as it is in the S. N. Of the tale of *The Go-between and the Dog*, here divided into two, I will speak in the following chapter.

When I say that the S. N. does not spring from a text of the *Sindibâd* independent of that from which the other versions proceed, I do not mean to say by this that all the differences which it presents should be attributed to its author. It is not at all improbable that the Persian prose version of the Arabic text upon which he worked might already contain some of the variants that are found again in the poem.

Seven Viziers.—From one identical corrupted text, interpolated and relatively modern, are derived the three Arabic versions of the *Seven Viziers* used by us, those of Habicht, of Scott, and of Bulaq, which have common to them all several tales quite foreign to the *Sindibâd*. The most complete of the three as regards the number of the tales is that of Bulaq. The following are the tales which it contains :—

The First Vizier	The Track of the Lion.
"	The Woman and the Parrot.
The Woman	The Calenderer and his Son.
"	The Blackguard.
The Second Vizier	The Loaves.
"	The Double Infidelity.
The Woman	The Lamia.
The Third Vizier	The Drop of Honey.
"	The Druggist.
The Woman	The Changed Sex.
The Fourth Vizier	The Bathman.
"	The Go-between and the Dog.
The Woman	Mahmud (the Jeweller).
The Fifth Vizier	Curiosity.
The Woman	The Lover in the Chest.

The Sixth Vizier	The Four Lovers.
”	The Three Wishes.
The Woman	The Thieving Magpie.
”	The Two Pigeons.
”	The Amazon.
The Seventh Vizier	The Burnt Cloth.
”	The Ring.
The Prince	The Poisoned Guests.
”	The Blind Old Man.
	The Boy of Three Years.
”	The Boy of Five Years.

Of these tales one only, *The Ring*, exclusively belongs to this text of Bulaq. The tales of Habicht's text are here all found again in the same place, with the exception of the last, *The Fox*, which is wanting.* But the text of Habicht wants the following original tales, which here reappear:—
1. *The Bathman;* 2. *The Two Pigeons;* 3. *The Boy of Three Years.*

Scott's text has exclusively its own the first tale, *Ahmed.* The order of the first tales in this text is as follows:—

The First Vizier	. Ahmed.
”	The Husband and the Parrot.
The Woman	The Calenderer and his Son.
”	. The Track of the Lion.
The Second Vizier	The Double Infidelity.
The Woman .	The Lamia.
The Third Vizier	The Drop of Honey.
The Woman	The Changed Sex.

And so consecutively as in the Bulaq text, except that here are wanting the following tales, besides that of *The Ring:* 1. *The Two Pigeons;* 2. *The Boy of Three Years;* 3.

* The tale of *The Three Wishes* is also in Habicht's text; on account of its obscenity, however, in the edition of Breslau mention only is made of its title, *Of Him who wished to know the Night of Al-kader*, under which title no one has recognized that tale. It bears the same title in the Bulaq text. On the subject of the *Night of Al-kader*, see Lane's *The Modern Egyptians*, p. 478.

The Boy of Five Years; 4. *The Blind Old Man.* As in the Bulaq text, so in this of Scott is wanting the tale of *The Fox*, which is in Habicht. Three tales are not given by Scott for reasons of delicacy; two of these are *The Bathman* and *The Three Wishes*. The other is the second tale of the third vizier, and should be *The Druggist*, which, however, is certainly not more free than others related by Scott. Perhaps it is the tale of *The Loaves*, which is not obscene, but nauseous, and may for that reason have been considered by the Englishman too indelicate for translation.

I will speak of the text of Nachschebî separately in the following chapter. Meanwhile, from the examination of each version in particular and from the comparison of all together, it seems to me to result clearly that the tales contained in the *Book of Sindibâd* are those that I have marked out in the scheme of this book, and in that order in which all reappear in the *Syntipas*. Here would be the place to seek the form which each of these tales had in the original, but, for the reason that I have already pointed out, I am obliged to waive for the present this part, which is less essential for the scope of the present work.

CHAPTER III.

CONCERNING THE EIGHTH NIGHT OF THE TUTI-NAMEH OF NACHSCHEBI, AND THE SECOND TALES OF THE VIZIERS IN THE BOOK OF SINDIBAD.

THAT all the known versions are derived from the *Book of Sindibâd*, such as I have described it in the preceding chapters, will now be readily conceded to me, subject to one exception in respect to the eighth night of the *Tûtî-nâmeh* of Nachschebi, regarding which there exists an opinion which we cannot here neglect. Professor Brockhaus, in making known that redaction for the first time, observed as follows: "From the character which this redaction of Nachschebî has, I should hold that it might be the oldest of those of the *Seven Sages*, since I know no others more simple, from which appears more clearly, or in a manner less disturbed by other additions, its true end—that of warning against the frauds of women. In fact, here we have nothing but the tâles of the viziers upon the subject of female wiles; and the tales which the girl tells in reply, in order to shake the king's confidence in his councillors, are wanting altogether. In this, strangely enough, the most ancient of the French versions, the *Dolopathos* of Herbers, agrees with the Persian redaction, no doubt by chance. Whether in the Indian *Book of the Parrot* there is the same cycle of tales I cannot, unfortunately, affirm, because I have not the original Sanscrit at hand; but of the separate novels I could say so almost with certainty. It would really be important to examine a manuscript of the *Çukasaptati*, and thus conclude the researches concerning this popular book."

Brockhaus wrote this in 1845; in 1851 the Greek translation of the first fifty-nine tales of the *Çukasaptati*, made from an Indian text by Galanos, was published; and the Indian text itself, though corrupt and imperfect, was used by Professor Benfey in his labours upon the *Pancatantra*, published in 1859. The hope of finding in India this text of the *Sindibâd* inserted in the *Çukasaptati*, as it is in the *Tûtînâmeh*, was frustrated. The novels which it contains are found, as Brockhaus had already asserted, in the *Çukasaptati*, but not the principal tale in which they are found inserted in Nachschebî. Benfey had remarked this before in his paper cited by me, which was first published in 1858. Yet the opinion of Brockhaus respecting the greater antiquity of the redaction mentioned by Nachschebî continued to be adopted, if not as certain, at least as probable, by Benfey himself, who many times had occasion to use this text in his introduction to the *Pancatantra*, and generally by all who have occupied themselves in these researches with the exception of Gödeke (*Or. u. Occ.*, iii. p. 388), who has, as if in passing, expressed a doubt, without, however, handling the question thoroughly. However sorry I may be to controvert the opinion of Professor Brockhaus and others of the same authority, I must say my strong conviction is that Nachschebî knew no redaction of the *Sindibâd* independent of that from which the other versions are derived.*

* Before undertaking these researches I also followed, in my paper upon the *Seven Sages*, the opinion which now, for reasons which I shall give, I have thought I ought to abandon.

THE BOOK OF SINDIBAD.

The opinion of Brockhaus, having found no support in the *Çukasaptati*, such at least as we at present know it, remains founded upon one single argument, which is the greater simplicity of this version, in which the viziers are the only persons who tell stories. By itself this is a very weak argument, and when we reflect that this redaction does not constitute a separate book, but forms part of that *Tûtî-nâmeh* in which it occupies *one single* night,—instead of imputing its greater simplicity to some more ancient version, it is more natural to consider it an abridgment, in which the author, suppressing several series of tales (the first ones of the viziers, those of the woman, those of the prince), has left only one series, in order to reduce the book into the lesser proportions which are compatible with being the tale of one single night. In a form much more ample the *Sindibâd* has been introduced into the *Thousand and One Nights;* but in these it occupies several nights in succession. I confess, too, that on reflection I do not see why in the first more ancient Indian form the book should not contain tales of the woman. Indeed, in order to give occasion to the tales of all the viziers, it was necessary that the condemnation should be renewed every day, and this, naturally, by the act of the woman, who accordingly, as also in Nachschebî, every day presents herself to ask again for justice. Now why should she in the earliest text present herself to demand justice *without telling any tale,* and not rather oppose tale to tale, since such were the arms given to the viziers against her object? Besides this, the asserted primitive simplicity of this redaction becomes suspicious by its appearing certainly exaggerated, when it is remarked that Nachschebî has seven viziers, while he only makes six of them speak, —a circumstance which Professor Brockhaus does not explain, yet which, rather than leading us to think of a more simple, because more ancient, text, would instead confirm the idea of its being an abridgment of the common text. Besides, if we suppose that of this more ancient redaction Nachschebî knew a Persian text, whether the latter already formed part (as I do not think probable) of the ancient *Tûtî-nâmeh* or was independent of it, it is very singular that such a text should have remained unknown down to the fourteenth century, and he only should then know it, whilst not long after, in the same century, the author of the *Sindibâd-nâmeh* is acquainted with no other than a Persian translation of the common text. What next dissuades one from believing in this greater antiquity is the great resemblance which is seen between the *Book of Sindibâd* and the text of Nachschebî in what they have in common. On comparing the principal tale in the two versions it is impossible not to perceive that in Nachschebî it is simply an abridgment of the usual form. A glance at the comparative table which I have drawn up of the various versions removes every doubt as to this. In some tales some differences are observed, but in the whole we are very far from finding that diversity which in similar cases may be expected by him who knows the changes to which these popular books are subject when they pass through divers phases, of the nature of those which the opinion of Professor Brockhaus supposes. This objection becomes still more grave if any one wishes to suppose that Nachschebî had before him an Indian text of that pretended more ancient version.*

Such are the more obvious and general reasons which I have for doubting that opinion. Other observations will better elucidate the true nature of this redaction. I note in the first place an important fact which up to this

* According to Pertsch (*l.c.*, p. 511), Nachschebî lived some time in India and knew some Indian dialects.

time has not been remarked. Seeing that in the *Book of Sindibâd* the viziers have two tales each, it is very natural that originally they may have had only one, and somebody may have added a second (entirely superfluous) to make the collection richer. Now, it is clear that this suspicion would lead one naturally to doubt the originality of the second, and not the first, stories of the viziers; and consequently in a more ancient redaction we should expect to find wanting those that in the others are *second* stories, and not those which in them are *first*. Now, in the redaction of Nachschebî precisely the contrary happens, and it is not the second but the first stories which are missing. Indeed, the five tales that reappear in the *Book of Sindibâd* are all second stories of the viziers. The following comparison shows this:—

The Double Infidelity	Second of the Second Vizier.
The Libertine Husband	Second of the Fourth Vizier.
The Young Elephant . . .	Second of the Sixth Vizier.
The Man who understood Female Wiles	Second of the Seventh Vizier.
The Woman and the Druggist . .	Second of the Third Vizier.

When we reflect that the six tales that are found in this redaction all reappear in the *Çukasaptati*,* every one will be ready to admit that, if they reappear in Nachschebî, they ought also to be found in the ancient *Tûtî-nâmeh* which he had before him. Accordingly, it is easy to

* Nachschebî	1st	Çukasaptati	26th
,,	2nd	,,	1st
	3rd		22nd
	4th		11th
,,	5th		15th
,,	6th	,,	32nd

The fourth tale of Nachschebî contains two stories, the second of which is foreign to the *Sindibâd* and to the *Çukasaptati*. Of the fifth tale the *Çukasaptati* has a second portion, which is foreign to the *Sindibâd* and also to the text of Nachschebî, and which is met with in other collections as a separate tale. (Cf. Benfey, *Pantsch.*, i. p. 457, and my *Virgilio Mago* in *Nuova Antologia*, 1867, August, p. 62, *et seq.*)

explain the origin of this redaction without thinking of a greater antiquity, and also without thinking of an abridgment, properly so called, of the *Book of Sindibâd*. Nachschebî remarked that those tales of the *Tûtî-nâmeh* were found again in the *Book of Sindibâd;* he therefore joined them together into one night, giving them for their framework the principal tale of the *Sindibâd* (abbreviated and the names removed), which latter was known to him probably in that same Persian version translated from the Arabic which was used by the author of the *Sindibâd-nâmeh*. This he could do conveniently because those tales which the *Sindibâd* has in common with the *Çukasaptati* or with the *Tûtî-nâmeh* constitute exactly a separate series, viz., that of the *second* stories of the viziers. In this way it is very well explained why the viziers have only six stories. In point of fact, the first of the second stories of the viziers being *The Woman and the Parrot*, itself almost identical with the principal tale of the *Tûtî-nâmeh*, he could not repeat it. He therefore has suppressed it, reducing the tales to six by the same expedient which we see adopted in the S. N., that is, by making the prince speak on the seventh day. Moreover, of the second tales of the viziers, one only, so far as we know, is foreign to the *Çukasaptati*, *The Burnt Cloth;* and this tale is not found in Nachschebî, who did not find it in the ancient *Tûtî-nâmeh*. Instead we find substituted the tale of *The Father-in-law*, which is foreign to the *Sindibâd*, but ought to have been in the ancient *Tûtî-nâmeh*, since besides being in Nachschebî it reappears in the *Çukasaptati*.

It is well known that the ancient Persian text which Nachschebî had before him was not a translation of the *Çukasaptati*, but a book for which the latter served as a groundwork. Besides this, however, other collections also had been used. Thus, indeed, it is well known that the text of Nachschebî is not properly a translation, but a free version or an adaptation of that ancient *Tûtî-nâmeh*, in which morever liberty may have been taken as regards the tales of the *Çukasaptati*, and for the version of the latter there may have been sometimes substituted one of another collection. We cannot therefore say with certainty whether Nachschebî, having before him for five tales the version of the *Sindibâd* and that of the ancient *Tûtî-nâmeh*, has always adhered to the latter, or has selected for each tale that version which pleased him best. As regards three of these tales the version of Nachschebî approaches nearer to the *Sindibâd* than to the *Çukasaptati*. They are *The Double Infidelity*, *The Man who understood Female Wiles*, and *The Woman and the Druggist*. I have already observed elsewhere that in the tale of *The Man who understood Female Wiles* there is in Nachschebî a second wile added to the tale of the ancient *Tûtî-nâmeh*, entirely foreign to the *Sindibâd*, and one which is only found again as a separate tale in that distant offshoot of the *Sindibâd*, the *Book of the Forty Viziers*, in which the tales are collected from a great variety of sources. It may be doubted whether this second wile is due to Nachschebî, or was not already added to the tale in the ancient *Tûtî-nâmeh*. The latter seems to me the more probable opinion, and the fact of that addition not being found in the *Çukasaptati* certainly does not exclude it, because, as I have said, that text contained also tales taken from other collections. That Nachschebî might find it added in the text of the *Sindibâd* known to him I would not believe unless, besides being in the latter, it were also in the ancient *Tûtî-nâmeh*. The tale of *The Young Elephant* is in Nachschebî a little nearer to the form which it has in the *Çukasaptati* than to that of the *Sindibâd*. But in the tale of *The Libertine Husband* (the latter part of *The*

Go-between and the Dog in the *Sindibâd*) Nachschebî is as much removed from the *Çukasaptati* as from the *Sindibâd*. Of this tale I shall shortly speak. In the mean time, I remark that the text of the *Sindibâd* being, as regards this tale, much more approximated to that of the *Çukasaptati* than the text of Nachschebî, is an argument against the pretended greater antiquity of this last-named redaction.

It will be proper here to consider a remarkable circumstance which, in regard to the second tales of the viziers, is elucidated by what I have just observed as to the tales of this version of Nachschebî. As I said before, if in all the *Book of Sindibâd* there are tales as to which it may be suspected that they would not be found in the primitive Indian text, such certainly are these second tales of the viziers, which, however, certainly were in the *Book of Sindibâd* from which the known versions spring. This suspicion is confirmed, and made almost a certainty, by the observation I have already made, viz., that the tales which Nachschebî has, and which are second tales of the viziers, are all found in the *Çukasaptati*. Of seven, which is the number of these second tales in the *Book of Sindibâd*, six are found in this collection, and, as if to exclude the suspicion of an accidental coincidence (very unlikely in itself, inasmuch as we have to deal not with here and there one or two tales, but with an entire series), that one of these six tales which is the first of the whole series, viz., the second tale of the first vizier, is *The Husband and the Parrot*, which, as Professor Benfey also remarks (*Pantsch.*, i. p. 273), corresponds in its ultimate analysis with the fundamental tale of the *Çukasaptati*. Of the various series of tales of the *Sindibâd*, this is the only one that presents a coincidence so important. Some other tales of the *Sindibâd* are found that may offer an analogy with the *Çukasaptati*, but slightly only, and, moreover, much less approximated to the form of the *Çukasaptati* than are those second tales of the viziers. Professor Benfey has already,* with his usual diligence and learning, illustrated two tales of the woman (*The Ape and the Wild Boar* and *The Thief and the Lion*) which resemble closely two stories of the *Çukasaptati*. A glance at the resemblances pointed out by this learned man is sufficient to convince us that they are very far from having with the *Çukasaptati* that clear and indisputable affinity of *derivation* which the second tales of the viziers present. It is clear that even in their more ancient and primitive form these Indian collections must, indeed, have had certain elements in common, whether they took them from popular narration or from more ancient writings or collections. Thence arise certain similarities, which do not always authorize us in supposing that one collection has lent to another. This, however, cannot in any way apply to the second tales of the viziers in this *Book of Sindibâd*, which, very like in form to tales in the *Çukasaptati*, and constituting a series at the head of which appears the principal tale of the *Çukasaptati*, bear evident character of being an addition made to the *Sindibâd* by some one who took them from a version of the *Çukasaptati*. This fact, already sufficiently clear of itself, is confirmed by an Arabian writer of the tenth century, Mohammed Ibn-el-Neddim-el-Werrak, who, as is well known, in a passage often cited, speaks of two texts of the *Book of Sindibâd*, one larger and another smaller, which is well explained by referring it to the text containing the considerable addition of seven tales, and to the other which is without it.†

* *Pantsch.*, i. § 173, 2, 11.

[† Nöldeke does not agree with me in this idea; he holds, on the contrary, that all the texts now in existence come from the lesser *Book of Sindibâd*. The observations of the learned Orientalist are very

Here the reader will ask me for an explanation of the presence of the tale of *The Burnt Cloth* (the second of the fifth vizier), which is the only one of all this series that is not to be found in the *Çukasaptati*. To account for this it is necessary to observe that the tale *immediately antecedent* in the same series, the second one of the fourth vizier (*The Go-between and the Dog*), corresponds not with one but with two tales of the *Çukasaptati*, which in this book are really placed one directly after the other (first and second night), but separate. Taking this into account, it seems to me we may believe, with every probability, that he who first added to the *Sindibâd* that new series of tales, taking them from the *Çukasaptati*, would give those two, one to the fourth and the other to the fifth vizier, so that all the second tales of the viziers came to be thus without exception taken from the *Çukasaptati*. There was some one, however, who wished to introduce the tale of *The Burnt Cloth*, and in order to do this he united the story of the fifth vizier with that of the fourth, and put the new tale in the vacant place. This union of two tales in order to leave room for a new one is a thing not at all unusual, as any one who is familiarly acquainted with the history of these popular books knows well, and the history itself of the *Sindibâd* offers other examples of it. Thus, as we have seen, in the Hebrew text for this very purpose there have been fused together two tales of the woman (*The Lamia* and *The Changed Sex*), which in all the other versions, as certainly in the original text, are separate.

noteworthy, but being unable to reproduce them here I invite the reader to study them in the *Zeitschrift der Deutsch. Morgenl. Gesellsch.*, xxxiii. p. 521, *et seqq.* The observation which he has been the first to make, that in two manuscripts of the *Fihrist* is indicated the title of the greater *Sindibâd*, which was *Aslam and Sindbâd,* is relevant. Of the first of these names no trace is found in the known text; perhaps it was the name of the prince, who has been left anonymous in the more compendious texts which we possess.]

So, indeed, in some of the Western texts, as the *Historia Septem Sapientum* (which I believe is very far from being the original of the vulgar Western versions) and others, there have been fused together two tales (*The Wife of the Seneschal* and *Janus in the Defence of Rome*) in order to make room for another tale, *The Three Lovers*. It would be an apparent support to this my opinion to find the two parts of the tale of *The Go-between and the Dog* separate, and attributed the one to the third and the other to the fourth vizier in the *Sindibâd-nâmeh*, which would lead to the belief that the S. N. comes from a more ancient version of the *Sindibâd*, in which the second tales of the viziers should have been already inserted, but the two with which we are occupied not yet fused together; the more so because the tale of *The Burnt Cloth* is not amongst those which this text offers. But this support is apparent merely. The absence in the S. N. of the tale of *The Burnt Cloth* proves nothing, since, as we have seen, others also are wanting that have evidently been suppressed, but were in the text from which the S. N., like the other versions, is derived. Among the missing stories is also *The Young Elephant*, viz., one of the second tales of the viziers which reappear in the *Çukasaptati*. As to the tale of *The Go-between and the Dog*, which we here find divided in two, it is clear that if the S. N. sprung from a version more ancient than that from which the others spring, the form of these two tales ought to be in it either more approximated to the form that they have in the *Çukasaptati* than their *ensemble* is in the later version, or at least just as near. Precisely the contrary is the fact. The tale of *The Libertine Husband* (which is the latter part of the tale of *The Go-between and the Dog*) is much nearer to the form it has in the *Çukasaptati* in those versions in which it is fused together with the other tale of *The Go-between and the Dog* than it is in the

S. N., in which it stands by itself, as in the *Çukasaptati*. The difference cannot be attributed to the caprice of the man who wrote the S. N., since, in the same form that it has in this latter, that tale recurs also in the eighth night of Nachschebî. But Nachschebî has not the other part or the other tale, in which the dog occurs, and it is observable that he not only has not it in the eighth night, but he has not it at all in his *Tûtî-nâmeh*, although, as I have said, the *Çukasaptati* has it. This other part is in the S. N., in which, as in the *Çukasaptati*, it constitutes a separate tale, of a form which approaches nearer to the *Sindibâd* (separating, of course, from it all that connects it with the other tale with which it has been united) than to the *Çukasaptati*.*

This circumstance of the go-between who employs the artifice of making a dog weep, &c., recurs in two tales of quite an opposite character: in the one (this of the *Sindibâd* and of the *Çukasaptati*) the subject is a woman who yields; in the other (Somadeva, p. 56, *et seq.*) the subject is a woman who resists the deceit of the go-between.† Both these tales

---

* Falconer communicates only the title; Dr. Sachau, however, has informed me of the contents, which I abridge as follows:—A man sees a beautiful woman at a window, and falls desperately in love with her, to which she, however, does not respond. He goes to an old woman to intercede for him, and the latter endeavours to persuade the woman to favour him, but in vain. Then the old woman has recourse to the expedient of the dog, &c., and the woman yields. In the *Çukasaptati* the woman who is tempted is the wife of a royal prince; a young man falls in love with her, and, loving her in silence, consumes and fades away to such a degree that his mother, in order not to see him die, determines to do her best that his love may be satisfied. The mother goes to the princess, and by the expedient of the dog persuades her not to be chary of herself towards men, and the princess having told her to find her some, the mother brings her into communication with her own son.

† See as to these two tales, much diffused in East and West, Loiseleur, *Essai*, p. 107; Hagen, *Gesammtabenteuer*, iii. p. lxxxiii, *et seqq.*; Maetzner, *Altenglische Sprachproben*, p. 103, *et seqq.*

reappear in Nachschebî, the one in the eighth night, the other in the fourth night (Kâdirî, No. 4; Rosen, i. p. 83); but in both the circumstance of the dog is wanting altogether, and it thence appears to have been deliberately left out, like other tales of the *Çukasaptati*. Nachschebî, as it appears, found in the ancient text of the *Tûtî-nâmeh* only the second part of the tale of *The Go-between and the Dog*; he placed it in the eighth night as he found it, viz., in a different form from that which it has both in the *Çukasaptati* and in the *Sindibâd*. As to the *Sindibâd-nâmeh*, as we have seen, its author has introduced tales taken from other collections, and has sometimes preferred versions different from those of the original. It is posterior to Nachschebî, and may consequently have taken that tale of *The Libertine Husband* from him, who is the only one in whom that tale is found in that form. Two other tales of the S. N., foreign to the other versions of the *Sindibâd*, reappear in Nachschebî (Nos. 5a and 35a).

That the addition of those second tales of the viziers was made in India cannot, it seems to me, be supposed with any likelihood if it be admitted as probable that the smaller text of the *Sindibâd*, of which the above-mentioned Arabian writer speaks, is that to which these tales had not yet been added. In point of fact it does not seem credible that two texts of the same book of different dimensions have come from India, and, passing through the Pehlvi (which is the accustomed way), have come into Arabic literature, and have maintained themselves therein distinct the one from the other up to the tenth century. Generally in these cases the richer collection overpowers and supersedes the other, just as happened afterwards to the *Sindibâd* itself, of which we find that all the known versions come from a text which contained the addition of those tales. One may believe that the Arabic version of

E

the smaller text was made from the Pehlvi in Persia, and there afterwards was increased by those tales which were taken from a Persian version of the *Çukasaptati*. What this latter was it is difficult to say, for of the vicissitudes of the *Çukasaptati* before Nachschebî, or before the fourteenth century, we do not know a great deal. Though the text of the *Tûtî-nâmeh* that Nachschebî had before him might be very ancient, so much so as to appear rude and antiquated, as Nachschebî himself says in his introduction,* that does not prove for certain that it reached the fourteenth century without having undergone the common lot of these books of tales, viz., that it preserved itself entirely in its earliest form. Three of the tales of the eighth night approach more nearly to the form of the *Sindibâd* than that of the *Çukasaptati*. It may be supposed that Nachschebî, between the versions that the ancient *Tûtî-nâmeh* and the *Sindibâd* offered, selected the latter in preference; but if, as I think, those tales have been added to the *Sindibâd* by taking them from a Persian version of the *Çukasaptati*, it is more natural to suppose that the coincidence is attributable to their being found in the ancient *Tûtî-nâmeh* such as they were in the *Sindibâd*. The differences, then, that two other tales present, and the absence of that of the dog, would be explained by the changes which the Persian *Tûtî-nâmeh* must have undergone before arriving at the fourteenth century. What has already been remarked† respecting the nature of that text which Nachschebî had before him is in full accord with these conjectures of mine. Some other observations may be added to consolidate them. The most ancient author's name that the versions of the *Sindibâd* offer us is,

* V. Kosegarten *apud* Iken; *Tûtî-nâmeh*, p. 195, *et seqq.*; and Rosen, *Tûtî-nâmeh*, i. p. ix.

† See the already cited article of Benfey in *Gott. Gel. Anz.*

in fact, the name of a Persian. Moreover, this Persian, Musa, is really the author of the most ancient text to which we are able to trace back these versions, viz., of that text from which directly, through the intermediate Syriac version, is derived the Greek text of the *Syntipas*, which is the most ancient, and, as results from our comparisons, the least remote from the original, of the known versions. The *Syntipas*, as I shall prove in the following chapter, was put into Greek by Andreopulos at the end of the eleventh century. Now if we consider that the Syriac version, from which Andreopulos translated, must naturally have been more ancient than this epoch, and that the text of the Persian Musa, from which that Syriac version was made, must have been more ancient still, we shall find, without any bold hypotheses, that this Persian Musa, author of a version in which we already find added the second tales of the viziers, may very well belong, and even be anterior, to the tenth century, in which for the first time mention is made in an Arabian writer of a greater *Book of Sindibâd*. How much that addition may be anterior to the last-named century it is difficult to say. But if indeed it was not made in that very century, it is not so anterior as to have thrown into oblivion the smaller collection, which we find was also known to the same Arabian writer. Masudi, who died thirty-one years before Mohammed, speaking of the *Sindibâd*, does not distinguish two texts of different dimensions. From this, however, nothing can be deduced, nor from his words can it be ever so little guessed which of the two redactions was known to him. In the *Syntipas* it is not said in what language the Persian Musa wrote, only the preface of the Syriac version is translated into Greek word for word (ὡς εἶχεν αὐταῖς λέξεσιν), and the words which have reference to this are, Ταύτην τὴν διήγησιν προϊστόρησε Μοῦσος ὁ Πέρσης. It is very likely that this latter wrote in Arabic, as the other Persian, Abdallah Ibn Almokaffa (translating from the Pehlvi), put the *Calila and Dimna* into Arabic. Can this Musa be really the author of that text from which are derived the known versions, and the original scheme of which we have been seeking?

CHAPTER IV.

UPON THE AGE OF THE SYNTIPAS AND OF THE HEBREW VERSION.

OF all the versions, that which best and to the greatest degree represents the original is the *Syntipas*, with the exception of the beginning, down to where the first education of the prince is told, in which other versions, as we have seen, abridge the original text less; through almost all the remainder the *Syntipas* finds a counterpart in one or more versions, and the comparison shows that it follows the original with greater fidelity than any other. The *Syntipas* is, therefore, the most remarkable of all the texts of the *Sindibâd* at present known, and it is worth our while to ascertain to what age it belongs. Though, however, even without a more minute collation of the various versions, one might easily perceive the importance which this version possesses, no one till now has endeavoured to fix the age of it in a positive manner. All that has seriously been said about it reduces itself to the following words, which Dacier wrote in the year 1780:—" A l'égard du temps auquel il faut rapporter la traduction grecque, si j'osais juger du style par celui des écrivains grecs du XIe siècle, je penserais qu'on peut lui assigner cette époque; mais l'expression est en général assez pure (!), la phrase parait être d'un temps où la langue avait dégénéré. Quoi qu'il en soit, il est vraisemblable que ce roman fut apporté chez nous au retour de la première croisade."* This vague, uncertain, contradictory judgment, founded upon no reason even apparently solid, could satisfy nobody; the less could it be considered as decisive since Dacier, who knew the *Syntipas* only from a bad Paris manuscript of the sixteenth century, was ignorant of the prologue in verse, afterwards published by Matthaei† from a more ancient manuscript at Moscow, wanting as well in the manuscript which Dacier read as in the others, in which prologue it is said by whom that translation was made from the Syriac into Greek, and by whose orders. But even after the document was published, neither Matthaei himself, nor Boissonade, nor Koraì, nor Keller, nor Sengelman, nor others amongst so many who had to deal with the *Syntipas* in their writings, could say anything more positive than Dacier had said. Boissonade, upon whom as the first publisher of the book it was incumbent to seek its age, gets out of his trouble by referring the reader to Dacier as regards this, which is equivalent to saying he knew nothing about it. More explicitly Loiseleur (*Essai*, p. 83, *et seq.*) says that the age of the *Syntipas* is unknown; he, however, considers it as more ancient than that the Hebrew version, which, in his belief, cannot be posterior to the end of the twelfth century. Up to the present time, therefore, what we know more positively concerning the age of the *Syntipas* is this: that it is certainly anterior to the thirteenth century—an age to which, in Matthaei's judgment, the Moscow codex, which is the most ancient known, may ascend. Respecting Andreopulos, who in the prologue in verse declares himself the author of the translation, Boissonade observes:—"Nominis ipsa desinentia recentiorem esse arguit." As far as I can at present recollect, names

---

* *Mém. de l'Académie des Inscrip.*, tom. xli. p. 556.

† *Syntipæ Philosophi Persæ Fabulæ*, Lips., 1781, p. viii, *et seq.*

of this form occur as early as the tenth century; and perhaps, if research be made, more ancient instances might be found.

The prologue before referred to is as follows:—

> Τοῦ μυθογράφου Συντίπα κατὰ Σύρους,
> Μᾶλλον δὲ Περσῶν τοὺς σοφοὺς λογογράφους
> Αὕτη πέφυκεν ἣν βλέπεις δέλτος, φίλε.
> Ἣν καὶ Συρικοῖς τοῖς λόγοις γεγραμμένην
> Εἰς τὴν παροῦσαν αὐτὸς Ἑλλάδα φράσιν
> Μετήγαγόν τε καὶ γέγραφα τὴν βίβλον,
> Τῶν γραμματικῶν ἔσχατός γε τυγχάνων,
> Ἀνδρεόπωλος Μιχαὴλ, Χριστοῦ λάτρις,
> Ἔργον τεθεικὼς προστεταγμένον τόδε
> Παρὰ Γαβριὴλ, τοῦ μεγιστάνων κλέους
> Δουκὸς σεβαστοῦ πόλεως μελωνύμου,
> Ὅς ἐστι Χριστοῦ θερμὸς ὄντως οἰκέτης.
> Ὅς καὶ διωρίσατο γραφῆναι τάδε
> Ὅτι γε μὴ πρόσεστι Ῥωμαίων βίβλοις.
> Ἡ συγγραφὴ γὰρ ἥδε τοὺς κακεργάτας
> Διασύρει μάλιστα, καὶ πρὸς τῷ τέλει
> Πράξεις ἐπαινεῖ τὰς καλῶς εἰργασμένας.

We know from this that the *Syntipas* was translated from the Syriac by a grammarian named Michael Andreopulos, by order of a gentleman named Gabriel, who was duke of a city which Andreopulos designates as μελώνυμος. Who this Michael Andreopulos was no one has been able to say, and I know no more than the others. It is not to be wondered at that nothing, except what he himself tells us, is known of an obscure grammarian who, as his book proves, was devoid of all merit. That Gabriel, however, who caused the translation to be made, being no ordinary person, but a man of very elevated position, invested with the government of a city, important so far as appears, decorated with the title of *Duke* and *Sebastos*,—there is room for believing that some record of him must be preserved in the numerous historians and chronologists we possess of the Byzantine middle ages. Matthaei, Koraì, and others have, in seeking after this Gabriel, suffered themselves to be misled by a false interpretation of that πόλεως μελωνύμου. Matthaei, believing that μελώνυμος must be the name of the city, and not finding any one of that name, imagined it to be an error of the copyist, and corrected it into Μελενίκου; and in this Koraì, with others, has followed him.* But, besides that this alteration is entirely arbitrary, and that there is no palæographical reason that can explain how Μελενίκου could be changed into μελωνύμου, not only no mention is found of any Gabriel who governed Melenicus, but it is not even known that there ever was a Duke of Melenicus. Melenicus is spoken of by the Byzantines for the most part as a φρούριον, as a rather strong castle, and the authority that governed it as an ἐπίτροπος, and not a duke.† Boissonade, therefore, who has adhered to the reading of the manuscript, has done well, he justly observing, which besides is easy to understand, that μελώνυμος is not the name, but the qualification of the name, of a city.‡ He has not stopped, however, to inquire what city this was and who Gabriel was. This research I undertook, and after a long rummaging of books, I have had the pleasure of finding out what I was looking for.

* *Prolegomena* (edit. 1815), p. 478.

† Φρούριον ὁ Μελένικος ἐπί τινος πέτρας ἱδρυμένον χρημνοῖς καὶ φάραγξι βαθυτάτοις πάντοθεν ἐστεφανωμένης (Cedren, 460, 20). Cf. Niceph. Greg., ix. cap. 5 ; Johann. Cantacuz., i. 43 ; iii. 37, 38, 41.

‡ He cites the example of Nicephorus Stefanopulos (*Notices et Extr.*, viii. 252), who says he was the brother, ἀνδρὸς κοσμίου καὶ τὴν περιώνυμον ἄγοντος πόλιν, Πόλιν μεγίστην νικεπωνυμουμένην, whcih city he believes to be Thessalonike, I Nikopolis.

The name of Gabriel is not very frequent among the Byzantines, still less with the title of duke. The only *Duke* Gabriel that I have found* was precisely Duke of *Melitene*, that is to say, of a city which excellently explains the μελώνυμος of Andreopulos, a compound for which no one will stop to criticize a Byzantine of his quality. Melitene was the *chef-lieu* of the third Armenia, which Duke Gabriel towards the end of the eleventh century governed in the name of the Byzantine empire,† on which he nominally depended, but in fact—as at the same epoch at Trebisond the Gabras, and others in other places of those distant regions—exercised an almost independent princely authority. Duke Gabriel was preceded in the government of Melitene by Philartes (Philaretes), who had retaken that city and the dependent territory from the Turks, for which the Byzantine emperor rewarded him with gifts and the title of *Sebastos*,‡ which we find borne also by Gabriel (Δουκὸς σεβαστοῦ). In A.D. 1100 Gabriel, threatened seriously by the Emir of Sebastia, who was already marching on Melitene, asked aid of Boemond, at that time besieging Aleppo, promising to cede to him the government of the country in case of victory. ‖ Boemond came to his assistance, but the Musulmans were victorious, and

* There can be no question here of Duke Angelo Gabriele of Crete (1280-1282).

† Sybel, *Geschichte der Ersten Kreuzzugs*, p. 302.

‡ Michael the Great by Petermann, *Beiträge zu der Geschichte der Kreuzzuge aus Armenischen Quellen* in *Transactions of the Berlin Academy*, 1860, p. 106.

‖ Albert Aquens, vii. 27, *et seqq*. (in *Gesta Dei per Francos*, p. 301, *et seq*.); Willerm. Tyr., ix. 21 (*ibid*., p. 774); Matthew Erets (in *Notices et Extraits*, ix. i. p. 315; Abulfarag., *Chron. Syr*., p. 282); Wilken, *Geschichte der Kreuzzüge*, ii. p. 14, *et seq*.; Hopf, *Gesch. Griechenlands im Mittelalter*, i. p. 135 (in *Ersch und Gruber's Encyklopädie*); Kugler, *Boemond und Tankred, Fürsten von Antiochien*, p. 16; Petermann, in the memoir above cited, pp. 111, 113.

gained possession of Melitene, which later on, in 1118, a Gabras of Trebisond attempted to retake.*

It does not seem to me possible to doubt that this is the Gabriel of whom Andreopulos speaks, so well all coincides with what Andreopulos points out to us about him. Gabriel had a brother-in-law, Thoros (Theodore), Governor of Edessa, a known centre of Syrian culture, and Melitene itself, placed upon the confines of Syria, was frequented by Syrians. Every one will see how well this accords with the statement that this translation was made at Gabriel's instance from a Syriac text. The great number of Mahometans who, in contact and in antagonism with the Christians, inhabited those countries, of which they shortly indeed became masters, explains quite well why Andreopulos (who certainly wrote in times long subsequent to the total destruction of paganism, in which Greek was the language of Christians), declares himself with so much earnestness to be a Christian, and declares also his patron Gabriel to be such.

Therefore the *Syntipas* belongs to the last years of the eleventh century. Thus we find that even in the Greek version the *Sindibâd* agrees with the *Calila and Dimna*, which, as is well known, was put into Greek verse by Simeon Seth for the Emperor Alexius Comnenus. But this latter, translated at Constantinople by a man of some merit, and much superior to Andreopulos, acquired a certain notoriety in the Byzantine world; so much so that in 1279 we find it cited by the Emperor Michael Paleologus in an assembly of ecclesiastical dignitaries, in which grave religious affairs were discussed.† The *Syntipas*, a writing of base alloy, by an obscure man, published in a

---

* Fallmereyer, *Gesch. d. Kaiserth. von Trapezunt*, p. 20; Finlay, *Medieval Greece and Trebizond*, p. 362.

† Pachymer, *Hist.*, vi. 18.

distant country, had another fate. It diffused itself in the East before it did in the West. One of the Paris manuscripts, as appears by a curious note of the copyist, was copied at Caffa, in the Crimea, whither the *Syntipas* must have been brought from Trebisond, which had commercial relations with both Caffa and Melitene. Later on a translation into Romaic obtained a certain vogue even in Greece.

Some will wish to ask if the language of the *Syntipas* really corresponds with its date as I found it. There is no doubt that the numerous neo-grecisms which it contains were already in use amongst the Greek lower orders at the end of the eleventh century, and even long before. It is well known how the vulgar Greek manifests itself in the first half of the twelfth century in Theodorus Prodromus, almost entirely equal to the modern. The only thing that can be doubted is whether all the neo-grecisms have really originated with Andreopulos. He says that he translates εἰς τὴν παροῦσαν Ἑλλάδα φράσιν; but it is clear that by these expressions he did not mean to say he translated into the Greek spoken in his own times, as Sengelman interprets; his quality of grammarian forbade his doing that, though, with modesty not exaggerated, he calls himself as such τῶν γραμματικῶν ἔσχατος. However much, therefore, whilst writing in the usual literary language of the Byzantines, he wished to affect a certain *recherche*, driven sometimes even into forming odd and ridiculous compounds (cf. for example p. 53), that does not prevent his book, in the form in which he wrote it, from leaving much to be desired as regards purity of language, and from containing, indeed, like so many other writings of that time, many neo-grecisms, whether in words, in forms, or in construction. In this respect we should be obliged to believe that he wished to justify himself, were it necessary to understand the word παροῦσαν as Sengelman understands it. But it is easy to perceive that in that passage *present* means simply *this*. He has written many words of vulgar use in their proper form and not in the popular form; such as he wrote them they have remained in the manuscripts, and cannot, therefore, be attributed to the copyists: thus ὀσπίτιον, not σπίτι; ἰδικός μου, not ἐδικός μου; ἐψητά, not ψητά; κραβάτιον, not κρεβάτι; ὀψάρια, not ψάρια, &c. But if in these cases the copyists have respected the text, in others they have corrupted it, introducing vulgar forms and gross absurdities where there certainly were none. Thus, for example, for the verb substantive we find the classical and regular forms generally employed, except a few cases in which we find the vulgar ἤσουν, ἦτον, and the like, which certainly were in use in the time of Andreopulos, but certainly have not been introduced into the text by him. However poor a grammarian he might be, it does not seem credible that he should not follow a certain constant system in writing, but should say promiscuously τοῦ καλουμένου σαχάρεως, and a little after τῆς σαχάρεως, and then τὸ σάχαρ, and so σιτάριον, σιτάριν, σιτάρι, so ἵνα and νά; nor that the same hand that wrote λαβεῖν ἕνα πίνακα γεμισμένον can have written in the same page δώσω σου εἰς πινάκιν γεμάτον (p. 127). It is necessary, therefore, to distinguish in the language of the *Syntipas* what belongs to Andreopulos from that which belongs to the copyists; not, however, in order to judge of the age of this text, since, as I have said, in that, even as we now know it, there is nothing that can hinder us from attributing it to the epoch that the prologue in verse assigns to it, according as I have elucidated it. But, now that this age is determined, a critical edition, such as Bode was preparing,* compiled with the aid not only of the two Paris manuscripts which Boissonade made use of, but of those of Venice, Vienna, and Moscow, and of others

* See Keller, *Li Romans des Sept Sages*, p. 23.

if there be any, would add one monument more to the history of neo-Greek, which certainly was revealing itself in the writing of Andreopulos.*

I do not know why some persons have wished to doubt the value of the description " Syrian " or " Syriac," which Andreopulos gives the text from which he has translated, some imagining that he has thus designated an Arabic text,† others a neo-Hebraic text.‡ They were wrong, inasmuch as a Syriac text has existed and does exist, and Rödiger has discovered it. As far back as February, 1866, he spoke of it to the Academy of Berlin,§ without, however, admitting the public into his confidence. He published last year [1868] a specimen of this text, consisting of the tale of *The Lamia*, in the second edition of his *Chrestomathia Syriaca* (p. 100, *et seqq.*), without giving any further notice of this find, but promising to speak of it in a special paper. Judging by the specimen published, this version is not precisely that which Andreopulos had before him. It is true that Andreopulos, as is shown by his own words, has used in his translation a certain liberty, limiting himself to translating *word by word* (ὡς εἶχεν αὐταῖς λέξεσιν) only the prologue of the Syriac version. It cannot, however, be

[* This wish has been gratified by Dr. Eberhard in his critical edition before mentioned (p. 5, note). Besides the manuscripts of the common text and the modern Greek version collated by him, he has, for the first time, communicated the entire text of a Munich MS. (unfortunately incomplete), which is most remarkable for the comparative purity and elegance of its Greek, and its remoteness from the vulgar language. I think we may say that this latter is the original version of Andreopulos, and that the common text was only a redaction of the eleventh century in a more popular form, made perhaps not long after the first.]

† Gödeke, in *Or. und Occ.*, iii. 393.

‡ Keller, *Li Romans*, &c., xxiii ; Sengelman, *Das Buch von den Sieben Weisen Meistern*, p. 18, *et seq.*

§ See *Monatsberichte der k. Akad. der Wiss. zu Berlin*, February, 1866, p. 61.

believed that all that the *Syntipas* contains in addition to the Syriac text published by Rödiger should be attributed to Andreopulos. Several things that are found in the *Syntipas* and are wanting in the Syriac text are found in other versions, and are therefore not due to the imagination of Andreopulos. Even these, however, are only small details, not essential matters. The tale is identical in the Greek and in the Syriac, only in the latter it is a little more abbreviated.*

* That those also who, like me, are ignorant of Syriac, may convince themselves of the accuracy of what I assert, I reproduce here that Syriac tale, translated literally by my learned friend and colleague Fausto Lasinio, whose cordial friendship and profound and solid acquaintance with Semitic matters have greatly assisted me in these researches:—"There was once a king, and he had a son, and he loved him much. And the son of the king said to the philosopher, 'Ask my father to permit me to go out hunting.' And the philosopher asked that of the king. And the king said to the philosopher, 'If you indeed go out with him I will permit him to go out.' And the philosopher went out with the king's son, and a wild ass came unexpectedly upon them. And the philosopher said, 'Pursue and chase this wild ass by yourself.' And the young man pursued the wild ass, and having left the philosopher far behind, and not knowing any longer where to go, he saw a road and went by it. And having travelled some distance, he found by the way a young woman who was weeping, and he said to her, 'What is the cause for which you weep?' And she said to him, 'I am the daughter of such-and-such a king, and I was riding an elephant, and I fell accidentally, and did not know where to go, and I ran until I got tired.' And the young man, seeing this, mounted the young girl behind him, until he brought her to some ruins. She said to him, 'I have something to do. I will alight and will enter these ruins.' And he found that she was a daughter of the Lilit (*lamiæ*, or witches), and heard her voice saying to her two female companions, 'Lo, I bring you a handsome young man riding on horseback.' They said to her, 'Bring him to such-and-such ruins.' When the king's son heard this he returned to where he had left the Lilit, and she came out to him, and the young man began to tremble from fear. She said to him, 'Why do you tremble?' He said to her, 'I remember one of my companions, and I fear much from him.' She said to him, 'Why do you not pacify him with the silver which you spoke of?' He said to her, 'He cannot

THE BOOK OF SINDIBAD. 63

The Moscow manuscript, besides the *Syntipas*, contains a certain number of Æsopic fables, attributed therein to the *philosopher Syntipas*. From this Matthaei, who has published them, has wished to deduce that they also have been translated from the Syriac by Andreopulos, who would have found them in the same manuscript as the Syriac *Syntipas*. This opinion has been already rightly combated by De Sacy, and wrongly supported again by Landsberger. Andreopulos says that Gabriel ordered him to make that translation from the Syriac because there was no such thing in the Greco-Roman literature, ὅτι γε μὴ πρόσεστι ‘Ρωμαίων βίβλοις, which is as true as regards the *Syntipas* as it is false as regards those Æsopic fables, which are found also even in the Syriac, but translated into this language from the Greek, as has been already remarked of those published by Landsberger.* In the manuscript in

be so appeased.' 'Lo,' she said to him, 'pray God for him, as you would speak to the king, and he will deliver you from his hands.' He said to her, 'You have said excellently well.' And he raised his eyes to heaven, and said, 'Lord, give me strength against this witch, and deliver me from her wickedness.' And when she heard this she cast herself down on the ground, and defiled herself in the dust. And she sought to rise, but could not, and the young man spurred his horse and escaped from the witch." [Now that the Syriac text is published (with a German translation) by Dr. Baethgen, and also a critical edition of the *Syntipas* has been issued by Dr. Eberhard, I believe that the part most abbreviated in the Syriac text is the introduction. I do not, however, think that the unique manuscript now known represents exactly this Syriac text, such as Andreopulos had before him in making his translation. As, however, the narrative is identical in both, I leave this question for some one else to occupy himself with; it is of minor importance as regards the main object of my researches.]

* *Die Fabeln des Sophos, Syrisches Original der Griechischen Fabeln des Syntipas*, vom Dr. Julius Landsberger, Posen, 1859. Cf. the article by the same author in *Zeitschrift der Deutschen Morgenl. Gesell.*, xii. p. 149, *et seqq.*, and Geiger, *ibid.*, xiv. p. 586, *et seqq.;* Benfey, *Or. u. Occ*, p. 354, *et seqq.;* Roth, in *Heidelberger Jahrbücher*, 1866, i p. 49, *et seqq.*

which Rödiger found the Syriac text of the *Syntipas* are found also some Syriac Æsopic fables ; but these also are translated from the Greek. Of the eight published by Rödiger in the second edition of his *Chrestomathia Syriaca*, p. 97, *et seqq.*, three only occur amongst those which Matthaei believed were translated from the Syriac by Andreopulos.*

The most interesting version after the *Syntipas* is the *Libro de los Engannos*, the age of which we know with certainty. After this in the order of importance comes the Hebrew text, whose age is not as yet determined in a manner really positive. What Sengelman has written concerning this I do not for the present stop to consider, for I am sorry to be obliged to say it is really a miracle of inaccuracy and of what is the opposite of true criticism. Professor Benfey, in his introduction to the *Pancatantra*, p. 11, *et seqq.*, has incidentally pointed out some relations between the Hebrew version of the *Sindibâd* and the Hebrew version of the *Calila and Dimna*, from which it would result that the Hebrew version of the *Sindibâd* is notably anterior to that of the *Calila and Dimna*. Professor Benfey endeavours to settle the question whether the Rabbi Joel, to whom De Rossi and a manuscript of the British Museum attribute the Hebrew text of the *Sindibâd*, is the same Rabbi Joel to whom Doni attributes the Hebrew *Calila and Dimna*. The fact that in the Hebrew *Calila and Dimna* the sage is named *Sendabar*, and besides this the occurring therein of two tales of the *Sindibâd* that form part of the Hebrew version of the latter book, and their non-occurrence in any version of the *Calila and Dimna* except the Hebrew,

---

* They are :—1. *The Sparrow and the Bird-catcher;* 2 *The Camel that asks Horns of Jupiter;* 3. *The Swallow and the Rook.*

might seem (as De Sacy* and Loiseleur† thought) to favour this idea. Against this apparent argument in favour of the two Joels, Benfey justly observes that the change of *Sindibâd* into *Sendabar* cannot in any way be owing to the author of the Hebrew version of the *Sindibâd*, who, having before him an Arabic text, could not certainly change a ד into a ר; and that besides this the two tales of the Hebrew *Calila and Dimna* differ so much from the two corresponding ones in the Hebrew *Sindibâd*, that it does not seem probable they could have been taken from the latter. And in this Professor Benfey is right. When, however, he wishes to demonstrate that in these coincidences not only is there no proof of the identity of the translator, but that rather they prove the contrary, and show that the Hebrew *Sindibâd* is much anterior to the Hebrew *Calila and Dimna*, to my sorrow I cannot follow him in this reasoning. He says that as the corruption *Sendabar* in the Hebrew *Sindibâd* cannot be attributed to the author, but only to the copyists, it follows of course that the author of the Hebrew *Calila and Dimna*, who has *Sendabar*, must have had before him a manuscript of the Hebrew *Sindibâd* very much posterior to the original, that that error should be already found in it fixed and firmly adopted. If it were so, therefore, the *Parables of Sandabar* would be much anterior to A.D. 1250, the approximative age of the Hebrew *Calila and Dimna*. But, in my belief, this reasoning of the learned professor of Göttingen is based upon two suppositions which are, at the very least, gratuitous, viz., 1. That in the Hebrew *Calila and Dimna* it is really the author himself who has written *Sendabar*, and not the copyists, as in the Hebrew *Sindibâd;* 2. That the author of the Hebrew *Calila and Dimna*, who translated

---

* *Notices et Extraits*, ix. pp 397 and 403.
† *Essai*, &c., p. 63.

from the Arabic, could not have had a direct knowledge of the *Sindibâd* in the Arabic text, but must have known it from the Hebrew version. To me it seems clear that with the same facility with which the copyists were able to change סנדבאד into סנדבאר in the Hebrew text of the *Sindibâd*, they were able to do the same thing in that of the *Calila and Dimna;* and it seems to me, moreover, very likely that he who translated *from the* Arabic the *Calila and Dimna* had means of knowing the Arabic text of the *Sindibâd;* and there is, therefore, reason to believe that he has given the true form of the name, corrupted afterwards by the copyists for the same obvious reason as in the other text. As to the two tales, the differences noticed by Benfey prove nothing against the identity of the translator if, as Benfey himself reasonably supposes, those two tales were not inserted by him in the Hebrew *Calila and Dimna*, but were found already in that Arabic text which he had before him. I conclude that there is no objection to the possibility that the two Joels are one and the same person.

The only chronological *data*, therefore, that we have respecting the *Parables of Sandabar* are :—first, the fact of their being certainly anterior to the *Igeret baale hayyim* of Kalonymos ben Kalonymos, in which they are found cited, and which was written about A.D. 1316;* second, the possibility that the author is the same Joel who made, about A.D. 1250, the Hebrew version of the *Calila and Dimna*—a matter which is made very probable not only by the identity of the name Joel, but also by the similarity between the two books as regards the subject in general, and

---

* Sengelman makes it belong to A.D. 1216, and not by a printer's error. Cf. Steinschneider, *Manna*, p. 112 ; Carmoly, *Paraboles de Sendabar*, p. 22; Zunz, in Geiger's *Zeitschrift für Judische Theologie*, ii. 319, *et seq.*; iv. 200, *et seq.*

by their being found also in other languages (in Greek in Persian,* and in Spanish) translated almost contemporaneously.

In order to determine anything respecting the age of the *Seven Viziers* it would be necessary to go into the very intricate question of the chronology of the various redactions of the *Thousand and One Nights*. But whatever might be the result of that investigation, it would be of little consequence for these researches, for which it is sufficient to know that this Arabic text, although not useless, is certainly much more recent, more remote from the original, and of less authority than the other text that we are acquainted with in a Spanish translation of ascertained date.

Such are the results of my researches. I know that the subject is not exhausted, and that further researches will add much more. If, however, what I have herein set forth shall meet with the approval of those men who seriously devote themselves to these studies, I shall be pleased to think that I have furthered the progress of an investigation which could scarcely be said to have been begun, and that I levelled and prepared the way for those who shall come after me.

The text that follows I publish only as a document in connexion with my work and the history of the *Sindibâd*. As such it is of great value, and I publish it accordingly exactly as it appears in the copy procured for me by the distinguished professor Amador de los Rios, to whom I am very grateful for the kindness which he has shown me on this occasion. I here transcribe the memor-

* Hakim Azraki, author of a Persian poetical translation of the *Sindibâd* now lost, died A.D. 1133; Bahrâm Shah, by whose order Nasr-Allah translated into Persian the *Calila and Dimna*, died A.D. 1151.

andum accompanying the copy which that gentleman had made for me:—" El MS. en que se contiene este libro es propriedad del Señor Conde de Puñonrostro. Es de letra del siglo XV. siendo de suponer y aun de creer positivamente que la copia está muy alterada, como sucede con el *Conde Lucanor*, que la precede. Pero, como si no bastara esto para desfigurar el original del siglo XIII., el poseedor ú otro que lo leyó en el XVI., ha enmendado sin discrecion ni criterio palabras y frases, á fin de hacerlo mas accessible á la ignorancia. La copia se ha ajustado en todo al primero traslado, desechando las enmiendas, ociosas siempre é innecesarias, y sobre todo agenas al texto primitivo." ("The MS. in which this book is contained is the property of Count de Puñonrostro. It is in the handwriting of the fifteenth century, but we may suppose, and even positively believe, that the copy is very corrupt, as is the case with the *Conde Lucanor* which precedes it. However, as if it were not sufficient to disfigure the original of the thirteenth century, the possessor, or some one else who read it in the sixteenth century, has corrected words and phrases without discretion or judgment, in order to make it more accessible to ignorance. The copy has been made conformable to the first translation, discarding the corrections, always idle and unnecessary, and above all foreign to the original text.") Only in the accents, of which the copyist has been very sparing, have I permitted myself any latitude. I have never supplied even evident omissions; some words that occur here and there in parentheses I have so found in the copy transmitted to me.

This text is so disfigured and corrupted that I must almost beg the pardon of the more delicate and susceptible scholars of the Romance languages for publishing it in this its unprepossessing form, which certainly will offend their refined tastes. But whoever has penetrated somewhat into these researches, and has thereby perceived how important is a text which, while it represents an Arabic text certainly anterior to A.D. 1253, more than any other agrees with the *Syntipas*, will approve of my having published it, such as it is, in its entirety, rather than in a mere abstract. The greatest corruption appears in that part of the book in which the dispute between the sages and Sindibâd is related. A collation of it with the Hebrew text, and, so far as regards the words which at the end of the dispute Sindibâd addresses to the king, with the *Syntipas* at p. 5, may throw some light on this passage.

Before concluding I must express my gratitude to Count de Puñonrostro, who so liberally permitted me to make a copy of the manuscript possessed by him. I owe also to Professors Benfey and Liebrecht many thanks for the kindness with which they have afforded me information respecting books not easy to find, but necessary for these researches, and not existing in my own library, which is too poor in Oriental matters. I have already intimated elsewhere how great a claim Professor Max Müller, Doctor Sachau, and my friend Fausto Lasinio have upon my gratitude.

LIBRO DE LOS ENGANNOS.

LIBRO DE LOS ENGANNOS ET LOS ASAYAMIENTOS DE LAS MUGERES.

DE ARÁVIGO EN CASTELLANO TRASLADADO POR EL INFANTE DON FADRIQUE,

FIJO DE DON FERRANDO ET DE DOÑA BEATRIS.

―◆―

PRÓLOGO.

El ynfante don Fadrique fijo del muy aventurado et muy noble rrey don Ferrando et de la muy santa reyna complida de todo bien doña Beatris, por quanto nunca se perdiese el buen nombre, oyendo las rrasones de los sabios que "quien bien fase, nunca se le muere la fama," et sabiendo que ninguna cosa non es mejor para aver de ganar la vida perdurable, sinon el bien obrar et el saber, pues el saber es una nave muy segura para poder pasar sin peligro, é juntamente con el bien obrar, para yr á la vida perdurable: et como el omme, como es de poca vida et la çiençia es fuerte et luenga, non puede aprender nin saber mas de lo que le es otorgado por gracia que le es dada et enviada de suso, con amor de aprovechar et faser bien et merced á los que la aman, plogo et tuvo por bien que aqueste libro fuese de arávigo en castellano trasladado para apercibir á los engannos et los asayamientos de las mugeres. Este libro fué trasladado en noventa et un años.

I. *Exemplo del consejo de la muger.*

Avia un rrey en Judea que avia nombre Alcos; é este rrey era señor de gran poder et amava mucho á los ommes de su tierra et de su regno et maneníalos en justiçia: et este rrey avia noventa mugeres. Estando con todas, segun era ley, non podia aver de ninguna dellas fijo, é estando una noche en su cama con una dellas comensó de cuydar que quien heredaria su rreyno despues de su muerte: et des y cuydó tanto en esto que fué muy triste et comensó de rrevolberse en la cama con muy gran cuydado que avia. Et á esto llegó una de sus mugeres aquella quél mas queria, et era cuerda et entendida et avíala él provado en algunas cosas; et llegóse á él por que lo veye estar triste, et díxol' que era onrrado et amado de los de su rregno et de los de su pueblo—¿por qué te veo estar triste et cuydadoso? si es por miedo, ó si te fise algun pesas, fásmelo saber et averé dolor contigo: et si es otra cosa, non deves aver pesar tant grande, ca gracias á Dios, amado eres de tus pueblos et todos disen bien de tí por el gran amor que te an; et Dios nunca te faga aver pesar é ayudes la su benediçion.—Estonce dixo el rrey á su muger: Piadosa bienaventurada, nunca quesiste nin quedeste de me conortar et me tolter todo cuydado, quando lo avia; mas esto,—dixo el rrey,—yo nin quanto poder hé nin quantos ay en mi rregno non podrian poner cobro en esto que yo estó triste. Yo querria dexar para quando muriese heredero para qué heredase el rregno: por esto estó triste. —Et la muger le dixo: Yo te daré consejo bueno á esto: ruega á Dios quél que de todos bienes es conplido, ca poderoso es, de te faser et de te dar fijo, si le pluguiere, ca él nunca cansó de faser merçed et nunca le demandaste cosa que la non diese: et despues quél sopiese que de tan corason le rruegas, darte a fijo. Mas tengo por bien, si tu quisieres, que nos levantemos et roguemos á Dios de todo corason et que le pidamos merçed que nos dé un fijo con que folguemos et fuique heredero despues de nos; ca bien fio por la su merced que si gelo rogamos que nos lo dará. Et si [no] nos lo diere devémosnos pagar et faser el su mandado et seer pagados del su juysio et entender la su merced, et saber que el poder todo es de Dios et en su mano, et á quien quier tolter et á quien quier matar.—Et despues que ovo dicho esto, pagóse él dello, et sopo que lo que ella dixo que era verdad. Et lavantáronse amos et fisiéronlo así, et tornáronse á su cama et yasió con ella el rrey, et empreñóse luego et despues que lo sopieron por verdad loaron á Dios la merced que les fisiera. Et quando fueron conplidos los nueve meses encaeció de un fijo sano et el rrey ovo gran gozo et alegria et mucho pagado dél: et la muger loó á Dios por ende. Des y enbió el rrey por quantos sabios avia en todo su rregno que viniesen á él et que catasen la ora et el punto en que nasiera su fijo; et despues que fueron llegados plógole mucho con ellos et mandólos entrar antél, et díxoles: Bien seades venidos. —Et estuvo con ellos una gran pieça alegrándose et solasándose, et dixo: Vosotros sabios, fágovos saber que Dios, cuyo nombre sea loado, me fiso merçed de un fijo que me dió con que me esforçase mi braso et con que aya alegria, et gracias sean dadas á él por siempre.—Et díxoles: Catad su estrella del mi fijo et vet qué verná su facienda. —Et ellos catáronle et fisiéronle saber que era de luenga vida et que seria de gran poder; mas a cabo de veynte annos quel' avia de acontecer con su padre, por que seria el peligro de muerte. Quando oyó desir esto fincó muy espantado, ovo gran pesar, et tornósele el alegria et dixo: Todo es en poder de Dios, que faga lo que él toviere por bien.—Et el ynfante creció et físose grande et fermoso, et dióle Dios muy buen entendimiento: en su tiempo non fué ome nascido tal como él fué. Et despues quando él llegó á edat de nueve annos, púsole el rrey á aprendel quel' mostrasen escrivir fasta que llegó a edat de quinse annos; é non aprendie ninguna cosa: et quando el rrey lo oyó ovo muy gran pesar et demandó por quantos sabios avia en su tierra; et vinieron todos á él: et díxoles: ¿Que vos semeja de la facienda de mi fijo?...¿non ay alguno de vos que le pueda enseñar? Et dalle hé quanto él demandase, et avia siempre mi amor.—Estonce se levantaron quatro dellos que y estavan, que eran nuevecientos omes, et dixo uno dellos: Yo le enseñaré de guisa que ninguno non sea mas sabidor quél.—Et dixo el rrey estonçe á un sabio quel' desian Cendubete: Por qué non le mostraste tu?—Dixo Cendubete: Diga cada uno lo que sabe.—Et des y fablaron en esto. Et despues díxoles Cendubete: ¿Sabedes ál sinon esto? Ca todo lo conoceré yo, et non curo ende nada, ca ninguno non ay mas sabydor que yo, et yo le quiero mostrar.—Et dixo al rrey: Dadme lo que yo pidiere: que yo le mostraré en seys meses que ninguno non sea mas sabidor quél. — Et estonce dixo uno de los quatro sabios: Atal es él que dise et non fase como el relámpago que non llueve: é pues ¿por qué non le enseñaste tu ninguna cosa en estos años que estuvo contigo, fasiéndote el rrey mucho bien?...—Por la gran piedad que avia dél non le pud enseñar: que avia gran duelo dél á lo apremiar; porque cuydava buscar otro mas sabio que yo, pues que veo que ninguno non sabe mas que yo mostrase.—Et estonçe se levantó el segundo maestro et dixo: Quatro cosas son que omme entendido non deve loar fasta que vea el cabo dellas; lo primero el comer fasta que vea el cabo de ello que lo aya espendido el estómago: et él que va a lydiar fasta que torne de la lit; la mies fasta que sea segada; et la muger fasta que sea preñada. Por ende non te devemos loar fasta que veamos por qué, et mostrar tus manos faser algo et de tu boca et desir algo, por qué faras de su consejo et su coraçon?...—Et dixo Cendubete que a su poder las manos con los pies et el oyr et el veer et todo el cuerpo; tal es el saber con el coraçon como el miésgano et el agua que salle de buena olor : otro sy el saber quando es en el coraçon, fase bueno todo el cuerpo.—Dixo el tercero de los quatro sabios : La cosa que non le tuelle el estómago despues come con sus manos quien non aprende en niñes saberes ; et la muger quando á su marido non a miedo nin teme, nunca puede ser buena : él que dise la rason, sinon la entiende, nin la sabe qué es, nunca tiene seso al que lo oye, nin lo puede despues entender : Et tu, Cendubete, pues que non podiste enseñar al niño en su niñes ¿come le puedes enseñar en su grandes ?...—Dixo Cendubete : Tu veras, sy Dios quisiere et yo bivo, quel' enseñaré en seys meses lo que non le enseñaria otrie en setenta annos.—Et dixo el quarto de los maestros : Sepades que los maestros quando se ajuntan, conosçen los unos á los otros et despuntéanse los unos á los otros et las sabidurías que an : non conosçe uno á otro lo que dise.—Et dixo : Faras lo que tu dises: quiero que me amuestres rrasson como pueda seer que lo así puedes faser ?—Dixo Cendubete : Yo te lo mostraré : dixo : mostrarle hé en seys meses lo que non le emostrará otrie en sesenta annos, por quissa que ninguno non sepa más quél : et yo non lo tardaré mas de una ora, ca me fisieron entender que en qualquier tierra que el rregno fuesse derechero, que él que non judgue los ommes que les libre por derecho que lo faga entender et non aya consejo que emiende á lo quel rrey fisiere, si lo provare. La rriquesa fué por una egualdat, et el físico fuere loçano con su fiesta que non la emuestre á los enfermos bien como tiene. Si estas cosas fueran en la tierra non devemos ay morar. Pues todo esto te hé castigado é te fis saber que los reys tales son como el fuego : Si te llegares á él quemarte as, et sy te arredrares esfriarte as. Quiero yo, Señor, que si te yo mostrare tu fijo que me des lo que te yo demandare.—Et el rrey dixo : Demanda lo que quisieres.—¿ Et si lo non pudieres?—Faserlo hé: que non a cosa peor que mentir, mas é mas á los reyes.—Et el rey dixo: Díme que quieres.—Et dixo Çendubete: Tu non quieras faser á otrie lo que non querries que fisiesen á tí.—Et el rrey dixo: Yo te lo otorgo.—Et fisieron carta del pleyto, é amos pusieron en qual mes é qual ora del dia se avia de acabar, é metieron en la carta quanto avia menester del dia. Eran pasadas dos oras del dia. Cendubete tomó este dia el ninno por la mano é fuése con él para su posada; et fiso faser un gran palaçio fermoso de muy grant guisa, et escribió por las paredes todos los saberes quel' avie de mostrar et de apprender, todas las estrellas et todas las feguras et todas las cosas. Des y díxole: Esta es mi siella et esta es la tuya, fasta que depprendas los saberes todos que yo aprendí en este palaçio: et desenbarga tu coraçon, et abiva tu engeño et tu oyr et tu veer.—Et asentóse con él á mostralle: et trayanles ally que comiesen et que beviesen, et ellos non sallian fuera, et ninguno otro non les entrava allá: et el ninno era de buen engeño et de buen entendymiento, de guisa que ante que llegase el plaso apprendió todos los saberes que Cendubete su maestro avia escripto del saber de los ommes. El rrey demandó por él los dias del plaso: quando llegó el mandadero del rrey díxole: El rrey te quiere tanto que vayas antél.—Díxol': Cendubete, que as fecho ó que tienes?...—Cendubete le dixo: Sennor, tengo lo que te plaserá: que tu fijo será cras dos oras pasadas del dia contigo.—Et el rrey le dixo: Cendubete, nunca fallesçió tal omme como tu de lo que prometiste; pues véte onrrado, ca meresçes aver gualardon de nos.—Et tornóse Cendubete al ninno et díxole: Yo quiero catar tu estrella.—Et católa, et vió quel ninno seria en gran cueyta de muerte, si fablase ante que pasasen los sieyte dias; et fué Cendubete en gran cueyta et dixo al moço: Yo hé muy grant pesar por el pleyto que con el rrey puse.—Et el moço: ¿Por qué has tu muy gran pesar? ca si me mandas que nunca fable, nunca fablaré; et mándame lo que tu quisieres ca yo todo lo faré.—Dixo Cendubete: Yo fis pleyto á tu padre que te vayas cras á él, et yo non le hé de fallescer del pleyto que puse con él: quando fueren pasadas dos oras del dia véte para tu padre, mas non fables fasta que sean pasados los syete dias, é yo esconderme hé en este comedio.—Et quando amansció otro dia mandó el rrey guisar de comer á todos los de su regno, et físoles faser estrados do estudiesen et menestryles quels trinxiesen delante. Et començó el ninno á venir fasta que llegó á su padre; et el padre llególo a sí et fablóle; et el moço non le fabló; et el rrey lo tovo por gran cosa; dixo al ninno: ¿Do es tu maestro?—Et el rrey mandó buscar á Cendubete et sallieron los mandaderos por lo buscar, é catáronlo á todas partes, et non lo pudieron fallar. Et dixo el rrey á los que estavan con él: Quiça por aventura a de mi miedo et non osa fablar; et fabláronle los consejeros del rrey et el ninno non fabló. Et dixo el rrey á los que estavan con él: Que vos semeja de fasienda deste moço? —Et ellos dixieron: Seméjanos que Cendubete su maestro le dió alguna cosa ó alguna melesina por que aprendiese algun saber, et aquella melesina le fiso perder la fabla. Et el rrey lo tovo por gran cosa et pesól' mucho de coraçon.

II. *Enxemplo de la muger en como apartó al ynfante en el ¡palacio, et como por lo quella le dixo olvidó lo que le castigara su maestro.*

El rrey avia una muger, la qual mas amava et onrrávala mas que á todas las otras mugeres quél avia; et quando le dixieron como le acaesciera al ninno, fuesse para el rrey et dixo: Señor, dixiéronme lo que avia acaesçido á tu fijo:

por aventura con gran verguença que de tí ovo non te osa fablar; mas, si quisieses dexarme con él aparte, quiça él me dirá su facienda: ca solia fablar sus poridades comigo, lo que non fasía con ninguna de las tus mugeres.—Et el rrey le dixo: Liévalo á tu palaçio et fabla con él.— Et ella físolo así: mas el ynfante non le respondie ninguna cosa quel' dixiese; et ella siguiólo mas et díxole: Non te fagas neçio, ca yo bien sé que non saldrás de mi mandado · matemos á tu padre et seras tu rrey et seré yo tu muger, ca tu padre es ya de muy gran hedat et flaco, et tu eres mancebo et comiénçase agora el tu bien, et tu debes aver esperança en todos bienes mas quél.—Et quando ella ovo dicho, tomó el moço gran saña et estonce se olvidó lo que le castigara su maestro et todo lo quel' mandara et dixo: Ay, enemiga de Dios, si fuesen pasados los syete dias, yo te responderia á esto que tu dises.—Despues que esto ovo dicho, entendió ella que seria en peligro de muerte, et dió boses et garpios et començó de mesar sus cabellos; et el rrey quando esto oyó, mandóla llamar et preguntóle qué oviera. Et ella dixo: Este que desides que non fabla, me quise forçar de todo en todo, et yo non lo tenia á él por tal.—Et el rrey quando esto oyó, creçiól' gran saña por matar su fijo et fué muy bravo et mandólo matar. Et este rrey avia syete pryvados, mucho sus consejeros de guisa que ninguna cosa non fasia menos de se aconsejar con ellos. Despues que vieron quel rrey mandava matar su fijo, á menos del su consejo, entendieron que lo fasia con saña porque creyera su muger: dixieron los unos á los otros: Si su fijo mata muchol' pesará et despues non s' tornará sinon á nos todos, pues que tenemos alguna rrason atal porque este ynfante non muera.—Et estonçe respondió uno de los quatro maestros et dixo: Yo vos excusaré, si Dios quisiere, de fablar con el rrey.—Este privado primero fuése para el rrey et fincó los ynojos antél et dixo: Señor, no deve faser ninguna cosa el omme fasta que sea cierto della, et si lo ante fisieres errallo as mas: et desirte hé un enxemplo de un rrey et de una su muger.—Et el rrey dixo: Pues dí agora et oýrtelo hé.—El privado dixo: Oy desir que un rrey que amava mucho las mugeres et non avia otra mala manera sinon esta: et seýe el rrey un dia ençima de un soberado muy alto et miró ayuso et vido una muger muy fermosa et pagóse mucho della; et enbió á domandar su amor, et ella díxol' que non lo podria faser, seyendo su marido en la villa. Et quando el rrey oyó esto, enbió á su marido á una hueste: et la muger era muy casta et muy buena et muy entendida et dixo: Señor, tu eres mi señor et yo só tu sierva, et lo que tu quisieres quiérolo yo; mas yrme hé á los vaños afeytar.—E quando tornó, diól' un libro de su marido en que avia leyes et juisios de los rreyes de como escarmentavan á las mugeres que fasian adulterio, et dixo: Señor, ley por ese libro fasta que me afeyte.—Et el rrey abrió el libro et falló en el primero capítulo como devia el adulterio seer defendido, et ovo gran verguença, et pesól' mucho de lo quél quisiera faser et puso el libro en tierra et sallióse por la puerta de la cámara et dexó los arcórcoles so el lecho en que estava asentado. Et en esto llegó su marido de la fueste et quando se asentó él en su casa, sospechó que y durmiera el rrey con su muger et ovo miedo, et non osó desir nada por miedo del rrey, et non osó entrar do ella estava. Et duró esto gran sason, et la muger díxolo á sus parientes que su marido que la avia dexado et non sabia por qual rrason. Et ellos dixiéronlo á su marido: ¿Por qué non te llegas á tu muger?—Et él dixo: Yo fallé los arcórcoles del rrey en mi casa é hé miedo, et por eso no me oso llegar á ella.— Et ellos dixieron: Vayamos al rrey, et agora démosle enxemplo de aqueste fecho de la muger, et non le declaremos el fecho de la muger; et si él entendido fuere, luego

G

lo entenderá.—Et estonçe entraron al rrey et dixiéronle · Señor, nos avíemos una tierra et diémosla á este ome bueno á labrar que la labrase et la defrutase del fruto della; et él físolo asy una gran sason, et dexóla una gran pieça por labrar.—Et el rrey dixo: ¿Qué dices tu á esto?—Et el omme bueno respondió et dixo: Verdat disen que me dieron una tierra así como ellos disen, et quando fuy un dia por la tierra fallé rastro del leon et ove miedo que me conbrie. Por ende dexé la tierra por labrar.—Et dixo el rrey: Verdat es que entró el leon en ella; mas non te fiso cosa que non te oviese de faser; nin te tornó mal dello. Por ende toma tu tierra et lábrala.—Et el omme bueno tornó á su muger, et preguntóle por qué fecho fuera aquello, et ella contógelo todo et díxole la verdat como le contesciera con él, et creyóla por las señales quel' dixiera el rrey, et despues se fiava en ella mas que non dante.

III. *Enxienplo del omme et de la muger et del papagayo et de su moça.*

Señor, oy desir que un onme que era celoso de su muger, et compró un papagayo et metiólo en una jabla, et púsolo en su casa et mandóle que le dixese todo quanto viese faser á su muger et que non le encobriese ende nada; et despues fué su via á recabdar su mandado. Et entró su amigo della en su casa do estava: el papagayo vió quanto ellos fisieron, et quando el omme bueno vino de su mandado, asentóse en su casa en guisa que non lo viese la muger, et mandó traer el papagayo et preguntóle todo lo que viera; et el papagayo contógelo todo lo que viera faser á la muger con su amigo: et el omme bueno fué muy sañudo contra su muger, et non entró mas do ella estava. Et la mugier coydó verdaderamente que la moça la descobriera, et llamóla estonce et dixo: Tu dexiste á mi marido todo quanto yo fise.—Et la moça juró que non lo dixiera; mas sabet que lo dixo el papagayo.—Et desçendiólo á tierra et commençóle á echar agua de suso como que era luvia; et tomó un espejo en la mano et parógelo sobre la jabla, et en la otra mano una candela et parávagela de suso; et cuydó el papagayo que era relámpago: et la muger començó á mover una muela, et el papagayo cuidó que eran truenos; et ella estovo así toda la noche, fasiendo así fasta que amanesçió. Et despues que fué la mañana vino el marido et preguntó al papagayo: ¿ Viste esta noche alguna cosa? —Et el papagayo dixo: Non pud' ver ninguna cosa con la gran luvia et truenos et relánpagos que esta noche fiso. —Et el omme dixo: ¿ En quanto me as dicho es verdat de mi muger así como esto? Non a cosa mas mintrosa que tu; et mandarte hé matar.—Et enbió por su muger et perdonóla et fisiéron pas. Et yo, Señor, non te dí este enxemplo, sinon porque sepas el engaño de las mugeres: que son muy fuertes sus artes et son muchos que non an cabo nin fin.—Et mandó el rrey que non matasen su fijo.

IV. *Enxemplo de como vino la muger al segundo dia antel rrey llorando, et dixo que matase su fijo.*

Et dixo: Señor, non debes tu perdonar tu fijo, pues fiso cosa por que muera; et si tu non lo matas et dexas á vida, aviendo fecho tal enemiga, ca si tu non lo matas non escarmentaria ninguno de faser otro tal, et yo, Señor, contarte hé el enxemplo del curador de los pannos é de su fijo. — Dixo el rrey: ¿ Como fué eso?—Et ella dixo· Era un curador de pannos et avia un fijo pequenno: este curador quando avie de curar sus pannos levava consigo su fijo, et el ninno començaba de jugar con el agua et el padre non gelo quiso castigar: et vino un dia quel ninno se afogó et el padre por sacar el fijo afogóse en el piélago, et afogáronse amos á dos. Et, Señor, si tu non te antuvias

á castigar tu fijo ante que mas enemiga te faga, matarte a.
—Et el rrey mandó matar su fijo.

V. *De como vino el segundo privado antel rrey por escusar al ynfante de muerte.*

Et vino el segundo privado et fincó les ynojos antel rrey et dixo: Señor, si tu avieses fijos, non devies querer mal á ninguno dellos: demas que non as mas de uno señero et mándaslo matar apriesa antes que sepas la verdat; et despues que le ovieres fecho, arrepentirte as et non lo podrás cobrar; et será el tu enxemplo tal como del mercador et de la muger et de la moça. — Dixo el rrey: ¿Como fué eso?—Dígote, Señor, que era un mercador muy rrico et era señerigo et apartado en su comer et en su bever; et fué en su mercaduría et levó un moço con él et posaron en una cibdat muy buena, et el mercador enbió su moço á mercar de comer, et falló una moça en el mercado que tenie dos panes de adargama et pagóse del pan et compról̃o para su señor et levólo; et pagóse su señor de aquel pan et dixo el mercador á su moço: Si te vala Dios que me compres de aquel pan cada dia á la moça; et comprávale aquel pan et levávalo á su señor; et un dia falló á la moça que non tenia pan, et tornóse á su señor et dixo que non fallava de aquel pan; et dixo el mercador que demandase á la moça como lo fasia aquel pan; et el moço fué buscar á la moça et fallóla et dixo: Amiga, mi señor te quiere alguna cosa que quiere.—Et ella fué et dixo: ¿Que vos plase?—Et el mercador le preguntó: Sennora, ¿cómo fasedes aquel pan? et yo faré faser otro tal.—Et ella dixo: Amigo señor, sallieron unas anpollas á mi padre en las espaldas, et el físigo nos dixo que tomásemos farina de adargama et que le amasássemos con manteca et con miel et que gela pusiésemos en aquellas anpollas, et quando oviésemos lavado et enxugado toda la podre, que gela tirásemos. Et yo tomava aquella masa con escuso et fasíala pan, et levávalo aqui al mercado á vender et vendíalo. Et, loado nuestro Señor, es ya sano, et dexámoslo de faser.—Et el mercador dió grandes boses del gran asco que avia de aquel pan que avia comido, et quando vido que provecho ninguno non tenia dixo contra su moço: Mesquino ¿que faré que busquemos con que lavemos nuestras manos et nuestros pies é nuostras bocas é nuestros cuerpos? ¿como los lavaremos? —Et, Señor, si tu matas tu fijo, miedo hé que te arrepentiras como el mercador: et, Señor, non fagas cosa por que te arrepientas fasta quo seas cierto della.

VI. *Enxiemplo del señor et del omme et de la muger et el marido de la muger, como se ayuntaron todos.*

Señor, fisiéronme entender de los engaños de las mugeres. Disen que era una muger que avia un amigo que era privado del rrey et avia aquella cibdat de mano del rrey en poder, et el amigo enbió un su omme á casa de su amiga que supiese si era y su marido, et entró aquel omme (á casa de su amiga), et pagóse dél et él della, por que era fermoso; et ella llamólo que jasiese con ella, et él físolo así. Et vido que detardava su señor el mancebo et fué á casa del entendera et llamó. Et dixo: ¿Qué faré (el mancebo) de mí?—Et ella dixo: Vé et escóndete en aquel rrencon.— Et el Señor dél entró á ella. Et non quiso quel amigo entrase en el rrencon con el mançebo. En esto vino el marido et llamó á la puerta. Et dixo al amigo: Toma tu espada en la mano et párate á la puerta del palacio et amenásame et vé tu carrera et non fables ninguna cosa.— Et físolo así. Et fué et abrió la puerta á su marido, et quando vió su marido estar el espada sacada al otro en la mano, fabló et dixo: ¿Ques esto?—Et él non rrespondió nada et fué su carrera; et el marido entró al palacio á su muger et dixo: Ay, maldita de tí ¿que ovo este omme contigo que te salle denostando et amenasando?...— Et ella dixo: Vino ese ome fuyendo con gran miedo dél, et falló la puerta abierta, et entró su señor en pos dél por lo matar et él dando boses quel' acorriese; et despues que s' arrimó á mí, paréme antél et apartélo dél que non lo matase, et por esto vá daquí denostando et amenasándome. Mas, si me vala Dios, non me ynchala.—El marido dixo: ¿Do está este mancebo?—En aquel rrencon está.—Et el marido salló á la puerta por ver si estava el señor del mançebo ó si era ydo: et quando vió que non estava allí, llamó al mançebo et dixo: Sal acá: que tu señor ydo es su carrera.—Et el marido se tornó á ella bien pagado, et dixo: Fesiste á guisa de buena muger et fesiste bien et gradéscotelo mucho.—Et, Señor, non te dí este enxemplo sinon que non mates tu fijo por dicho de una muger, ca las mugeres ayuntados en sí ay muchos engaños.—Et mandó el rrey que non matasen su fijo.

VII. *Enxiemplo de como vino la muger al rrey al tercero dia, disiéndole que matase su fijo.*

Et vino la muger al tercero dia et lloró et dió boses antel rrey et dixo: Señor, estos tus privados son malos et matar te an así como mató un privado á un rrey una bes.— Et el rrey dixo: ¿Como fué eso?—Et ella dixo: Era un rrey et avia un fijo que amava mucho caçar y el privado fiso en guisa que fuese á su padre et pidiese liçençia que les dexase yr á caça; et ellos ydos amos á dos, travesó un venado delante et díxole el privado al ninno: Vé en pos de aquel venado fasta que lo alcanses et lo mates, et levárloas á tu padre. Et el ninno fué en pos del venado atanto que se perdió de su conpaña; et yendo así falló una senda et ençima de la senda falló una moça que llorava et el ninno dixo: ¿Quien eres tu?...—Et la moça dixo:

Yo so fija de un rrey de fulana tierra, et venia cavallera en un marfil con mis parientes, et tomóme sueño et caý dél et mis parientes non me vieron et yo desperté et non sope por do yr; et madrugando en pos dellos fasta que perdí los pies.—Et el ninno ovo duelo della et levóla en pos de sí. Et ellos yendo así, entraron en una aldea despoblada et dixo la moça: Descéndeme aqui que lo he menester, et venirme hé luego para tí.—Et el ninno físolo así et ella entró en el casar et estudo una gran pieça; et quando vió el ninno que detardava desçendió de su cavallo et subió en una paret et paró mientes et vió que era diabla que estava con sus parientes et desíales: Un moço me trayo en su cavallo et félo aqui do lo traygo.—Et ellos dixieron: Véte adelante con él á otro casar, fasta que te alcançemos.—Et quando el moço esto oyó ovo grant miedo et desçendió de la paret et saltó en su cavallo; et la moça vínose á él, et cavalgóla en pos dél et comensó á tremar con el miedo della et ella dixo: ¿Qué as que tremes?— Et él le dixo: Espántome de mi conpañero: que hé miedo que me verná dél mal.—Et ella dixo: ¿Non lo puedes tu adobar con tu aver? que tu te alabaste que eras fijo de rrey et que tenia gran aver tu padre.—Él le dixo: Non tiene aver.—É mas te alabaste que eras rrey et gran prýncipe.—Et el diablo le dixo: Ruega á Dios que te ayude contra él et seras librado.—Et dixo él: Verdat dises, et faserlo hé, et alçó sus manos contra Dios, et dixo: Ay Señor Dios, rruégote et pídote por merçed que me libres deste diablo et de sus compañeros.—Et cayó el diablo detras et començó enbarduñar en tierra et queríase levantar et non podia. Et estonce començó el moço de correr quanto podie fasta que llegó al padre muerto de sed, et era mucho espantado de lo que viera. Et, Señor, non te dí este enxemplo sinon que non te esfuerçes en tus malos privados. Si non me dieres derecho de quien mal me fiso, yo me mataré con mis manos. Et el rrey mandó matar su fijo.

VIII. *Enxemplo del tercero privado del caçador et de las aldeas.*

Et vino el terçero privado ante el rrey et finçó los ynojos antél et dixo: Señor, de las cosas, quando el omme non para mientes en ellas, viene ende gran daño, et es atal como el enxemplo del caçador et de las aldeas.—Et el rrey dixo: ¿ Como fué eso ?...—Dixol' él : Oy desir que un caçador que andava caçando por el monte et falló en un arbol un enxanbre et tomóla et metióla en un odre que tenia para traer su agua : et este caçador tenia un perro et trayalo consigo; et traxo la miel á un mercador de un aldea que era acerca de aquel monte para la vender, et quando el caçador abrió el odre para lo mostrar al tendero, cayó dél una gota et posóse en ella una abeja ; et aquel tendero tenia un gato et dió un salto en el abeja et matóla ; et el perro del caçador dió salto en el gato et matólo; et vino el dueño del gato et mató al perro; et estonces levantóse el dueño del perro et mató al tendero por quel' matara al perro. Et estonces vinieron los del aldea del tendero et mataron al caçador, dueño del perro, et vinieron los del aldea del caçador á los del tendero et tomáronse unos con otros et matáronse todos que non fincó y ninguno. Et así se mataron unos con otros por una gota de miel. Et, Señor, non te dí este enxenplo sinon que non mates tu fijo, fasta que la verdat, por que non te arrepientas.

IX. *Enxenplo de como vino la muger et dixo que matase el rrey á su fijo et dióle enxenplo de un fijo de un rrey et de un su privado como lo engañó.*

Et dixole la muger: Era un rrey et avia un privado et avia un fijo et casólo con fija de otro rrey. Et el rrey padre de la ynfante enbió desir al otro rrey: enbíame tu fijo et faremos bodas con mi fija et despues enbiarte hé mandado.—Et el rrey guisar su fijo muy bien et que fuese faser sus bodas et que estudiese con ella quanto quesiese. Et des y enbió el rrey aquel privado con su fijo; et assy fablando uno con otro, alongáronse mucho de su compaña et fallaron una fuente, et avia tal virtud que cualquier omme que beviese della que luego se tornava muger; et el privado sabia la virtud que tenia la fuente et non lo quiso desir al ynfante et dixo: Está aqui agora fasta que vaga á buscar carrera, andándola á buscar.—Et fuese por ella et falló al padre del ynfante, et el rrey fué muy mal espantado et díxol': ¿Como vienes así sin mi fijo ó que fué dél?—El privado dixo: Creo que lo comieron las bestias fieras.—Et quando vió el ynfante que detardava el privado et que non tornava por él, desçendió á la fuente á lavar las manos et la cara, et bevió del agua et físose muger et estuvo en guisa que non sabia que faser nin que desir nin do yr. En esto llegó á él un diablo et díxol'—que quien era él—et él le dixo: Fijo de un rrey de fulana tierra—et díxol' el nombre derecho et catol' la falsedat quel' fisiera el privado de su padre. Et el diablo ovo piedat dél porque era tan fermoso et díxol': Tornarme hé yo dueña como tu eres, et á cabo de quatro meses tornarme hé como dantes era.—Et el ynfante lo oyó et fisieron pleyto, et fué. Y el diablo otrosí vino en lugar de muger preñada; et dixo el diablo: Amigo, tórnate como dantes et yo tornarme hé como dante era.—Et dixo el ynfante: ¿Como me tornaré yo asy, que quando yo te fise pleyto et omenage, yo era donsella et virgen et tu eres agora muger preñada?—Et estonce se rrasonó el ynfante con el diablo ant sus alcalles, et fallaron por derecho que venciera el ynfante al diablo. Estonce se tornó el ynfante onme, et fuése para su muger et levóla para casa de su padre et contógelo todo como le aconteciera. Et el rrey mandó matar al privado por que dexara al ynfante en la fuente. Et por ende yo hé fiusa que me ayudará Dios contra tus malos privados.—Et el rrey mandó matar su fijo.

X. *Enxenplo del quarto privado et del bañador et de su muger.*

Et vino el quarto privado et entró al rrey et fincó los yuojos antel rrey et díxol': Señor, non deve faser omme en ninguna cosa fasta que sea bien çierto de la verdat, ca quien lo fase ante que sepa la verdat, yerra et fase muy mal, como acaesçió á un bañador que se arrepyntió quando non le tovo pro.—El rrey le preguntó: ¿Como fué eso?— Dixo: Señor, fué un ynfante un dia por entrar en el baño: era mancebo, et era tan grueso que non podia ver sus mienbros por do era; et quando se descubrió, viólo el bañador et començó de llorar, et díxole el ynfante: ¿Por qué lloras?—Et díxol': Por tu seer fijo de rrey, como lo eres, et non aviendo otro fijo sinon á tí et non seer señor de tus mienbros asy como son otros varones; ca yo bien creo que non puedes jaser con muger.—Et el ynfante díxol': ¿Que faré yo, que mi padre me quiere casar? Non sé si podré (aver) fasimiento con muger.—Et el ynfante díxol': Toma agora dies tanto et béme buscar una muger fermosa.—Et el bañador dixo en su coraçon: Terné estos dies maravedis et entre mi muger con él; ca bien sé que non podrá dormir con ella.—Et estonce fué por ella; et el ynfante dormió con ella; et el bañador començó de atalear como yasia con su muger; et el ynfante rrióse: et el vañador fallóse ende mal et dixo: Yo mesmo me lo fis: et estonce llamó su muger et díxol': Véte para casa.—Et ella díxol': ¿Como yré? ca le fis pleyto que durmiria con él toda esta noche.—Et quando él esto oyó, con cueyta et con pesar fuese á enforcar, et así se mató.—Et, Señor, non te dí este enxenplo si non que non mates tu fijo.

XI. *Enxienplo del onme et de la muger et de la vieja et de la perrilla.*

Señor, oy desir que un omme et su muger fisieron pleyto et omenage que se toviesen fieldat: et el marido puso plaso á que viniese, et non vino á él. Et estonçe salió á la carrera, et estando así vino un omme de su carrera et vióla et pagóse della et demandól' su amor; et ella que en ninguna guisa que lo non faria. Estonçe fué á una vieja que morava cerca della et contógelo todo como le conteciera con aquella muger, et rrogóle que gela fisiese aver et quel' daria quanto quisiese. Et la vieja dixo quel' plasie et que gela faria aver. Et la vieja fuése á su casa et tomó miel et masa et pymienta, et amasólo todo en uno et fiso della panes. Estonçe fuése para su casa daquella muger; et llamó una perrilla que tenie et echóle d'aquel pan en guisa que non lo viese la muger. Et despues que la perrilla lo comió, empeçó de yr tras la vieja, falagándosela quel' diese mas et llorándole los ojos con la pimienta que avie en el pan. Et quando la muger la vido así, maravillóse et dixo á la vieja: Amiga ¿viestes llorar así á otras perras así como á esta?—Dixo la vieja: Fase derecho, qu'esta perra fué muger et muy fermosa, et morava aqui cabo mí, et enamoróse un omme della et ella non se pagó dél; et estonçe maldíxola aquel omme que l' amava et tornóse luego perra: et agora quando me vió menbrósele della et començóse de llorar.—Et estonçe dixo la muger: Ay mesquina ¿que faré yo que el otro dia me vido un omme en la carrera et demandóme mi amor et yo non quis? Et agora he miedo que me tornaré perra si me maldixo: et agora vé et rruégale por mí quel' daré quanto él quisiese.—Estonçe dixo la vieja: Yo te lo trayeré. —Et estonçe se levantó la vieja et fuése para el omme; et levantóse la muger et afeytóse. Et estonçe se asomó á casa de la vieja si avia fallado aquel omme que fuera buscar, et la vieja dixo: Non lo puedo fallar.—Et estonçe dixo la muger: Pues ¿qué faré yo?...—Estonçe la vieja fué, et falló al omme et díxol': Anda acá: que ya fará la muger todo, todo quanto yo quisiese.—Et era el omme su marido, et non lo conosçia la vieja que venia estonçes del su camino. Et la vieja l' dixo: ¿Que daras á quien buena posada te diere et muger moça et fermosa et buen comer et buen bever, si quieres tu?—Et él dixo: Por Dios si querria.—Et fuese ella delante et él en pos della, et vió que lo levava á su casa é para su muger mesma; et sospechó que lo fasia así toda via quando él salliera de su casa. Et la vieja mala entró en su casa et dixo: Entrat.—Despues quel omme entró (en su casa), dixo (la muger): Asentatvos aqui.—Et catól' al rrostro; et quando vió que su marido era, non sopo ál que faser sinon dar salto en sus cabellos, et dixo: Ay, don putero malo, estō es lo que yo et vos posiemos et el pleyto et omenage que fisiemos? Agora veo que guardades las malas mugeres et las malas alcauetas.—Et él dixo: Ay de tí ¿qué oviste comigo?—Et dixo su muger: Dixiéronme agora que vinies et afeytéme, et dixe á esta vieja que salliese a ty por tal que te provase si usavas las malas mugeres, et veo que ayna seguiste la alcautería: mas jamas nunca nos ayuntaremos nin llegaras mas á mí.—Et dixo él: Asy me dé Dios la su graçia et aya la tuya, como non cuydé que me traye á otra casa si non la tuya et mia, sinon

non fuera con ella, et aun pesóme mucho quando me metió en tu casa que cuydé questo mesmo faras con los otros.—Et quando ovo dicho, rrascós' en su rrostro et rrompiólo todo con sus manos, et dixo: Bien sé questo cuydaries tu de mí; et ensañóse contra él, et quando vió qu' era sannosa, començóla de falagar et de rrogar quel' perdonase et ella non lo quiso perdonar fasta quel' diese gran algo; et él mandóle en arras un aldea que avia. Et, Señor, non te dí este enxenplo si non que los engaños de las mugeres que non an cabo nin fin.—Et mandó el rrey que non matasen su fixo.

XII. *Enxenplo de como vino al quinto dia la muger et dió enxenplo del puerco et del ximio.*

Et vino la muger al quinto dia et dixo al rrey: Si me non das derecho de aquel ynfante et veras que pro te ternan estos tus malos privados: despues que yo sea muerta, veremos qué faras con estos tus consejeros, et quando ante Dios fueres ¿qué diras que fasiendo atan gran tuerto en dexar á tu fijo á vida por tus malos consegeros et por tus malos privados, et dexas de faser lo que tiene pro en este siglo?...Mas yo sé que te será demandado ante Dios; et desirte hé lo que acaesçió á un puerco una vez.—Et dixo el rrey: ¿Como fué eso?—Dígote, Señor, que era un puerco et yasia sienpre so una figuera et comia sienpre de aquellos figos que cayen della, et vino un dia á comer et falló ençima á un ximio comiendo figos; et el ximio quando vido estar al puerco en fondon de la figuera, echol' un figo, et comiólo et sópole mejor que los quél fallava en tierra; et alçava la cabeça á ver si le echarie mas; et el puerco estudo así atendiendo al ximio fasta que se le secaron las venas del pescueço et murió daquello.—Et quando esto ovo dicho, ovo miedo el rrey ques' matara con el tósigo que tenie en la mano et mandó matar su fijo.

XIII. *Enxenplo del quinto privado et del perro et de la culebra et del ninno.*

Et vino el quinto privado antel rrey et dixo: Loado sea Dios: tu eres entendido et mesurado et tu sabes que ninguna cosa apresuradamente ante ques' sepa la verdat es bien fecha, et si (omme) lo fisiere fará locura, et quandol' quisiere emendar non podrá; et contecerle ha así como á un dueño de un perro una ves.—Et dixo el rrey: ¿Como fué eso?...—Et él dixo: Sennor, oy desir que un omme que era criado de un rrey, et aquel omme avia un perro de caça muy bueno et mucho entendido, et nunca le mandava faser cosa que la non fisiese. Et vino un dia que su muger fué á veer sus parientes et fué con ella toda su compaña; et dixo ella á su marido: Sey con tu fijo que yase durmiendo en la cama, ca non tardaré allá, ca luego seré aquí. —El omme asentóse cabo su fijo: él seyendo allí llegó un omme de cas del rrey quel' mandava llamar á gran priesa: et el omme bueno dixo al perro: Guarda bien este ninno, et non te partas dél fasta que yo venga; et el omme cerró su puerta, et fuése para el rrey. Et el perro yasiendo çerca del ninno vino á él una culebra muy grande et quísol' matar por el olor de la leche de la madre: et quando la vido el perro, dió salto en ella et despedaçóla toda. Et el omme tornó ayna por amor de su fijo que dexava solo, et quando abrió la puerta, abriéndola sallió el perro á falagarse á su señor por lo que avia fecho: et traia la boca é los pechos sangrientos. Et quando lo vió tal, cuydóse que avia matado su fijo, et metió mano á un espada et dió un gran golpe al perro et matólo: et fué mas adelante á la cama et falló su fijo durmiendo et la culebra despedaçada á sus pies. Et quando esto vido, dió palmadas en su rrostro et rrompióselo et non pudo ál faser. Et tóvose por mal andante que lo avia errado. Et, Señor, non te contesa atal en tus fechos, ca despues non te podras rrepentir: non mates tu fijo que los engaños de las mugeres non an cabo nin ffin.

XIV. *Enxenplo de la muger et del alcaueta, del omme et del mercador et de la muger que vendió el panno.*

Señor, oy desir que avia un omme que quando oya fablar de mugeres que se perdia por ellas con cueyta de las aver: et oyó desir de una muger fermosa et fuéla buscar et falló el lugar donde era. Et estonçe fué á un alcaueta et díxole que moria por aquella muger. Et dixo la vieja alcaueta: Non fisieste nada en venir acá: ca es buena muger; et non ayas fiusa ninguna en ella, si te vala Dios.—Et él le dixo: Fas en guisa que la aya, et yo te daré quanto tu quisieres.—Et la vieja díxol' que lo faria, si pudiese; mas díxol': Vé á su marido ques mercador, sil' puedes conprar de un panno que trae cubierto.—Et el fué al mercador et rrogógelo que gelo vendiese; et el óvogelo mucho aduro de vender; et adúxolo á la vieja et tomó el panno et quemólo en tres lugares et díxol': Estáte aqui agora en esta mi casa que non te vea aqui ninguno: et ella tomó el panno et doblólo et metiólo so sí, et fué alli do seye la muger del mercador, et fablando con ella, metió el panno so el cabeçal et fuése. —Et quando vino el mercador, tomó el cabeçal para se asentar et falló el panno, et tomólo et cuydó quél que lo mercara quera amigo de su muger é que se l'olvidara allí el panno. Et levantóse el mercador et firió á su muger muy mal, et non le dixo por qué ni por qué non. Et levó el panno en su mano. Et cubrio su cabeça la muger et fué para sus parientes. Et sópolo la vieja alcaueta, et fuéla ver et dixo: ¿Porqué te firió tu marido de balde?— Et dixo la buena muger: Non sé, á buena fé.—Dixo la vieja: Algunos fechisos te dieron malos; mas, amiga

¿quieres que te diga verdat?...Darte hé buen consejo: en mi casa ay un omme de los sabios del mundo é si quisieredes yr á ora de viéspera comigo á él, él te dará consejo.—Et la buena muger dixo quel' plasia.—Et venida fué ora de viésperas, et vino la vieja por ella, et levóla consigo para su casa et metióla en la cámara adonde estava aquel omme, et levantóse á ella et yasió con ella; et la muger con miedo é con vergüença et callóse; et despues quel omme yasió con ella, fuése para sus parientes, et el omme dixo á la vieja: Gradéscotelo mucho et darte hé algo.—Et dixo ella: Non ayas tu cuydado que lo que tu fesiste yo lo aduré á bien; mas vé tu via et fáste pasadiso por su casa, do está su marido, et quando él te viere, llamarte a et preguntarte a por el panno que qué lo fesiste. Et tu díle que te posiste cabo el fuego et que se te quemó en tres lugares et que lo dieste á una vieja que lo levase á sorsir, et que lo non vieste mas nin sabes dél, et faserme hé yo pasadisa por aý, et tu: A aquella dí el panno—et llámame, ca yo te escusaré de todo. Et estonçe fué et falló al mercador et dixo ¿Qué fesiste el panno que te yo vendí?—Et dixo él· Asentéme al fuego et non paré mientes, et quemóseme en tres logares, et dílo á una vieja mi vesina que lo levase á sorsir et non lo vide despues.—Et ellos estando en esto, llegó la vieja el llamóla et dixo al mercador: Esta es la vieja, a quien yo dí el panno;—et dixo ella: A buena fé, si me vala Dios, este mancebo me dió un paño á sorsir et entré con ello so mi manto en tu casa et en verdat non sé si se me cayó en tu casa ó por la carrera.—Et dixo: Yo lo fallé: toma tu panno et véte en buena ventura. —Estonçe fué el mercador á su casa et enbió por su muger á casa de sus parientes et rrogóla quel' perdonase et ella físolo así.—Et, Señor, non te dí este enxenplo si non que sepas el engaño de las mugeres ques muy grande et sin ffin. Et el rrey mandó que non matasen su fijo.

XV. *Enxenplo de como vino la muger al seseno dia et dióľ enxenplo del ladron et del leon en como cavalgó en él.*

Et vino la muger al seseno dia et dixo al rrey: Yo fio en Dios que me amparará de tus malos privados como anparó una ves un omme de un leon.—Et el rrey dixo: ¿Como fué eso?...—Et ella dixo: Pasava un gran recuero por cabo de una aldea et entró en ella un gran ladron et muy mal fechor; et ellos yendo así, tomóles la noche et llovió sobrellos muy gran luvya, et dixo el recuero: Paremos mientes en nuestras cosas, non nos faga algund mal el ladron.—Et á esto vino un ladron et entró entre las bestias, et ellos non lo vieron con la grant escuredat; et començó de apalpar qual era la mas gruesa para levarla, et puso la mano sobre un leon et non falló ninguna mas gruesa, nin de mas gordo pescueço quél. Et cavalgó en él; et el leon: Esta es la tempestat que disen los ommes.—Et corrió con él toda la noche fasta la mañana: et quando se conosçieron el uno al otro, avíanse miedo; et el leon llegó á un árbor muy cansado, et el ladron travóse á una rrama et subióse al árbor con gran miedo del leon. Et el leon fuése muy espantado et fallóse con un ximio et díxoľ: ¿Qué as, leon, ó como vienes así?—Et el leon díxoľ: Esta noche me tomó la tempestat et cavalgó en mi fasta en la mañana nunca cansó de me correr.—El ximio le dixo: ¿Do es aquella tenpestat?—Et el leon le mostró el omme ençima del árbor; et el ximio subió ençima del árbor et el leon atendió por oyr et veer qué faria. Et el ximio vió quera omme et fiso senal al leon que viniese: et el leon vino corriendo. Et estonçe abaxóse un poco el omme, et echól' mano de sus cojones del ximio, et apretógelos tanto fasta que lo mató, et echólo al leon. Et des y quando el leon

H

esto vido, echó á foyr, et dixo: Loado sea Dios que me escapó desta tenpestat.—Et dixo la muger: Fio por Dios que me ayudará contra tus malos privados así como ayudó al ladron contral ximio.—El rrey mandó matar su fijo.

XVI. *Enxenplo del seseno privado del palomo et de la paloma que ayuntaron en uno el trigo en su nido.*

Et vino el seseno privado et fincó los ynoios antel rrey et dixo: Si fijo non ovieses devies rogar á Dios que te lo diese. Pues ¿como puedes matar este fijo que Dios te dió et non aviendo mas deste? ca si lo mates, fallarte as ende mal, como se falló una ves un palomo.—Dixo el rrey: ¿Como fué eso?—Dixo: Señor, era un palomo et morava en un monte et avia y su nido; et en el tiempo del agosto, cogieron su trigo et guardáronlo en su nido, et fuése el palomo en su mandado et dixo á la paloma que non comiese del trigo grano mientras que turase el verano, mas díxol': Véte á esos campos et come deso que fallares; et quando viniere el ynvierno comeras del trigo et folgaras.—Et despues venieron los grandes calores et secáronse los granos et encogiéronse et pegáronse, et quando vino el palomo dixo: ¿Non te dixe que non comieses grano, que lo guardases para el ynvierno?—Et ella juróle que non comiera grano, nin lo començara poco nin mucho; et el palomo non lo quiso creer, et començóla de picar et de ferirla de los onbros et de los alas atanto que la mató. Et paró mientes el palomo al trigo et vió que cresçia con el rrelente et que non avia menos nin más, et él fallóse mal, porque mató á la paloma.—Et, Señor, hé miedo que te fallaras ende mal, así como se falló este palomo, si matas tu fijo: quel engaño de las mugeres es la mayor cosa del mundo.

XVII. *Enxenplo del marido et del segador et de la muger et de los ladrones que la tomaron ä trayçion.*

Señor, oy desir un enxenplo de un omme et de una muger et morava en una aldea: et el omme fué arar et la muger físole de comer de paniso un pan, et levógelo á do arava, et yendo por gelo dar, dieron salto en ella los ladrones et tomáronle el paniso; et uno de los ladrones fiso una ymágen de marfil por escarnio et metióla en la cesta, et ella non lo vió. Et dexáronla yr, et fuése para su marido, et quando abrió el marido la cesta, vió aquello et díxol': ¿Ques aquesto que aqui traes?—Et ella cató, et vió que los ladrones lo avian fecho, et ella dixo: Ensonava esta noche entre sueños questavas ante un alfayate et que te pesava muy mal; et estonçe fuy á unos ommes que me lo ensolviesen este ensueño, et ellos me dixieron que fisiese una ymágen de paniso, et que la comieses, et que serias librado de quanto te podria venyr.—Et este ensueño, dixo el marido que podria seer verdat. Et tal es el engaño et las artes de las mugeres quo non han cabo nin fin.—Et el rrey mandó que non matasen su fijo.

XVIII. *Enxenplo de como vino la muger al seteno dia antel rrey, quexando, et dixo que se queria quemar, et el rrey mandó matar su fijo apriesa antes quella se quemase.*

Et quando vino (la muger) al seteno dia dixo: Si este mancebo oy non es muerto, oy seré descubierta.—Et esto dixo la muger: Non ay sinon la muerte.—Todo quanto aver pudo diólo por Dios á pobres et mandó traer mucha leña et asentóse sobre ella et mandó dar fuego enderredor et desir que se queria quemar ella. Et el rrey, quando esto oyó, ante que se quemase, mandó matar al moço. Et llegó el seteno privado et metióse delante del moço et d'aquel quel' queria matar et omillósel' al rrey et díxol': Señor, non mates tu fijo por dicho de una muger : que non sabes si miente ó si dise verdat ; et tu avias atanta cobdiçia de aver un fijo como tu sabes, et pues que Dios te fiso plaser, non le fagas tu pesar.

XIX. *Del enxenplo de la diablesa et del omme et de la muger et de como el omme demandó los tres dones.*

Señor, oy desir que era un omme que nunca se partia de una diablesa et ovo della un fijo; et fué así un dia quella que se queria yr, et dixo: Miedo hé que nunca me veré contigo; mas ante quiero que sepas tres oraçiones de mí, que quando pidieses a Dios tres cosas averlas as; et mostról' las oraçiones et fuése la diablesa et él fuese, muy triste, por que se le fué la diablesa, para su muger, et díxol': Sepas que la diablesa que me tenia que se me fué, et pesóme ende mucho del bien que sabia por ella, et emostróme tres oraciones con que demandase tres cosas á Dios que las averia, et agora conseiame qué pida á Dios, et averlo hé.—Et la muger le dixo: Bien sabes verdaderamente que puramente aman los ommes á las mugeres et páganse mucho de su solás : por ende rruega á Dios que te otorgue muchas dellas.—Et quando se vido cargado dellas, dixo á la muger: Confóndate Dios: que esto por el tu conseio se fiso.—Et dixo ella: ¿Aun non te quedan dos oraciones? Et agora rruega á Dios que te las tuelga, pues tanto pesas con ellas.—Et el fiso oraçion et tolliéronse luego todas et non fincó y ninguna. Et él quando esto vió començó de desir mal á su muger, et díxol' ella : Non me maldigas: que aun tienes una oraçion et rruega á Dios que te torne como de primero;—et tornóle como de primero. Et así se perdieron las oraçiones todas. Por ende te dó por conseio que non mates tu fijo; que las maldades de las mugeres non an cabo nin fin.—Et desto darte hé un enxenplo.—Et dixo el rrey : ¿Como fué eso ?

XX. *Enxenplo de un mancebo que non queria casar fasta que sopiese las maldades de las mugeres.*

Et, Señor, dixiéronme que un omme que non queria casar fasta que sopiese et apprendiese las maldades de las mugeres et los sus engaños. Et anduvo tanto fasta que llegó á un aldea, et dixiéronle que avie buenos sabios del engaño de las mugeres, et costól' mucho apprender las artes. Díxol' aquel que era mas sabidor: ¿Quieres que te diga?...Jamas, nunqua sabras nin apprenderas acabadamente los engaños de las mugeres fasta que te asientes tres dias sobre la cenisa et non comas sinon un poco de pan de ordio et sal: et apprenderas.—Et él le dixo quel' plasia et físolo así. Estonçe posóse sobre la çenisa et fiso muchos libros de las artes de las mugeres, et despues questo ovo fecho dixo que se queria tornar para su tierra et posó en casa de un omme bueno; et el huespet le preguntó de todo aquello que levava et él dixo donde era, et como se avia asentado sobre la çeniza de mientra trasladara aquellos libros, et como comiera el pan de ordio, et como pasava mucha cueyta et mucha laseria, et trasladó aquellas artes. Et despues questo le ovo contado, tomólo el huespet por la mano el levólo á su muger et díxol': Un omme bueno hé fallado que viene cansado de su camino.—Et contól' toda su fasienda et rrogól' quel' fisiese algo fasta que se fuese esforçado, ca estonçe era flaco. Et despues questo ovo dicho fuése á su mandado, et la muger fiso bien lo quel' castigara. Estonçe començó ella de preguntalle que omme era ó como andava; et él contógelo todo, et ella quandol' vió tóvolo por omme de poco seso et de poco recabdo, por que entendió que nunqua podia acabar aquello que començare, et dixo: Bien creo verdaderamente que nunca muger del mundo te pueda engañar, nin es á enparejar con aquestos libros que as adobado; et dixo ella en su coraçon: Sea agora que un sabidor quisiere que yo le faré conosçer el su poco seso, en que anda engañado: yo só aquella que lo sabré faser.—Estonçe lo llamó et dixo: Amigo, yo só muger manceba et fermosa et en buena sason et mi marido es muy viejo et cansado, et de muy grant tienpo pasado que non yasió comigo: por ende si tu quisieses et yasieses conmigo, que eres omme cuerdo et entendido; et non lo digas á nadie.—Et quando ella ovo dicho, cuydóse quel' desia verdat, et levantóse et quiso travar della et díxol': Espera un poco et desnudémonos.—Et él desnudóse, et ella dió grandes boses et garpios, et recudieron luego los vesinos et ella dixo ante que entrasen: Tiéndete en tierra, sinon muerto eres.—Et él físolo así; et ella metiól' un gran bocado de pan en la boca et quando los ommes entraron pescuidaron que qué mal oviera, et ella dixo: Este omme es nuestro huéspet et quísose afogar con un bocado de pan, et bolvíensele los ojos.—Estonçe descubrió' et echól' del agua por que acordase: él non acordava, en todo esto echándol' agua fria et alynpiándole el rrostro con un panno blanco. Estonçe sallyéronse los ommes et fuéronse su carrera et ella díxol': Amigo ¿en tus libros ay alguna tal arte como esta?—Et dixo él: En buena fe nunca la ví, nin la fallé tal como esta.— Et dixo ella: Tu gasteste y mucho laseria et mucho maldia, et nunca esperes ende ál: que esto que tu demandas nunca lo acabaras tu nin omme de quantos son nasçidos.—Et él quando esto vió, tomó todos sus libros et metiólos en el fuego, et dixo que demas avia despendido sus dias. Et yo, Señor, non te dí este enxenplo sinon que non mates tu fijo por palabras de una muger.— Et el rrey mandó que non matasen su fijo.

XXI. *De como al otavo dia fabló el ynfante et fué antel rrey.*

Quando vino el otavo dia en la mañana ante que saliese el sol, llamó el ynfante á la muger quel' servia en aquellos dias que non fablava, et díxol': Vé et llama á fulano ques mas privado del rrey et díl' que venga quanto pudier'.—Et la muger en que vido que fablava el ynfante, fués' muy corriendo et llamó al privado; et él levántóse et vino muy ayna al ynfante; et él loró con él, et contól' por qué non fablara aquellos dias, et todo quantol' conteciera con su madrastra.—Et non guaresçí de muerte sinon por Dios et por tí, et por tus conpanneros que me curaron de ayudar bien et legalmente á drecho. Dios vos dé buen gualardon, et yo vos lo daré, si bivo et veo lo que cobdicio. Et quiero que vayas corriendo á mi padre et que le digas mis nuevas ante que llegue la puta falsa de mi madrastra, ca yo sé que madrugará.—El privado fué muy rresio corriendo desde quel' vido así fablar, et fué al rrey, et dixo: Señor, dáme albrycias por el bien et merced que te a Dios fecho que non quiso que matases tu fijo, ca ya fabla; et él me enbió á tí.—Et non le dixo todo lo quel ynfante le dixiera, et dixo el rrey: Vé muy ayna et díl' que se venga muy para mí el ynfante.—Et él vino et omillósele et dixo el rrey: ¿Qué fué que estos dias non fablaste, que viste tu muerte á ojo?—Et díxol' el ynfante: Yo vos lo diré.—Et contól' todo como le acaesçiera et comol' defendiera su maestro Cendubete que non fablase siete dias:—Mas de la muger te digo que quando me apartó que me queria castigar et yo díxol' que yo non podia rresponder fasta que fuesen pasados los siete dias, et quando esto oyó, non sopo otro consejo (tomar) sinon que me fisiésedes matar ante que yo fablase. Enpero, Señor, pídovos por merced, si vos quisieredes et lo tovieredes por bien, que mandases ayuntar todos los sabios de vuestro regno et de vuestros pueblos; ca querria decir mi rrason entre ellos.—Et quando el ynfante esto dixo, el rrey fué muy alegre et dixo: Loado sea Dios por quanto bien me fiso que me non dexó faser tan gran yerro que matase mi fijo.—Et el rrey mandó llegar su gente et su corte; et despues que fueron llegados, llegó Cendubete et entró al rrey, et dixo: Omíllome, Señor.—Et dixo el rrey: ¿Qué fué de tí, mal Cendubete, estos dias? Ca poco fincó que non mate mi fijo por lo que le tu castigaste.—Et dixo Cendubete: Tanto te dió Dios de merced et de enseñamiento por que tu deves faser la cosa quando supieres la verdat, mas que mas los rreyes señaladamente por derecho devedes seer seguros de la verdat que los otros; et él non lexó de faser lo que le yo castigué; et tu, Señor, non devieras mandar matar tu fijo por dicho de una muger.—Et dixo el rrey: Loado sea Dios que non maté mi fijo: que perdiera este sieglo et el otro; et, vosotros sabios, si matara el mi fijo ¿cuya seria la culpa? Si seria mia ó de mi fijo ó de mi muger ó del maestro.—Levantáronse quatro sabios et dixo el uno: Quando Cendubete vido el estrella del moço en como avia de seer su fasienda, non se deviera esconder.—Et dixo otro: Non es así como tu dises: que Cendubete non avia y culpa, ca tenia puesto tal pleyto con el rrey que non avia de fallescer: deviera ser la culpa del rrey que mandava matar su fijo por dicho de una muger et non sabiendo si era verdat ó si era mentira.—Dixo el terçero sabio: Non es así como vosotros desides, ca el rrey non avia y culpa: que non ay en el mundo fuste mas frio quel sándalo nin cosa mas fria que la carofoja, et quando los buelven uno con otro ánse de escalentar tanto que salle dellos fuego, et si el rrey fuese firme en su sesso, non se bolverie por sesso de una muger; mas pues era muger quel rrey amava, non podie estar que non la oyese. Mas la culpa era de la muger por que con sus palabras lo engannava et fasia desir que matase su fijo.—Et el quarto dixo: La culpa non era de la muger, mas que era del ynfante que non quiso guardar lo que mandara su maestro; ca la muger quando vido al niño tan fermoso et apuesto ovo sabor dél, mas que mas quando se apartó con él et ella entendió que seria descubierta á cabo de los syete dias de lo que el ynfante desia, et ovo miedo que la mataria por ello, et curó de lo faser matar ante que fablase.—Et Cendubete dixo· Non es así como vos desides que el mayor saber que en el mundo ay es desir.—Et el ynfante dixo: Fablaré, si me vos mandaredes.—Et el rrey dixo:...Dios á tí loado, que me fesiste ver este dia et esta ora, que me dexeste mostrar mi fasienda et mi rrason! Menester es de entender la mi rrason: que quiero desir el mi saber et yo quiérovos desir el enxenplo desto.

XXII. *Enxenplo del omme et de los que conbidó et de la manceba que enbió por la leche et de la culebra que cayó la ponçoña.*

Et los maestros le dixieron que dixiese, et él dixo: Disen que un omme que adobó su yantar et conbidó sus huéspedes et sus amigos et enbió su moça al mercado por leche que comiesen; et ella compróla et levóla sobre la cabeça, et pasó un milano por sobre ella, et levava entre sus manos una culebra, et apretóla tanto de rresio con las manos que salyó el venino della et cayó en la leche, et comiéronla et murieron todos con ella. Et agora me desit ¿cuya fué la culpa por que murieron todos aquellos ommes?—Et dixo uno de los quatro sabios: La culpa fué en aquel que los conbidó que non cató la leche que les dava á comer.—Et el otro maestro dixo: Non es así como vos desides: quél que los huéspedes conbida non puede todo catar, nin gostar de quanto les dava á comer; mas la culpa fué en el milano que apretó tanto la culebra con las manos que ovo de caer aquella ponçoña.—Et el otro rrespondió: Non es así como vosotros desides: ca el milano non avia y culpa por que comia lo que solia comer, demas non fasiendo á su nescesidat; mas la culebra ha la culpa que echó de sí la ponçoña.—Et el quarto dixo: Non es así como vos otros desides: que la culebra non a culpa; mas la culpa avia la moça que non cubrió la leche quando la traxo del mercado.—Dixo Cendubete: Non es así como vosotros desides: que la moça non avia y culpa, ca non le mandaron cobrir la leche, nin el milano non avia y culpa, ca comia lo que avia de comer, nin la culebra non avia y culpa, ca yva en poder ageno, nin el huéspet non ovo y culpa: quel omme non puede gostar tantos comeres quantos manda guisar.—Estonçe dixo el rrey á su fijo: Todos estos disen nada: mas díme tu cuya es la culpa.— El ynfante dixo: Ninguno destos non ovo culpa, mas acertóseles la ora en que avien á morir todos.—Et quando el rrey oyó esto dixo: Loado sea Dios que me non dexó matar mi fijo.—Estonçe dixo á Cendubete el rrey: Tu has fecho mucho bien et nos as fecho para faserte mucha mercet; pero tu sabes si a el moço mas de aprender: amuéstragelo et avras buen galardon. — Estonçe dixo Cendubete: Señor, yo non sé cosa en el mundo que yo non le mostré, et bien creo que non la ay en el mundo, et non ay mas sabio quél.—Estonçe dixo el rrey á los sabios que estavan enderredor: ¿Es verdat lo que dise Cendubete?—Estonçe dixieron que non devia omme desir mal de lo que bien paresce.—Et dixo el ynfante: El que bien fase, buen gualardon meresçe.—El ynfante dixo: Yo te diré quien sabe mas que yo.—El rrey díxol': ¿Quien?...

XXIII. *Enxenplo de los dos ninnos sabios et de su madre et del mancebo.*

Señor, disen que dos moços, el uno de quatro años et el otro de cinco años, ciegos et contrechos et todos disen que eran mas sabios que yo.—Et dixo su padre : ¿Como fueron estos mas sabios que tu?—Oy desir que un omme que nunca oye desir de muger fermosa que non se perderia por ella, et oyó desir de una muger fermosa et enbiól' su omme á desir que la queria muy gran bien ; et aquella muger avia un fijo de quatro años; et despues quel mandadero se tornó con la rrespuesta que queria faser lo quél toviese por bien, fuése para ella el señor, et dixo ella : Espera un poco et faré á mi fijo que coma, et luego me verné para tí.—Mas dixo el omme : Fas lo que yo quisiere et despues que yo fuere ydo, dalle as á comer.—Et dixo la muger : Si tu sopieses quan sabio es, non diries eso.—Et levantóse ella et puso una caldera sobre el fuego et metió arros et coxólo et tomó un poco en la cuchara et púsogelo delante. Et lloró et dixo: Dáme mas, que esto poco es.—Et ella díxol': ¿Mas quieres?—Et díxol': Mas.—Et dixo quel' echase aseyte de alcuça.—Et lloró mas et por todo esto non callava.—Et dixo el moço: ¡Guay de tí!...Nunca ví mas loco que tu nin de poco sesso.—Dixo el omme : ¿En qué te semejo loco et de poco sesso?—Et dixo el moço : Yo non lloro sinon por mi pro ¿Qué te duelen mis lágremas de mis oios? Et sana mi cabeça ; et mas mandóme mi padre por el mi llorar arros que coma quanto quisiere ; mas quél es loco et de poco sesso et de mal entendimiento él que salle de su tierra et dexa sus fijos et su aver et sus parientes por fornicar por las tierras, buscando de lo que fase daño et enflaquesiendo su cuerpo et cayendo en yra de Dios.—Et quando esto ovo dicho el moço, entendiendo que era mas cuerdo quel vieio, et él llegóse á él et abraçól' el falagól' et dixo por buena fé: Verdat dises: non cuydé que tan sesudo eras et tan sabydor eras, et só mucho maraviellado de quanto as dicho.—Et rrepintióse et fiso penitençia.—Et, Señor, dixo el ynfante; esta es la estoria del ninno de los quatro años.

XXIV. *Enxenplo del niño de los cinco años et de los compañeros que dieron el aver á la vieja.*

Et, Señor, desirte hé del niño de los cinco annos.—Dixo el rrey: Pues dí.—Dixo: Oy desir que eran tres compañeros en una mercaduría et salieron con grant aver. Et todos tres anduvieron en el camino; et acaesçió que posaron con una vieja et diéronle sus averes á guardar et dixiéronle: Non lo deres á ninguno en su cabo fasta que seamos todos ayuntados en uno.—Et díxoles ella: Pláseme.—Et des y entraron ellos en una huerta de la vieja por bañarse en una aluerca que y avia et dixieron los dos al uno: Vé á la vieja et díle que te dé un peyne con que nos peynemos.—Et el físolo así et fuése para la vieja et díxol': Mandáronme mis conpañeros que me diésedes el aver que lo queremos contar.—Dixo: Non te lo daré fasta que todos vos ayuntedes en uno, así como lo posiestes comigo.—Dixo él: Llégate fasta la puerta.—Et dixo: Catad la vieja que dise si me lo mandades vos.—Et dixieron ellos: Busat et dátgelo.—Et ella fué et dióle el aver et él tomólo et fué su carrera, et desta guisa engannó á sus compañeros. Et quando ellos vieron que detardava, fueron á la vieja et dixieron: ¿Por qué fases detardar á nuestro conpañero?...—Et dixo ella: Dado le hé el aver que me mandastes.—Et dixeron ellos: ¡Guay de tí!...que nos non te mandamos dar el aver, sinon un peyne.—Et ella dixo: Levado a el aver que me diestes.—Et pusiéronla delant' el alcalle et fueron antél et ovieron sus rrasones, et judgó el alcalle que pagase el aver la vieja, pues que así lo conosciera. Et la vieja lorando, encontró con el ninno de los cinco annos, et díxol' el ninno: ¿Por qué lloras?—Et dixo ella: Lloro por mi mala ventura et por mi grant mal que me vino; et por Dios, déxame estar.—Et fué el ninno en pos della fasta quel' dixo por qué llorava et díxol': Yo te daré consejo a esta cueyta que as, si me dieres un dinero con que conpre dátiles.—Et dixo el ninno: Tórnate al alcalle et dí quel aver tu lo tienes, et dí: Alcalle, mandat que trayan su conpañero, et sinon, non les daré nada fasta que se ayunten todos tres en uno como pusieron comigo.—Et ella tornos' para el alcalle et díxol' lo que le conseiara el ninno, et entendió el alcalle que otrie gelo avia consejado et dixo el alcalle: Ruégote por Dios, vieia, que me digas quien fué aquel que te conseió.—Et ella dixo: Un ninno que me fallé en la carrera.—Et enbió el alcalle á buscar al ninno et duxiéronle antel alcalle et díxol': ¿Tu conseieste aquesta vieia?...—Et dixo el niño: Yo gelo mostré.—Et el alcalle fué y muy pagado del niño et tomólo para si et guardól' mucho para su consejo.—Et fué pagado el rrey de su estoria del niño de los cinco annos.

XXV. *Enxenplo del mercador del sándalo et del otro mercador.*

Et dixo el rrey: ¿Como fué eso?—Señor, disen de la estoria del viejo; et oy desir una vegada que era un mercador muy rrico que mercava sándalo et preguntó en aquella tierra do era el sándalo mas caro et fuése para allá et cargó sus bestias de sándalo para aquella tierra; et pasó por cerca de una cibdat muy buena, et dixo entre su coraçon: Non entraré en esta cibdat fasta que amanesia; et él seyendo en aquel lugar, pasó una mançeba que traye su ganado de paçer; et quando ella vido la rrecua, preguntól' que qué traye é donde era. Et fué la mançeba para su señor et díxol' como estavan mercadores á la puerta de la villa que trayen sándalo mucho. Et fué aquel omme et lo que tenia echólo en el fuego, et el mercador sintiólo quera fumo de sándalo, et ovo grant miedo, et dixo á sus ommes: Catad vuestras cargas que non llegue fuego á ellas, ca yo huelo fumo de sándalo.—Et ellos cataron las cargas et non fallaron nada. Et levantóse el mercador et fué á los pastores á ver si eran levantados; et aquel que quemava el sándalo vino al mercador et díxol': ¿Quien sodes ó como andades, et que mercaduría traedes?—Et dixo él: Somos mercadores que traemos sándalo.—Et dixo el omme: Ay buen omme, esta tierra non quemamos ál sinon sándalo.—Dixo el mercador: ¿Como puede ser? que yo pregunté et dixiéronme que non avia tierra mas cara que esta nin que tanto valiese el sándalo.—Dixo el omme: Quien te lo dixo, engañarte quiso.—Et començó el mercador de quexarse et de maldesirse et fiso grant duelo et dixo el omme: Por buena fé yo hé grant duelo de tí.— Mas dixo: Ya que así es, conprártelo hé et darte hé lo que quisieres, et liévate et otórgamelo.—Et otorgógelo el mercador, et tomó el omme el sándalo, et levólo á su casa et quando amanesçió entró el mercador á la villa et posó en casa de una muger vieja et preguntól' como valia el sándalo en esta cibdat.—Dixo ella: Vale á peso de oro.— Et arrepintióse el mercador mucho quando lo oyó, et dixo la vieja: Ya, omme bueno, los desta viella son engannadores é malos baratadores, et nunca viene omme extraño quellos non lo escarnescan et guardatvos dellos.—Et fuése el mercador fasta el mercado et falló unos que jugavan los dados et paróse ally, et mirólos; et dixo el uno: ¿Sabes jugar este juego?—Dixo él: Si sé.—Dixo: Pues pósate; mas dixo: Cata que sea atal condiçion quél que ganare quel otro sea tenudo de faser lo quel otro quesiere et mandare.—Dixo él: Si otorgo.—Des y asentóse él et perdió el mercador, et dixo aquel que ganó: Tu has de

faser lo que yo te mandare.—Díxol' él: Otorgo ques verdat.
—Díxol': Pues mándote que bevas toda el agua de la mar,
et non dexes cosa ninguna, nin destello.—Et dixo el
mercador: Pláseme.—Dixo él: Dáme fiadores que lo fagas.
—Et fuése el mercador por la calle et fallós' con un omme
que non avia sinon un oio et trabó del mercador et dixo:
Tu me furteste mi oio: anda acá comigo antel alcalle.—
Et dixo su huéspeda la vieja: Yo só su fiador de la fas quel
traiya cras ante vos.—Et levólo consigo á su posada, et
díxol' la vieja: ¿Non te dixe et te castigué que los ommes
desta villa eran ommes malos et de mala rrepuelta? Mas
pues non me quisiste creer en lo primero que te yo defendí,
non seas tu agora torpe de lo que te agora diré.—Et dixo el
mercador: A buena fé nunca te saldré de mandado de lo
que tu mandares et me consejares.—Dixo la vieja: Sepas
quellos an por maestro un viejo ciego et es muy sabidor;
et ayúntanse con él todos cada noche, et dise cada uno
quanto a fecho de dia. Mas si tu pudieses entrar con ellos
á bueltas et asentarte con ellos, y diran lo que fisieron á tí
cada uno dellos et oyras lo que les dise el viejo por lo que
á tí fisieron; ca non puede seer quellos non lo digan todo
al viejo.—Et des y fué el omme para allá et entró á bueltas
dellos et posóse, et oyó quanto desian al viejo. Et dixo el
primero, que avia comprado el sándalo a mercador' de que
guisa lo conprara et quel' daria quanto él quisiese.—Et
dixo el viejo: Mal fesiste á guisa de omme torpe: ¿que te
semeja si él te demanda pulgas, las medias fembras, et los
medios machos, et las unas çiegas et las otras coxas et las
otras verdes et las otras cárdenas et las otras bermejas et
blancas et que non aya mas de una sana?...¿Cuydas si
lo podras esto conplir?...—Dixo el omme: Non se le
menbrará á él deso: que non demandará sinon dinieros.—
Et levantóse aquel que jugara á los dados con el mercador
et dixo: Yo jugué con ese mercador et dixe así que si yo

ganase á los dados que fisiese lo quel' yo mandase faser. Et yo mandéle que beviese toda el agua de la mar.—Et dixo el viejo: Tan mal as fecho como el otro. ¿ Qué te semeja si el otro dise: Yo te fis pleyto de bever toda el agua de la mar ; mas vieda tu que no entre en ella rrio nin fuente que non caya en la mar; estonçe la beveré.—...? Cata si lo podras tu faser todo esto.—Levantóse él del oio et dixo · Yo me encontré con ese mesmo mercador et ví que avia los oios tales como yo, et díxele : Tu que me furtaste mi oio, non te partas de mí fasta que me des mi oio lo que val. —Et dixo el viejo : Non fuste maestro nin sopiste que te fesçiste. ¿ Qué te semeja si te dixiera : Saca el tuyo que te fincó et sacaré yo el mio, et veremos si se semejan et pesémoslos, et si fueren eguales es tuyo, et si non, non—...? Et si tu esto fisieres, seras çiego et el otro fincará con un oio et tu non con ninguno. Et faras mayor pérdida que non él.—Et quando el mercador oyó esto, plógol' et apprendiólo todo, et fuése para la posada et díxol' todo lo que le conteçiera, et tóvose por bien consejado della ; et folgó esa noche en su casa, et quando amanesçió, vido aquel quel' conprara el sándalo et díxol' : Dáme mi sándalo ó dáme lo que posiste comigo.—Et dixo: Escoge lo que quisieres.—Et díxol' el mercador: Dáme una fanega de pulgas llena, la meytat fembras et la meytat machos, et la meytat bermejas, et la meytat verdes, et la meytat cárdenas et la meytat amarillas et la meytat blancas.—Et dixo el omme : Darte hé dineros.—Dixo el mercador : Non quiero sinon las pulgas.—Emplasó el mercador al omme, et fueron antel alcalle ; et mandó el alcalle quel' diese las pulgas.— Et dixo el omme que tomase su sándalo.—Et así cobró el mercador su sándalo por consejo del viejo. Et vino el otro que avia jugado á los dados et díxol' : Cunple el pleyto que pusiste comigo que bevas toda el agua de la mar.—Et dixo él : Pláseme con condiçion que tu que viedes todas las fuentes et rrios que entren en la mar.—Et dixo: Vayamos ante el alcalle.—Et dixo el alcalle: ¿Es así esto?—Et dixieron ellos que sí.—Et dixo: Pues vieda tu que non entre mas agua, él dise que la beverá.—Dixo él: Non puede seer.—Et el alcalle mandó dar por quito al mercador.—Et luego vino el de el oio, et dixo: Dáme mi oio.—Et dixo él: Pláseme: saca tu ese tuyo et sacaré yo este mio; et veremos si se semejan, et pesémoslos, et si fueren eguales es tuyo, et si non es tuyo, págame lo que manda el derecho.—Et dixo el alcalle: ¿Qué dises tu?—Dixo: ¿Como sacaré yo el mi oio que luego non terné ninguno?—Dixo el alcalle: Pues derecho te pide.—Et dixo el omme que lo non queria sacar. Et dió al mercador por quito.—Et así acaesçió al mercador con los ommes daquel lugar.—Et dixo el ynfante: Sennor, non te dí este enxenplo sinon por que sepas las artes del mundo.

XXVI. *Enxenplo de la muger et del clérigo et del frayle.*

Et dixo el rrey: ¿Como fué eso?—Et dixo el ynfante Oy desir de una muger que fué su marido fuera á librar su facienda et ella enbió al abat á desir quel marido non era en la viella et que veniese para la noche á su posada. Et el abat vino et entró en casa et quando vino, fasia la media noche. Vino el marido et llamó á la puerta. Et dixo él: ¿Qué será?—Et dixo ella: Véte et ascóndete en aquel palacio fasta de dia.—Et entró el marido et echóse en su cama, et quando vino el dia, levantóse la muger et fué a un frayle su amigo et rrogóle que levase un ábito que sacase al abat questava en su casa. Et fué el frayle et dixo: ¿Qué es de fulano?—Et dixo ella: Non es levantado.—Et entró et preguntóle por nuevas onde venia, et estovo allí fasta que fué vestido; et dixo el frayle: Perdóname: que me quiero acoger.—Dixo él: Vayades en ora buena.—Et en egualando con el palaçio sallió el abat vestido como frayle et fuése con él fasta su orden, et fuése.—Señor, non te dí este enxenplo sinon que non creyas á las mugeres que son malas. Et dise el sabio que aunque se tornase la tierra papel, la mar tinta, et los peces della péndolas, que non podrian escrevir las maldades de las mugeres.—Et el rrey mandóla quemar en una caldera en seco.

BOOK OF THE DECEITS
AND
TRICKS OF WOMEN.

BOOK OF THE DECEITS AND TRICKS OF WOMEN.

TRANSLATED FROM THE ARABIC INTO CASTILIAN FOR THE INFANTE DON FADRIQUE,

SON OF DON FERRANDO AND OF DOÑA BEATRIS.

PROLOGUE.

THE Infante Don Fadrique, son of the very prosperous and very noble king Don Ferrando and of the very holy queen, replete with every excellence, Doña Beatris, in order that his good name might never be lost, hearing the reasons of the wise men that "the fame of a man who does well never dies," and knowing that nothing is better adapted for gaining a lasting life than good works and knowledge, since knowledge is a ship very safe to enable a person to go forward without danger and, in conjunction with good works, to attain unto the lasting life,—and inasmuch as man, being of little life, and science being hard and long, can learn no knowledge more than is granted to him by the grace which is given to him and sent from above,—with love of improving and benefiting and favouring those who are fond of it, was pleased and thought it good that this book should be translated from Arabic into Castilian, in order to its being a warning against the deceits and tricks of women.

This book was translated in the year ninety-one.

I. *An Example of the Woman's Counsel.*

There was a king in India named Alcos, and this king was a lord of great power, and loved much the men of his land and maintained them in justice; and this king had ninety wives. Though cohabiting with all of them, as was the law, he had no son by any of them, and being one night in his bed with one of them, he began to meditate who should inherit his kingdom after his death; and he had meditated so much on this that he became very sorrowful, and began to turn in his bed with the great care that he had. And there came to him one of his wives whom he most loved, and she was sensible and judicious, and he had tried her in some things. And she came to him because she saw that he was sorrowful, and said to him that he was honoured and loved by those of his kingdom and by his own people: —Why do I see thee sorrowful and full of care? If it is from fear, or if any one does thee wrongs, let me know and condole with thee. And if it is aught else, thou oughtest not to feel so much annoyance, for, thanks to God, thou art beloved of thy peoples, and all speak well of thee for the great love which they bear thee. And may God never permit thee to have sorrow, but help thee with his blessing.

Then the king said to his wife: Pious and blessed woman, you have ever comforted me, and removed from me all care when I had it; but, said the king, all the power I have and all that there is in my kingdom are powerless to provide a remedy for what I grieve for. I would fain leave an heir when I die who may inherit my kingdom.

And the woman said to him: I will give thee counsel good for this. Ask of God, who is full of all goodness, for he is powerful, to give thee a son, should it so please him; for he has not wearied of showing mercy and thou never askedst aught of him that he did not give thee; and when he shall know that thou heartily seekest it, he will give thee a son. But I think it good, if thou art pleased, that we should rise and pray to God with our whole heart, and ask of him to grant us the favour of a son who shall be heir after us, for I feel confident that in his mercy he will give us one; should he [not] give us him, then we ought to be pleased and do his command, and be satisfied with his decision, and comprehend his favour, and know that all power is of God and is in his hand, and some he likes to deprive, to some he likes to give more.

And after she had said this he was pleased with it, and knew that what she said was the truth, and they both arose and did so; and they returned to their bed, and the king lay with her, and she was with child forthwith, and after they knew it for truth they praised God for the favour which he had done them.

And when the nine months were completed she was delivered of a healthy son; and the king had great joy and gladness and was pleased therewith, and the wife praised God therefor. Then the king sent for all the wise men of his kingdom to come to him and examine the hour and the minute of his son's birth; and after they were come he sent for them into his presence and said: Ye are welcome. And he was with them a long time, cheering and solacing himself, and he said: Ye wise men, I let you know that God, whose name be praised, has granted me the favour of a son, whom he has given me to strengthen my arm, and with whom I shall have joy; and thanks be given to him for ever. And he said to them: Examine into my son's star, and see what shall be his fortune. And they examined into it, and let him know that he (the son) should have a long life and great powers, but at the end of twenty years something should happen between him and his father through which he should be in danger of death. When he heard this he was much affrighted and felt great pain, and his cheerfulness was over, and he said: All is in God's power, and he will do what he shall think right.

And the prince grew and became tall and handsome, and God gave him a very good understanding. In his time was no man born such as he was; and afterwards, when he attained the age of nine years, the king set him to learn to write until he attained the age of fifteen years; and he learned nothing. And when the king heard that he had great sorrow, and asked for all the wise men in his land. And they came all to him, and he said to them: What think ye of the state of my son? Is there none of you that can teach him? I will give him all that he can ask for, and he shall enjoy my love for ever.

Then there rose four of them who were there (and there were nine hundred men), and one of them said: I will teach him so that no one shall have more knowledge than he. And the king said to a wise man whom they called Cendubete: Why didst thou not teach him? Cendubete said: Let every one say what he knows. And afterwards they talked over this. Cendubete said to them: Do you know anything else than this? for this is all known to me and it is nothing to me, since no one has more knowledge than I, and I will show it. And he said to the king: Give me what I shall ask, for I will so teach him in six months that no one shall have more knowledge than he.

And then said one of the four wise men: He that says and does not act is like the lightning that has no rain with it. Why didst thou teach him nothing in those years that he was with thee, the king doing thee much good?—For the great pity that I had for him. I could not teach him because I had great reluctance to compel him, and I was anxiously seeking some one wiser than I. But now

I see that no one knows more than I, I shall be able to teach him.

And then arose the second master and said: There are four things that a sensible man will not praise until he sees the end of them. The first is food, until he sees what the stomach finally does with it; he that goes to a lawsuit until he returns from it; the harvest until it is cut; and a wife until she is pregnant. Therefore we must not praise thee until we see a reason why—until thou hast shown that thy hands can do something and thy mouth can say something. And Cendubete said: The hands with the feet and hearing and seeing and all the body have each its own power. Knowledge in the heart is like scented water in a barrel (?); if knowledge is in the heart it makes all the body good.

The third of the wise men said: He who does not learn knowledge in his childhood is like the man who eats what does not agree with his stomach; and the wife when she has no fear of her husband never can be good. He that says reason, but does not understand it and does not know what it is, never can convey it to the hearer's mind nor make it intelligible to him. And thou, Cendubete, since thou couldst not teach him in his boyhood, how canst thou teach him when he is older? Cendubete said: Thou shalt see if God will, and I live, that I will teach him in six months what another would not teach him in seventy years.

And the fourth of the masters said · * Cendubete said :......* If these things were in the land, we ought not to stay in it. Therefore all this I have told thee, and I let thee know that kings are like fire: if thou comest

---

* I have omitted this unimportant part, where the Spanish text is hopelessly corrupt.

to it thou wilt burn thyself, and if thou retirest from it thou gettest cold. I desire, lord, that if I shall teach thy son thou wilt give me what I shall ask of thee. And the king said: Ask what thou desirest.—What if thou canst not (do it)?—I will do it, for there is nothing worse than lying, especially in kings. And the king said: Tell me what thou desirest. And Cendubete said: Thou shouldst not do to another what thou wouldst not he should do unto thee. And the king said: I grant it thee. And they drew up a written contract, and they put in it in what month and what hour of the day it was to be completed, and they inserted in the deed what was wanted about the day. Two hours of the day were passed.

Cendubete took the child this day by the hand and went with him to his inn; and he had a beautiful and magnificent palace made, and wrote over the walls all the kinds of knowledge which he had to teach him, all the stars and all the figures and all things. Then he said to him: This is my seat and this is thine until thou learnest all the sciences that I have been teaching thee in this palace; and relieve thy heart and freshen thy mind and thy hearing and thy seeing. And he sat down with him to teach him, and they (the servants) brought them there what they should eat and what they should drink, and they did not go out, and no one else entered there. And the boy was of good mind and of good understanding, so that before the time arrived he learnt all the sciences that Cendubete, his master, had written of the knowledge of man.

The king sent for him on the appointed day. When the king's messenger came, he said to him: The king desires much that thou shouldst attend him. He said to him: Cendubete, what hast thou done, or what hast thou got? Cendubete said to him: I have got what shall please thee—that thy son shall be to-morrow with thee when two hours of the day are passed. And the king said to him: Never has such a man as thou failed in his promise. Then go with honour, for thou deservest to have a reward of us. And Cendubete returned to the boy and said to him: I desire to examine into thy star. And he examined into it, and saw that the child would be in great peril of death if he should speak before seven days had passed, and he said to the boy: I am very much troubled about the agreement I made with the king. And the boy (said): Why art thou much troubled? For if thou commandest me never to speak, I will never speak. And command me whatever thou desirest, I will do it all. Cendubete said: I have made an agreement with thy father that thou shalt go to him to-morrow, and I must not fail in the agreement that I made with him. When two hours of the day shall have passed, go to thy father, but speak not until the seven days be passed, and I will hide myself in the meanwhile.

And when the next day dawned, the king ordered dinner to be prepared for all (the nobles) of his kingdom, and he ordered places to be made for them, and servants to attend and carve before them; and the boy came into his father's presence, and the father came forward to him and spoke to him. And the boy did not speak to him. The king was amazed and said to the boy: Where is thy master? And the king sent for Cendubete, and the messengers went out to seek him, and they searched for him everywhere and could not find him. And the king said to those that were with him: Perhaps he is afraid of me and dares not speak. And the king's counsellors spoke to him, and the child did not speak. And the king said to those that were with him: What think ye of the state of this boy? And they said: We think Cendubete, his master, has given him something or some medicine whereby he should learn some science, and that medicine has made him lose his speech. And the king was amazed and had much sorrow thereat.

II. *Example of the Woman, how she took the Prince to her Apartment, and how through what she said to him he forgot what his Master had taught him.*

The king had a wife whom he loved and honoured more than all the other wives that he had, and when they told her what had happened to the prince, she went to the king and said: Lord, they told me what has happened to thy son. Peradventure for the awe that he has of thee he dares not speak. But if thou wilt leave him alone with me, perhaps he will tell me his business. For he was wont to tell me his secrets, which he did with no other of thy wives. And the king said to her: Take him to thy apartment and talk with him. And she did so. But the prince answered her nought, whatever she might say, and she pursued him the more and said to him: Do not be silly, for I know that thou wilt not reject my proposal. Let us kill thy father, and thou wilt be king and I will be thy wife, for thy father is already of very advanced age and weak, and thou art a young man, and now thy happiness is beginning and thou must have more expectation of happiness than he. And when she had said [this] the young man became greatly enraged, and then he forgot what his master had taught him and all that he had commanded him. And he said: O enemy of God, if the seven days were passed, I would answer this that thou sayest.

After he had said this she knew that she was in danger of death. And she cried aloud and began to tear her hair. And the king, when he heard this, ordered her to be called, and asked her what she might ail. And she said: This man that thou saidst did not speak wished to force me, and I never had such an opinion of him. And when the king heard this he desired much to kill his son, and was very savage, and ordered him to be killed.

And this king had seven favourites, his great counsellors, so that he did nothing without consulting them. After they saw that the king had ordered his son to be killed without their advice, they understood that he did so out of rage because he believed his wife. They said one to another: If he kills his son, it will [hereafter] pain him much, and then his wrath shall be turned against nobody else than ourselves, for we have some reason why this prince should not die. And then answered one of the four [*sic*] masters and said: I will excuse you, if God will, from speaking with the king.

This first favourite went to the king and knelt before him and said: Man should do nothing until he be certain of it, and if thou shouldst act before that, thou wilt err. And I will tell thee an example of a king and of a wife of his. And the king said: Then tell it now and I will hear it of thee.

And the favourite said: I have heard that there was a king who loved women much and had no evil custom but this. And one day the king was sitting on a very high terrace, and looked down and saw a very beautiful woman, and was much pleased with her. And he sent to ask her love. And she told him that she could not do so, her husband being in the town. And when the king heard this he sent her husband to the army on a campaign. And the wife was very chaste and very good and very intelligent, and she said: Lord, thou art my lord and I am thy slave, and whatever thou desirest I desire also. But I must go to the bath and paint myself up. And when she returned she gave him a book of her husband's, one that contained laws and judgments of the kings, concerning how they castigated the woman that committed adultery, and she said: Lord, read through this book whilst I paint myself up. And the king opened the book and found in the first chapter how adultery ought to be prohibited, and he had great shame, and he grieved much at what he had wished to do. And he put the book down on the ground, and went out through the door of the chamber, and left his sandals under the bed on which he was seated.

And at this time came her (*i. e.*, the lady's) husband from the cámpaigning army. And when he sat down in his house he suspected that the king had slept there with his wife, and he feared and dared say nothing for fear of the king. And he dared not go in where she was. And this lasted a great season, and the wife told her relations that her husband had left her, and she knew not for what reason. And they said to her husband: Why dost thou not come to thy wife? And he said: I found the king's sandals in my house and I fear, and therefore I dare not come to her. And they said: Let us go to the king and give him an example of this action of the wife, and not declare it to him as the action of the wife. And if he be intelligent he will straightway understand it.

And then they went in unto the king and said to him: Lord, we had an estate, and we gave it to this good man that he should cultivate it and gather the fruits thereof. And he did so for a long season, but has long left off cultivating it. And the king said: What sayest thou to this? And the good man answered and said: They say truth, for they did give me an estate as they say. And when I went one day through the land I found the track of a lion, and I feared that he would destroy me. Therefore I left off cultivating the land. And the king said: It is true that the lion entered on the land, but he did nothing to thee that thou wouldst not wish. No ill came to thee from him, therefore take thy land and cultivate it.

And the good man returned to his wife and asked her what the occurrence had been, and she told him all, and told him the truth of what had happened between her and him (*i. e.*, the king). And he believed her for the signs which the king had told; and afterwards he trusted her more than before.

III. *Example of the Man and the Woman and the Parrot and their Maidservant.*

Lord, I have heard that (there was) a man who was jealous of his wife, and he bought a parrot and put it into a cage. And he placed it in his house, and he ordered it to tell him all that his wife should do, and never to conceal anything thereof from him; and afterwards he went away on business of his own.

And a friend of hers entered the house where she was. The parrot saw all that they did; and when the good man came home, he sat down, unseen by his wife, and ordered the parrot to be brought, and asked him all that he had seen, and the parrot told him all that he had seen the woman do with her friend. And the good man was very much incensed against his wife, and went no longer into the place where she was (viz., the harem). And the wife believed truly that the maid had told about her. And then she called her and said: Thou didst tell my husband all that I did. And the girl swore that she had not told it, but knew that the parrot had told it.

And she [the wife] took it down and began to throw water upon it, just as if it were rain. And she took a mirror in her hand and held it over the cage, and in the other hand [she held] a candle, and she held that over [also]. And the parrot thought that it was lightning. And the wife began to move a grindstone, and the parrot thought that it was thunder. And she occupied herself all night doing this until morning. And after it was morning the husband came and asked the parrot: Hast thou seen anything this night? And the parrot said: I could see nothing for the great rain and the thunder and lightning that there were this night. And the man said: Hath what thou hast told me of my wife as much truth as this? There is nothing more lying than thou, and I will order thee to be killed. And he sent for his wife and pardoned her, and they made peace.

And I, lord, have told thee this example only that thou mayst know the deceit of women; that their arts are very strong, and are many, so that they have no end.

And the king commanded that they should not kill his son.

IV. *Example of how the Woman came on the Second Day before the King weeping, and told him to kill his Son.*

And she said: Lord, thou oughtest not to pardon thy son, since he has done a thing for which he should die. And if thou dost not kill him, but leavest him alive, having done such an evil thing, then nobody will be deterred from doing another such act; and I, lord, can tell thee the example of the calenderer and of his son. The king said: How was that?

And she said: There was a calenderer and he had a son still a little child. When he had to go to his work of fulling the clothes, he used to take his son with him; and the child began to play with the water, and the father would not punish him for it. And there came a day when the child sank into the water, and the father, trying to catch hold of the child, sank too, and both were drowned.

And, lord, if thou art not beforehand in chastising thy son before he does thee more harm, he will kill thee.

And the king gave orders to kill his son.

V. *Of how the Second Favourite came before the King to save the Prince from Death.*

And the second favourite came and knelt before the king and said: Lord, if thou hadst many children thou oughtest not to wish evil to any one of them; the less so that thou hast only a single one, and yet thou commandest him hastily to be killed before thou knowest the truth; and after thou shalt have done so, thou wilt repent and wilt not be able to bring him back. And thy example will be like that of the merchant and the woman and the girl. Said the king: How was that?

I tell thee, lord, there was a very rich merchant, and he was particular and fidgety about his eating and his drinking. And he left on his trade, and took a boy with him, and they stopped in a very good town. And the merchant sent his boy to buy something to eat, and he found a girl in the market who had two loaves, and he liked the bread, and bought it for his master and took it away. And his master liked that bread. And the merchant said to his boy: For God's sake, do buy some of that bread every day of the girl. And he bought that bread and took it to his master.

And one day he found that the girl had no bread, and he went back to his master and said that he found none of that bread; and the merchant said that he should ask the girl how she made that bread. And the boy went to seek the girl, and he found her, and said: Friend, my master desires something of thee. And she went to the merchant and said: What is your pleasure? And the merchant asked her: Madam, how do you make that bread? I intend to have some made like it. And she said: Friend and master, some blisters came out on my father's shoulders, and the physician told us to take fine flour, and to knead it with butter and honey and put it on those blisters, and when we should have washed and wiped off all the pus, to take it off (and change it). And I took that dough and made it into bread, and carried it to the market to sell, and I sold it. And, praised be our Lord, he is now whole, and we cease to make it. And the merchant cried aloud for the great sickness that he had of that bread which he had eaten. And when he saw that it availed nought, he said to his boy: What shall I do, that we may seek wherewith to wash our hands and our feet and our mouths and our bodies? How shall we wash them?

And, lord, if thou killest thy son, I fear that thou wilt be like the merchant. And, lord, do nothing of which thou mayst repent until thou art certain of it.

VI. *Example of the Lord and the Man and the Woman and the Woman's Husband, how they all met together.*

Lord, I have heard of the deceits of women. They say that there was a woman that had a friend who was a favourite of a king. And from the king he had received a town under his power. And the friend sent a man of his to the lady's house to learn if her husband was there. And that man entered the lady's house, and she was pleased with him and he with her, for he was handsome. And she invited him to lie with her, and he did so.

And his master saw that the young man was late, and went to the house to hear from him, and called out. And the young man said: What shall I do with myself? And the woman said: Go and hide thyself in that recess. And his lord came in; and she managed that her friend should not go into the recess where the young man was.

At this time the husband came and called at the door; and she said to her friend: Take thy sword in thy hand, and stay at the door of the apartment (harem) and threaten me, and go out, and say nothing. And he did so. And he went and opened the door to the husband; and when the husband saw the other with his drawn sword in his hand, he spoke and said: What is this? And he answered nought, and went out. And the husband went into the apartment to his wife, and said: Oh, curses upon theè! What business had this man with thee, that he went out bullying and threatening thee? And she said: This man came fleeing with great fear, and he found the door open; and his lord entered after him to kill him, and he cried out for help. And after he approached me I stood before him and prevented the other from killing him. And therefore he goes hence bullying and threatening me. But if God protect me I do not mind. And the husband said: Where is this young man?—He is in that corner. And the husband went to the door, to see if the lord of the young man was (there) or if he had gone. And when he saw that he was not there, he called the young man, and said: Go hence, for thy lord has gone away. And the husband returned to her (his wife) well pleased, and said: Thou hast acted like a good woman and done well; and I am much satisfied with thee therefor.

And, lord, I have told thee this example only that thou mayst not kill thy son for the saying of a woman, for women have a large store of deceits in themselves.

And the king ordered that they should not kill his son.

VII. *Example of how the Woman came to the King on the Third Day, telling him to kill his Son.*

And the woman came on the third day, and wept and cried aloud before the king, and said: Lord, these thy favourites are wicked, and will kill thee as a favourite once killed a king. And the king said: How was that?

And she said: There was a king and he had a son who loved much to hunt. And the favourite contrived that he (*i.e.*, the son) should go to his father and ask leave for them to go hunting. And they having both gone out, a deer passed right before them. And the favourite said to the child: Go after that deer until thou overtakest and killest it, and thou shalt take it to thy father.

And the child went after the deer until he lost sight of his attendants. And being in this situation he found a path, and at the end of the path he found a girl who was weeping. And the boy said: Who art thou? And the girl said: I am the daughter of the king of such-and-such a land, and I was riding an elephant with my relations, and sleep overtook me, and I fell from it. And my relations did not see me. And I awoke and did not know where to go. And I hastened after them until I could not walk any further.

And the boy was grieved for her and took her behind him. And going in this manner they entered a deserted village. And the girl said: Put me down here, for I have need, and I will come presently to thee. And the boy did so; and she entered the village and was (there) a long time. And when the boy saw that she delayed, he got off his horse, and mounted upon a wall and looked about him, and saw that she was a devil and was with her relations and was saying to them: A boy has brought me on his horse, and I have brought him here. And they said: Go forward with him to another village until we overtake thee. And when the boy heard this he was much frightened and got off the wall and jumped on his horse.

And the girl came to him, and he took her up behind him, and he began to tremble from fear of her. And she said: What hast thou to tremble for? And he said to her: I am frightened about my companion, that ill will come to me through him. And she said: Canst thou not soothe him by thy wealth? For thou didst boast that

THE BOOK OF SINDIBAD. 133

thou wast the son of a king and that thy father had great wealth. And he said to her: He has no wealth.—But thou didst boast that thou wast a king and a great prince.

And the devil said to him: Pray God to help thee against him and thou wilt be delivered. And he said: Thou sayest truth, and I will do so. And he raised his hands to God and said: O Lord God, I pray thee and ask thee for thy favour to deliver me from this devil and her companions. And the devil fell down behind and began to wallow in the dust, and wished to rise and could not.

And then the boy began to run as fast as he could until he came to his father, dead with thirst, and he was much frightened with what he had seen.

And, lord, I have told thee this example only that thou mayst not rely on thy wicked favourites. If thou wilt not do me justice upon him who has done me ill, I will kill myself with my own hands.

And the king ordered his son to be killed.

VIII. *The Third Favourite's Example of the Huntsman and the Villages.*

And the third favourite came before the king and knelt before him and said: Lord, of things to which a man does not give heed cometh great harm. And the example of the huntsman and the villages is to that effect. And the king said: How was that?

He said to him: I have heard that there was a huntsman who went hunting through the forest, and he found in a tree a hive. And he took it, and put it into a skin that he had for carrying his water. And this huntsman had a dog which he took out with him. And he took the honey to a merchant in a village that was near that forest to sell it. And when the huntsman opened the skin to show it to the tradesman, there fell a drop from it, and a bee settled down upon it. And that tradesman had a cat, and it jumped upon the bee and killed it. And the huntsman's dog jumped upon the cat and killed it. And the master of the cat came and killed the dog. And then the master of the dog rose up and killed the tradesman because he had killed the dog. And then came the people of the tradesman's village and killed the huntsman, the owner of the dog. And the people of the huntsman's village came to the tradesman's people and fell out with each other. And they all killed each other, so that no one was left there, and thus they killed each other for a drop of honey.

And, lord, I have told thee this example only that thou mayst not kill thy son until the truth (is made known), in order that thou mayst not repent.

IX. *Example of how the Woman came and said that the King should kill his Son, and gave him an Example of a King's Son, and of a Favourite of his, how he deceived him.*

And the woman said to him: There was a king who had a favourite; and he had a son, and married him to a daughter of another king. And the king, father of the princess, sent word to the other king: Send me thy son, and we will have the marriage performed with my daughter and will afterwards send him back to thee. And the king furnished forth his son very well, in order that he should be married and be with her (the bride) as long as he wished. And then the king sent that favourite with his son. And talking one with another they got separated from their retinue, and they found a fountain. And it had such a virtue that whatever man should drink thereof straightway became a woman. And the favourite knew the virtue that the fountain had, and he would not tell it to the prince. And he said: Stay here now whilst I go and seek our way, for we must seek it. And he went in search of it. And he found the prince's father, and the king was very frightened, and said to him: How comest thou here without my son, or what has become of him? And the favourite said: I believe the wild beasts have eaten him.

And when the prince saw that the favourite delayed and did not return for him, he got down to the fountain to wash his hands and face. And he drank of the water and became a woman, and he knew not what to do or where to go. At this a devil came to him and asked him who he was. And he told him that he was the son of the king of such-and-such a land, and told him his right name, and the falseness which his father's favourite had shown him. And the devil had pity on him because he was so handsome, and said to him: I will turn myself into a woman as thou art, and at the end of four months I will turn myself into what I was before. And the prince heard him, and they made a compact, and he (the prince) went away.

And (at the end of the four months) the devil came in the position of a pregnant mother. And the devil said · Friend, become again what thou wast, and I will become again what I was. And the prince said: How can I become such again? For when I made (the) compact with thee I was a maid and a virgin, and thou art now a pregnant woman. And then the prince referred the matter between himself and the devil to his judges, and they decided that the prince had beaten the devil. Then the prince became a man again, and went to his wife and took her away to his father's house, and told her all that had happened. And the king ordered the favourite to be killed because he had left the prince at the fountain.

And therefore I have confidence that God will help me against thy wicked favourites.

And the king ordered his son to be killed.

X. *Example of the Fourth Favourite and of the Bathing Man and his Wife.*

And the fourth favourite came and went in unto the king and knelt before the king and said to him: Lord, no man ought to act in anything until he be very certain of the truth; for he who does so before he knows the truth errs and does very ill, as befell a bathing man who repented when it was no use. And the king asked him: How was this?

He said: Lord, a prince was one day about to enter his bath. He was a young man, and was so fat that he could not see his limbs wherever he was. And when he uncovered himself the bathing man saw him. And he began to weep, and the prince said to him: Why dost thou weep? And he said to him: To see a king's son as thou art, and (he) having no son but thee, and not to be lord of thy limbs as are other men. And the prince said to him: What shall I do? for my father wishes to marry me. And the prince said to him: Go and pick me a handsome woman. And the bathing man contrived an intrigue between his wife and the prince, but being disappointed in the result he went and hanged himself.*

And, lord, I have told thee this example only that thou mayst not kill thy son.

XI. *Example of the Man and the Woman and the Old Woman and the little She-Dog.*

Lord, I have heard that a man and his wife made an agreement that they should keep faithful to each other. And the husband made an appointment that she should come (to him), and she came not. And she went out into

* I have purposely abridged my translation for obvious reasons.

the street, and a man met her and saw her and was pleased with her, and asked of her her love. And she (said) that in no wise would she do so. Then he went to an old woman that dwelt near her, and told her all that had befallen him with that woman, and begged her to obtain her for him, and (said) that he would give her whatever she should ask. And the old woman said that she was willing and would obtain her for him.

And the old woman went to her home, and took honey and dough and pepper, and kneaded it together, and made loaves of it. Then she went to that woman's house, and called to a little she-dog which she had, and threw it some of that bread, unseen by the woman. And after the little she-dog had eaten it she began to go after the old woman, caressing her to give her more, and her eyes full of tears from the pepper that was in the bread. And when the wife saw her in this state she wondered, and said to the old woman: Friend, have you ever seen other she-dogs weep like this one? The old woman said: She does right, for this dog was a woman and very handsome, and lived here near me, and a man fell in love with her and she did not like him. And then that man who loved her cursed her, and straightway she became a she-dog. And now when she saw me she remembered it and began to weep.

And then the woman said: Ah, the wretch! What shall I do? The other day I saw a man in the street, and he asked me for my love, and I would not (grant it). And now I am afraid that I shall become a she-dog if he cursed me. And now go and beg him for me to give me what he pleases. Then said the old woman: I will bring him to thee.

And then the old woman rose and went after the man. And the woman rose and painted her face. And then she suddenly came to the old woman's house (to see) if she had found that man of whom she went in search. And the old woman said: I cannot find him. And then the woman said: Then what shall I do? Then the old woman went and found the man, and said to him: Come here, for the woman will do all that I shall desire. And the man was her husband, and the old woman did not know him. And the old woman said to him: What wilt thou give to whoever shall give thee good lodging, a young beautiful woman, and good eating and good drinking if thou desirest? And he said: Yes, by God I should like it.

And she went before, and he behind her, and saw that she was taking him to his house to his own wife. And he suspected that she was doing so all the way when he went out of his own house. And the bad old woman entered his house and said: Enter. After the man entered his house, the wife said: Sit down here. And she examined his face, and when she saw that it was her husband, she did not know what to do except to jump up and to say: Thou stinking bad fellow, is this what I and thou agreed to do? Now I see that thou hast maintained wicked women and wicked procuresses. And he said · Woe unto thee! What is thy complaint against me?

And his wife said: They told me just now that thou wast come, and I painted myself up. And I told this old woman to go out to thee, that she might test thee whether thou didst consort with bad women, and I see that thou wast quick in following her proposals. Never more shall we meet. Never more shalt thou come to me. And he said: So God give me his grace and I have thine as I imagined not but she was taking me to my house and thine; otherwise I would not have gone with her. And it grieved me much when I set foot in thy house and thought that thou wouldst act thus with other men. And when he had said this she scratched her face and disfigured it with her hands and said: Well I knew that thou wouldst think this of me. And she was enraged against him. And when he saw that she was in a rage he began to caress her and to beg her to pardon him. And she would not pardon him until he gave her some very valuable present. And he bequeathed her as dower a farm that he had.

And, lord, I do tell thee this only as an example of the deceits of women, that have no end.

And the king commanded that they should not kill his son.

XII. *Example of how the Woman came on the Fifth Day, and gave the Example of the Pig and the Ape.*

And the woman came on the fifth day and said to the king: If thou dost me not right upon that prince, thou wilt see what good thy wicked favourites will be to thee. After I am dead, we shall see what thou wilt do with thy counsellors. And when thou shalt be before God, what wilt thou say when, doing such a great wrong in letting thy son live through thy wicked counsellors and thy wicked favourites, thou failest to do what is good in this world? But I know what will be asked of thee before God. And I will tell thee what once happened to a pig. And the king said: How was that?

I tell thee, lord, that there was a pig, and he lay always under a fig tree, and ate always of those figs that fell from it. And one day he came in order to eat, and he found up (in the tree) an ape eating figs. And the ape, when he saw the pig at the foot of the fig tree, threw him a fig. And he ate it and liked it better than those which he found on the ground. And he raised his head to see if he would throw him more. And the pig thus waited on the ape until the veins of his neck dried up and he died therefrom.

And when she had said this the king feared that she would kill herself with the poison which she held in her hand, and he ordered his son to be killed.

XIII. *Example of the Fifth Favourite and of the Dog and the Snake and the Child.*

And the fifth favourite came before the king and said : Praised be God, thou art intelligent and moderate, and thou knowest that nothing hastily done before the truth is known is well done. And if a man does so, he will do foolishly; and when he shall wish to correct it he will not be able. And it will happen to him just as it did once to an owner of a dog. And the king said : How was that?

And he said : Lord, I have heard that there was a man who was servant of a king. And that man had a dog for hunting very good and very intelligent. And he never commanded him to do a thing that he did not do it. And it fell out one day that his wife went to see her relations, and all her companions went with her. And she said to her husband : Be with thy son, who lies sleeping in the bed; for I will not be long there, but will soon be here. The man sat down by his son. He being there, there came a man of the king's household, who commanded him to come in great haste. And the good man said to the dog: Guard well this child, and do not leave him till I come. And the man closed his door and went to the king. And the dog lying near the child, there came to him a very large snake and wished to eat him for the smell of the mother's milk. And when the dog saw it he jumped on to it and tore it all in pieces. And the man soon came back for love of his son whom he had left alone. And when he opened the door the dog immediately came out to ingratiate himself with his master for what he had done, and his mouth and breast were bloody. And when he saw him in such a state, he thought that he had killed his son, and he put his hand to his sword, and gave the dog a great blow and killed him. And he proceeded to the bed, and found his son sleeping and the snake torn in pieces at his feet. And when he saw this he beat his own face with his hands and was in despair. And he reproached himself for the wrong which he had done.

And, lord, act not thus thyself, for repentance afterwards will not avail thee. Do not kill thy son, for the deceits of women have no end.

XIV. *Example of the Woman and the Procuress, of the Man and the Merchant, and of the Woman that sold the Cloth.*

Lord, I have heard that there was a man who, when he heard women talked of, lost himself for love of them out of desire to have them. And he heard of a beautiful woman, and went in search of her. And he found the place where she was; and then he went to a procuress and told her that he was dying for that woman. And the old procuress said: Thou hast done nought in coming here, for she is a good woman. Have no expectation of her (unless) God help thee. And he said to her: Assist me to get her and thou shalt have what thou wilt. And the old woman said that she would do it if she could. But she said to him: Go to her husband, who is a merchant, and (try) if thou canst buy of him a cloth that he keeps hidden. And he went to the merchant and asked him to sell it to him. And he sold it, though with great reluctance. And he (the man) brought it to the old woman. And she burnt the cloth in three places and said to him: Stay here now in this my house, and let no one see thee here. And she took the cloth, folded it, put it under her dress, and went where was the wife of the merchant. And talking with her she put the cloth under the pillow and went away.

And when the merchant came he took up the pillow to sit down, and found the cloth. And he took it, and thought that he who had bought it was a friend of his wife, and that he had left the cloth there out of forgetfulness. And the merchant rose up and beat his wife very rudely without saying why. And he took away the cloth in his hand. And the woman covered her head and went to her relations.

And the old procuress knew it and went to see her, and said: Why did thy husband beat thee so evilly? And the good woman said: I know not, by my fay. The old woman said: Some enchantments have done thee these ills, but, friend, wishest thou that I should tell thee the truth? I will give thee good counsel. In my house is a man, one of the sages of the world, and shouldst thou wish to go at eventime with me to him, he will give thee counsel. And the good woman said that she would.

And when the hour of evening was come, the old woman came for her, and took her away with her to her house, and put her in the chamber where that man was. And he rose up to meet her, and lay with her. And the woman from fear and shame was silent. And afterwards she went away to her relations.

And the man said to the old woman: I am under a great favour to thee, and will give thee something. And she said: Have no care. What thou hast done I will give a good colour to. But depart and walk near the house where her husband is. And when he shall see thee, he will ask thee about the cloth that thou didst leave. And tell him that thou wast sitting near the fire, and that it was burnt in three places, and that thou gavest it to an old woman to take it away and mend it, and that thou didst not see it any more and knowest nothing of it. And I will go and walk that way, and thou wilt say: This is the woman to whom I gave the cloth. And call me, and I will excuse thee altogether.

And then he went and met the merchant, and he said: Where didst thou leave the cloth that I sold thee? And he said: I sat down by the fire, and did not pay attention, and it got burnt in three places. And I gave it to an old woman, my neighbour, to take it away and mend it, and I have never seen her since. And whilst they were thus talking came the old woman. And he called her, and said to the merchant: This is the old woman to whom I gave the cloth. And she said: By my fay, so God help me, this young man gave me a cloth to mend, and I went with it under my mantle to thy house. And in truth I know not if it fell down in the house or in the street. And he (the merchant) said: I found it. Take thy cloth and go away. Then the merchant went home and sent for his wife from her relations, and begged her to pardon him, and she did so.

And, lord, I have told this example only that thou mayst know the deceit of women, which is very great and without end.

And the king commanded that they should not kill his son.

XV. *Example of how the Woman came on the Sixth Day, and gave him the Example of the Thief and the Lion, how he rode upon him.*

And the woman came on the sixth day and said to the king: I trust in God that he will protect me from thy wicked favourites, as he once protected a man from a lion. And the king said: How was that?

And she said: A rich herdsman was passing (with a caravan) by the end of a village, and there came into it (the caravan) a great thief and great evildoer; and they being in this position night overtook them, and a great rain fell upon them, and the herdsman said: Let us look after our things lest the thief do us some harm.

And then came (a lion) and got in amongst the beasts, and they did not see him through the great darkness. And (the thief) began to feel which was the largest (of the beasts), in order to take it away. And he put his hand upon the lion, and found none larger, none that had a plumper neck than he. And he mounted him, and the lion said: This is the (demon) Tempest that men speak of. And he ran with him all the night until the morning. And when they knew each other, they were afraid. And the lion came to a tree, very weary, and the thief took hold of a branch and mounted up into the tree with great fear of the lion.

And the lion was very frightened; and he met with an ape, and he said to him: What ails thee, lion, or how didst thou come thus? And the lion said to him: This night the (demon) Tempest caught me, and rode on me until the morning. He never wearied of making me run. The ape said to him: Where is that Tempest? And the lion showed the man up in the tree. And the ape mounted to the top of the tree, and the lion waited to hear and see what he would do. And the ape saw that it was a man, and beckoned to the lion to come. And the lion came running. And then the man lowered himself a little, and caught hold of the ape's......and compressed them until he killed him, and threw him to the lion. And when the lion saw this he fled and said: Blessed be God who has liberated me from this Tempest.

And the woman said: I trust in God that he will assist me against thy wicked favourites, as he assisted the thief against the ape.

And the king ordered his son to be killed.

XVI. *Example of the Sixth Favourite, of the Two Pigeons that jointly collected the Wheat in their Nest.*

And the sixth favourite came and knelt before the king and said: If thou hadst no son thou oughtest to petition God that he would grant thee one. Then how canst thou kill that son whom God gave thee, having no more than that one? If thou killest him thou wilt incur evil therefrom, as once upon a time a pigeon did. The king said: How was that?

He said: Lord, there was a pigeon, and he dwelt in a wood and had his nest there. And in the time of August they (*i.e.* the pigeon and his mate) collected their wheat and kept it in their nest, and the cock pigeon went away and told the hen pigeon that she should eat none of the wheat whilst the summer lasted. He also said to her: Go to these fields and eat of what thou shalt find. And when the winter shall come thou wilt eat of the wheat and make merry.

And afterwards the great heat came and the corn dried up and shrivelled and stuck together. And when the cock pigeon came he said: Did not I tell thee not to eat corn, but to keep it for the winter? And she swore to him that she had not been eating the corn, that she had not begun it either with little or much. And the cock pigeon would not believe her. And he began to peck her and strike her with his claws and his wings until he killed her. And the cock pigeon kept the corn and saw that it grew with the damp, and that there was neither less nor more of it. And he grew sad because he had killed the hen pigeon.

And, lord, I fear that thou wilt grieve therefor, as the cock pigeon did, if thou killest thy son. That deceit of women is the greatest thing in the world.

XVII. *Example of the Husband and the Reaper and the Woman and the Thieves that took her by Treason.*

Lord, I have heard an example of a man and a woman who lived in a village. And the man went to plough, and the woman made him a loaf of panic grass to eat, and brought it to him where he was ploughing. And whilst she was on her way to give it to him, robbers attacked her and took the loaf away from her. And one of the robbers made an image of an elephant by way of scoff, and put it into the basket, and she did not see it. And they let her go, and she went to her husband. And when he opened the basket he saw that, and he said to her: What is that which thou bringest here? And she looked and saw what the robbers had done, and she said: I dreamed this night that thou wast before a botcher and that thou wast much grieved. And then I went to some men that they might solve this dream for me. And they told me that I should make an image of panic, and that thou shouldst eat it, and that thou wouldst be freed from what might happen to thee. And this dream, said the husband, may be true. And such is the deceit and the arts of women that have no end.

And the king commanded that they should not kill his son.

XVIII. *Example of how the Woman came on the Seventh Day before the King, complaining and saying that she wished to be burnt. And the King ordered his Son to be killed in haste rather than she should complain.*

And when the woman came on the seventh day, she said: If this young man dies not to-day, to-day I shall be discovered. And the woman said this (also): There is no course open but death.

All whatever she had she gave to the poor for God's sake, and ordered much wood to be brought, and ordered it to be set on fire, and said that she would burn herself.

And the king when he heard this, before she could burn herself, ordered the youth to be killed.

And the seventh favourite came and set himself between the youth and the man who was to kill him. And he humbled himself before the king and said: Lord, kill not thy son for the saying of a woman, for thou knowest not whether she lies or tells the truth. And thou didst so greatly covet to have a son, as thou knowest, and since God gave pleasure to thee, do not grieve him.

XIX. *Of the Example of the She-Devil, and of the Man and the Woman, and of how the Man asked Three Gifts.*

Lord, I have heard that there was a man who never went away from a she-devil and had by her one son. And one day she wished to go and said: I fear that I shall never see thee again. But I will that thou learn of me three prayers, and when thou shalt ask three things of God thou shalt have them. And she taught him the prayers and the she-devil went away.

And he was very sorrowful because she went away, and he went to his wife and said to her: Know that the she-devil that held me has gone away, and I sorrow much for the good that I knew through her, and she taught me three prayers by which, if I should ask three things of God, I should have them. And now advise me what I shall ask of God, and I shall have it. And the wife said to him: Thou knowest truly that men love women above all things, and are much gratified with their solace therefore ask God that he would grant thee many of them. And when he saw himself loaded with them, he said to the wife: God confound thee, because this has been done by thy counsel. And she said: Do not two prayers still remain unto thee? Now ask God to take them away from thee, since thou art so annoyed with them. And he prayed, and straightway all were taken away and there remained none. And when he saw this, he began to revile his wife; and she said to him: Do not revile me, for thou hast still another prayer, and ask God to restore what was before. And it was restored. And thus all the prayers were lost.

Therefore I give thee the advice not to kill thy son; for the wickednesses of women have no end, and of this I will give thee an example. And the king said: How was that?

XX. *Example of a Young Man who would not marry until he knew the Wickednesses of Women.*

And, lord, they told me that a man would not marry until he knew and had learnt the wickednesses of women and their deceit. And he went on until he came to a hamlet, and they told him that there were men wise in the deceit of women, and he spent much money to learn the arts.

He that was most knowing said to him: Desirest thou that I tell thee? Never, never wilt thou learn completely the deceits of women until thou sittest three days upon ashes and eatest nothing but a little barley bread and salt; and then thou wilt learn. And he told him that it pleased him, and he did so. Then he sat down upon the ashes and made many books of the arts of women.

And after he had done this, he said that he would return to his country. And he took up his abode in the house of a good man. And the host asked him about all that he brought, and he told (from) where he was, and how he had sat upon the ashes while he translated those books, and how he ate the barley bread, and how he suffered much care and much discomfort, and translated those arts.

And after he had told him this, the host took him by the hand and brought him to his wife, and said to her: A good man I have found who is wearied of his road. And he told her all about him, and asked her to do something that the man might be refreshed or strengthened, for then he was weak. And after he had said this he went away, and the woman did all well according to his directions. Then she began to ask the man what he was or how he was travelling. And he told her all, and she took him to be a man of small brains and of small gifts because she knew that he never could achieve what he had undertaken, and said: I believe truly that no woman in the world can deceive thee. There is nothing to equal those books that thou hast made. And she said in her heart: Here is a sage who wants me to let him know how silly he is in his delusion. I am the woman to do it.

Then she called him and said: Friend, I am a young and beautiful woman, and at a good time of life, and my husband is very old and worn, and for a long time has not lain with me. Therefore, as I see that thou art a judicious and intelligent man, if thou desirest, thou shalt lie with me. And don't tell it to anybody. And when she had said (this), he imagined that she spoke truth. And he arose and wanted to lay hold of her, and said to her: Wait a little and let us undress ourselves. And he undressed himself, and she uttered loud cries and howls. And straightway the neighbours gathered together, and she said before they entered: Lie down on the ground, otherwise thou art dead. And he did so, and she put a great morsel of bread in his mouth. And when the men entered, they asked what evil had occurred. And she said: This man is our guest, and he was nearly choked by a morsel of bread and he was rolling his eyes. Then she uncovered him and threw water over him that he might come to his senses. He did not come to his senses, though she threw cold water over him all this time and wiped his face with a white cloth

Then the men went out. And when they were gone out she said to him: Friend, in thy books is there any art like this? And he said: By my fay, I never saw it; I never found any such as this. And she said: Thou hast incurred much trouble and difficulty for it, and never expect any better profit from it. That which thou desirest thou wilt never so obtain, neither thou nor any other man of all that ever were born. And when he saw this he took all his books and put them into the fire, and said that he had spent his days to no purpose.

And I, lord, have told thee this example only in order that thou shalt not kill thy son for the words of a woman.

And the king commanded that they should not kill his son.

XXI. *Of how on the Eighth Day the Prince spoke and went before the King.*

When the eighth day came, in the morning, before the sun rose, the prince called the woman who attended him in those days when he did not speak, and said to her: Go and call such a one, who is one of the greatest favourites of the king, and tell him to come as soon as he can.

And the woman, when she saw that the prince spoke, ran fast and called the favourite. And he arose and came speedily to the prince. And he wept with him, and told him why he had not spoken during those days, and he told him what had happened with his stepmother:—And I have escaped death only through God and through thee and through thy companions, who have helped me well and loyally to justice. God give thee good reward, and I will give it thee if I live and see what I desire. And I wish thee to run off to my father and tell him the news of me before my false stepmother comes, for I know that she will be early.

And the favourite ran off quickly when he saw him speak thus, and went to the king and said: Lord, give me largesse for the benefit and favour that God has done thee, because thou didst not kill thy son; for he now speaks, and he has sent me to thee. And he did not tell him all that the prince had said to him.

And the king said: Go very quickly and tell the prince to come straightway to me. And he came and humbled himself to him, and the king said: Why was it that during those days thou didst not speak though thou sawest death before thee? And the prince said: I will tell you it.

And he told him all that had happened to him, and how his master Cendubete had prohibited him from speaking for seven days. Moreover, of the woman I tell thee, said he, that when she took me aside to give good counsel to me, I told her that I could not answer until the seven days had passed. And when she heard this, she knew no other counsel than that thou shouldst cause me to be killed before I might speak. Yet, lord, I ask of you as a favour, if you would and should think fit, to order all the wise men of your kingdom and of your towns to assemble, for I would state my case before them.

And when the prince said this the king was very glad and said: Praised be God for all the good which he has done me, in that he did not let me commit so great an error as to kill my son.

And the king ordered his people and his court to come. And after they were come, Cendubete came and went in unto the king and said: I humble myself, lord. And the king said: What hast thou been doing, wicked Cendubete, these seven days? For I was very near killing my son through the suggestion thou madest him. And Cendubete said: God gave thee so much grace and instruction in order that thou shouldst act after knowing the truth. More especially you kings should be surer of the truth than others. And he (the prince) did not fail to do what I had taught him. And thou, lord, shouldst not have ordered thy son to be killed for the saying of a woman. And the king said: Praised be God that I did not kill my son, for I should have lost this world and the other. And (I ask) you wise men, if I had killed my son, whose fault would it have been? Would it have been mine, or my son's, or my wife's, or the master's?

Four wise men rose up, and one said: When Cendubete saw the young man's star, how his fate would be, he should not have hidden himself.

And another said: It is not so as you say. Cendubete was not to blame, for he had made a compact with the king and he was not to fail. It would have been the fault of the king, who ordered his son to be killed for the saying of a woman, not knowing if it was true or if she lied.

The third wise man said: It is not so as you say, for the king was not to blame. For there is no wood in the world colder than sandalwood, and nothing colder than camphorwood, and when they roll one against the other they will be so heated that fire will issue from them. And if the king were strong in his brain, he would not turn his mind for a woman's brain. But as it was a woman that the king loved, it could not be but that he should listen to her. But the fault was the woman's, because with her words she deceived him, and made him say that he would kill his son.

And the fourth said: The fault was not the woman's,

but the prince's, who would not regard what his master had commanded. For the woman, when she saw the boy so nice and handsome, immediately took a liking to him, and more so when she was in private with him. But when she understood from what the prince said that she would be discovered at the end of the seven days, she feared that he would kill her for that, and took measures to have him killed before he should speak.

And Cendubete said: It is not so as you say, for the greatest science that is in the world is to speak.

And the prince said: I will speak if you should command me.

And the king said:......(And the prince said:) God, be thou praised, because thou hast caused me to see this day and this hour, when thou hast let me show forth my case and my right. It is necessary to hear my case, for I desire to say what I know and to tell you this example.

XXII. *Example of the Man and of those whom he invited, and of the Young Maid whom he sent for the Milk, and of the Snake from whom fell Poison.*

And the masters told him to tell (it). And he said: They say that (there was) a man who prepared his breakfast and invited his guests and his friends, and sent his maid to the market for milk for them. And she brought it and carried it on her head. And a kite passed over her, and he was carrying in his claws a snake, and he squeezed it so strongly with his claws that the poison came out of it and fell into the milk. And they drank it and all died of it. And now tell me, whose fault was it that all those men died?

And one of the four wise men said: The fault was in him that invited them, that he did not examine the milk that he gave them to drink.

And the other master said: It is not so as you say. He who invites guests cannot examine everything nor taste of all that he has provided. But the fault was in the kite that squeezed the snake so hard with his claws that it let the poison fall.

And the other answered: It is not so as you say. For the kite was not to blame for it, because he ate what he was used to eat, according to his necessity. But the snake is to blame because it threw the poison out of itself.

And the fourth said: It is not so as you others say. For the snake is not to blame. But the maid was to blame that she did not cover the milk when she brought it from the market.

Cendubete said: It is not so as you others say. For the maid was not to blame, for they did not order her to cover the milk. Nor was the kite to blame, for he ate what he had to eat. Nor was the snake to blame, for he was in another's power. Nor was the host to blame. Such a man cannot taste all the eatables that he orders to be dressed.

Then the king said to his son: All these say nothing. But tell me, thou, whose fault it is.

The prince said: None of these was to blame. But the time had arrived at which they were all to die.

And when the king heard this he said: Blessed be God that he did not let me kill my son.

Then said the king to Cendubete: Thou hast done much good, and what thou hast done entitles thee to much favour from us. But thou knowest if the young man has more to learn. Teach it him and thou wilt have a good reward.

Then Cendubete said: Lord, I know nothing in the world that I did not teach him. And I well believe that there is no such thing in the world and that there is none wiser than he.

Then said the king to the wise men who were present: Is it true what Cendubete says? Then they said that no man ought to depreciate what was evidently good. And the prince said: He that does well deserves good reward.

The prince said: I will tell thee who knows more than I. The king said: Who?

XXIII. *Example of the Two Wise Children and their Mother and the Young Man.*

Lord, they say that there were two boys, one four years old and the other five years, blind and deformed, and all say that they were wiser than I. And his father said: How were they wiser than thou?

The prince said: I have heard that there was a man who never heard of a beautiful woman but he would lose himself for her. And he heard of a beautiful woman and sent his man to her to say that he was very fond of her. And that woman had a son four years old. And after that messenger returned with the answer that she would do what he thought best, the lord went to her, and she said: Wait a bit and I will give my son his dinner, and presently I will come to thee. But the man said: Do what I desire, and after I shall have gone hence give him his dinner. And the woman said: If thou knewest how wise he is, thou wouldst not say this.

And she rose up and put a kettle upon the fire, and put rice in and boiled it, and took a little in the spoon and put it before him. And he wept and said: Give me more, for this is little. And she said to him: Dost thou desire more? And he said to her: More. And he told her to throw into it some oil from the bottle. And he wept more, and for all this was not silent.

And the boy said: Woe to thee!......Never saw I one

more mad than thou, for thou hast little brains. The man said: In what do I seem to thee mad and of little brains? And the boy said: I am only weeping for my own good. How do my tears from my own eyes pain thee? And my mind is sound, since my father sent me for my weeping as much rice to eat as I could wish. But he is mad and of little brains and of bad understanding who goes out of his country, and leaves his children and his property and his relations, to lead a loose life in the world, seeking to do mischief and to weaken his own body, and falling into God's wrath.

And when the boy had said this, perceiving that he was more shrewd than his years, he came to him and embraced him and caressed him, and said in good faith: Thou sayest truth. I did not think that thou wast so judicious and so knowing, and I am much amazed at what thou hast said. And he repented and did penance.

And, lord, said the prince, this is the story of the child of four years of age.

XXIV. *Example of the Child of Five Years of Age, and of the Partners who gave the Money to the Old Woman.*

And, lord, I will tell thee of the child of five years of age. The king said: Then tell (it).

He said: I have heard that there were three partners in a trade, and they obtained great wealth, and all three set out on a journey. And it happened that they lodged at an old woman's house. And they gave her their money to guard, and said to her: Thou shalt give it to no one separately until we all join together. And she said to them: I will do so.

And then they went into the old woman's kitchen garden, in order to bathe in a tank that was there. And the two said to the one: Go to the old woman and tell her to give thee a comb with which we may comb ourselves. And he did so, and went to the old woman and said to her: My companions have sent me in order that thou shouldst give me the money, for we wish to count it. She said: I will not give it thee until all of you join together, just as you settled it with me. He said: Come to the door. And he said: Observe the old woman; she wants to know if you have sent me. And they said: Give it him. And she went and gave him the money, and he took it and departed. And in this manner he deceived his companions. And when they saw that he did not come, they went to the old woman and said: Why hast thou detained our companion? And she said: I have given him the money as you commanded me. And they said: Woe unto thee! We did not command thee to give him the money, but a comb. And she said: He has taken away the money which you gave me. And they summoned her before the magistrate, and they attended him and stated their case. And the magistrate decided that the old woman should pay the money, for she knew the condition.

And the old woman weeping met a child of five years of age, and the child said to her: Why weepest thou? And she said: I weep for my bad fortune and for the great ill that has come to me. And for God's sake leave me alone. And the child followed her until she told him why she wept. And he said to her: I will give thee counsel touching this trouble that thou hast, if thou wilt give me a coin wherewith to buy dates. And the child said to her: Go back to the magistrate and say that thou hast the money, and say: Magistrate, order them to bring their companion. And if not, I will give them nothing until all three join together as they settled it with me.

And she went back to the magistrate and said to him

what the child had advised her. And the magistrate knew that another had advised her this, and he said: I pray thee for God's sake to tell me who he was that advised thee. And she said: A child that I met on the road. And the magistrate sent for the child. And they brought him before the magistrate, and he said to him: Thou didst advise this old woman? And the child said: I taught it her. And the magistrate was much pleased with the child, and took him home, and took much care of him for his advice.

And the king was pleased with the history of the child of five years of age.

XXV. *Example of the Merchant of Sandalwood and the other Merchant.*

And the king said: How was that?

They tell the story of the old man, and I hear it said that once upon a time there was a very rich merchant who traded in sandalwood, and he inquired in what land sandalwood was most dear. And he went and loaded his beasts with sandalwood for that land. And he passed near to a very fine city, and he said in his heart: I will not enter into this city until it be day.

And he being in that place there passed a young woman who was taking her herd to pasture. And when she saw the (merchant's) beasts she asked him what he was bringing and (from) where he was. And the young woman went to her master and told him how there were merchants at the gate of the town who were bringing much sandalwood. And that man took all (the sandalwood) that he had and threw it into the fire. And the merchant perceived that it was smoke of sandalwood, and he was much afraid, and said to his men: Look to your pàcks, that the fire do not reach them, for I smell smoke of·

sandalwood. And they examined their packs, and found nothing.

And the merchant rose and went to the shepherds to see if they were risen; and he that burnt the sandalwood came to the merchant and said to him: Who are you, and how did you come, and what merchandise do you bring? And he said: We are merchants that bring sandalwood. And the man said: Ah, good man, in this land we burn nought but sandalwood. Said the merchant: How can that be? For I inquired and they told me that there was no land more remunerative than this, and none where sandalwood would be worth so much. The man said: Whoever told thee so wished to deceive thee.

And the merchant began to lament and to curse himself, and he made great complaint; and the man said: By my fay, I have great grief for thee. Moreover he said: Since it is so, I will buy it of thee and give thee what thou shalt wish. And now get up and give it to me. And the merchant agreed to it, and the man took the sandalwood and carried it to his home.

And when it was daylight the merchant entered the town, and put up in the house of an old woman, and inquired of her what was the value of sandalwood in that city. She said: It is worth its weight in gold. And the merchant repented much when he heard it. And the old woman said: Indeed, good man, the inhabitants of this town are deceivers and wicked cheats, and there never comes a foreigner but they mock him; and beware ye of them.

And the merchant went to the market, and found some men playing at dice, and he stopped there and looked at them. And one (of them) said: Knowest thou how to play this game? He said: Yes, I know how. He said: Then sit down. But he said: Mind that there be this condition—whoever shall win, the other shall be bound to do what the former shall desire and command. The other said: I agree. Then the merchant sat down, and lost. And he that won said: Thou must do what I shall command thee. He said: I acknowledge that this is true He said to him: Then I command thee to drink up all the water of the sea, and leave nothing—not a drop. And the merchant said: I will. The other said: Give me sureties that thou wilt do it.

And the merchant went through the street, and he met with a man who had but one eye. And he laid hold of the merchant and said: Thou didst rob me of my eye. Go hither with me before the magistrate. And the old woman his hostess said: I am his surety to bring him before you to-morrow.

And the old woman took him with her to her inn, and said to him: Did I not tell thee and warn thee that the men of this town were bad men and of bad character? But thou wouldst not believe my first warning. Neglect not now what I shall tell thee. And the merchant said: By my fay, I will never fail to do what thou shalt command and advise me. The old woman said: Know that those men have for their master an old blind man, and he is very knowing. And they all meet together with him every night, and each one tells what he has done in the day. Now if thou couldst go in amongst them and sit down there unperceived, they will tell what they did to thee each one of them, and thou wilt hear what the old man says about what they did to thee. It cannot be but that they will tell it all to the old man.

And so the man (the merchant) went there, and sat down unperceived by them, and heard what they said to the old man. And the first said that he had bought sandalwood of a merchant and told how he had bought it, saying that he would give as much as he pleased. And the old man said: Thou hast acted like a stupid fellow. What wilt thou think if he asks of thee fleas, half female and half male, and some blind, and others lame, and others green, and others livid, and others red and white, and that there be no more than one sound one amongst them? Dost thou think it is possible for thee to accomplish this? The man said: He will never think of this; he will ask nothing but money.

And he that played at dice with the merchant rose and said: I played with that merchant, and said that if I won at the dice he should do what I should order him to do; and I ordered him to drink up all the water of the sea. And the old man said: Thou hast done as ill as the other. What wilt thou think if he says: I agree with thee to drink up all the water of the sea; but look thou that there enter into it no river, nor that any fountain fall into the sea· then I will drink it. Consider whether thou wilt be able to do all this.

He of the eye rose and said: I fell in with this same merchant and saw that he had eyes such as my (single one), and I said to him: Thou that stolest from me my eye shalt not part from me till thou givest me the worth of my eye. And the old man said to him: Thou wast not a master; thou didst not know what thou didst. What wilt thou think if he shall say to thee: Take out thine that has remained, and I will take out mine, and we will see if they are like each other, and weigh them. And if they shall be equal, it is thine; and if not, not. And if thou shalt do this, thou wilt be blind, and the other will have one eye left, and thou none. And thou wilt suffer a greater loss than he.

And when the merchant heard this, he had learnt

everything, and went to the inn and told it all to her (*i.e.*, his hostess), and held himself to have been well counselled by her. And he rested that night in her house.

And when the day broke, he saw the man who would buy the sandalwood, and he said to him: Give me my sandalwood, or give me what thou didst covenant with me. And he said: Choose what thou wilt. And the merchant said to him: Give me a bushel full of fleas, half females and half males, and half red, and half green, and half livid, and half yellow, and half white. And the man said: I will give thee money. The merchant said: I want nothing but the fleas. The merchant summoned the man, and they went before the magistrate. And the magistrate ordered that he should give the fleas. And the man said that he (the merchant) might take his sandalwood. And so the merchant recovered his sandalwood by the advice of the old man.

And the other came that had played at dice, and said to him: Perform the contract that thou didst make with me, that thou wilt drink all the water of the sea. And he said: I will do so, on condition that thou shalt prevent all the fountains and rivers from entering into the sea. And he said: Let us go before the magistrate. And the magistrate said: Is this so? And they said: Yes. And he said Then see thou that no more water enter (into the sea), and (then) he says that he will drink it. He said: It cannot be. And the magistrate released the merchant from his obligation.

And straightway came he of the eye and said: Give me my eye. And he said: I will. Take out thine own and I will take out mine, and we will see if they are alike, and weigh them. And if they shall be equal, it is thine; and if it is not thine, pay me what the law commands. And the magistrate said: What sayest thou? He said: How shall I take out my eye without having straightway none? The magistrate said: The law demands (it) of thee. And the man said that he would not take it out. And the magistrate released the merchant from his obligation.

And thus it befell the merchant with the men of that town.

And the prince said: Lord, I only gave thee this example that thou mayst know the arts of the world.

XXVI. *Example of the Woman and the Clerk and the Friar.*

And the king said: How was that?

And the prince said: I have heard of a woman whose husband went away on some business. And she sent to the abbot to say that her husband was not at home, and that he should come for the night to her dwelling. And the abbot came and entered the house. And when he came it was midnight. The husband came and called at the door. And he (*i.e.*, the abbot) said: How shall it be? And she said: Go and hide thyself in that apartment till daylight.

And the husband entered, and threw himself on his bed. And when day came the woman arose, and went to a friar her friend, and asked him for a habit that he might get the abbot away who was in her house. And the friar went and said: What has become of such a one? And she said: He is not yet risen. And he went in and asked him (the husband) whence he came, and was there until he (the abbot) was dressed. And the friar said: Pardon me, I wish to retire. He said: You must go, and be well. And joining the other in the apartment, the abbot went out dressed like a friar, and in that dress went with him to his convent.

Lord, I do tell thee this example only in order that thou mayst not believe women that are bad.

And the wise man said that even if the earth became paper, the sea ink, and its fishes pens, they could not write all the wickednesses of women.

And the king ordered her to be burnt in a dry caldron.

THE END.

INDEX.

'Abbot, The,' tale of, 163-164
'Absalom,' tale of, told in Hebrew version of Sindibad, 28
Æsopic fables, MSS. of, 63-64
'Ahmed,' tale of, 35
Alcos, name of king in Sindibad story, 10
'Amazon, The,' tale of, 35
Andreopulos (Michael), translation of Syntipas by, 5, 51, 54, 59
'Ape and the Wild Boar,' tale of, 19, 25, 28, 31, 45, 139-140
Arabic texts of Sindibad, 5, 6, 7, 8
Arabic writers, first mention of Sindibad by, 4
Aslam and Sindbad, title of the greater Sindibad, 46
Ass, guilty woman condemned to ride on, story incident, 22
Astrologers called at birth of king's son, story incident, 11

Baethgen (Dr.), Syriac text of Sindibad by, 5, 63
Bahrâm Shah, 67
Baibor, name of king in Sindibad story, 10
Bandello, novel of, told in Spanish version of Sindibad, 27
'Bathman,' tale of, 18, 25, 28, 31, 34, 136
Benfey (Dr.), researches upon the Sindibad, 3, 30, 38
Bengalee MS. of the Seven Viziers, 7
Birth, extraordinary, story incident, 11
'Blackguard, The,' tale of, 34
'Blind Old Man,' story of, 20, 25, 28, 31, 35
'Boar, Wild,' tale of. *See* "Ape."
Boissonade, edition of Sindibad by, 5, 54

Boolak version of 'Thousand and One Nights,' 7
'Boy of Three Years,' tale of, 20, 25, 35, 155-156.
'Boy of Five Years,' tale of, 20, 25, 31, 35, 156-158
British Museum, MS. of Hebrew version of Sindibad at, 64
Brockhaus (H.) on text of Nachschebi, 7, 37-39
Buddhistic origin of Sindibad, 3, 30
'Burnt Cloth,' story of. *See* "Cloth."

Caffa, in Crimea, Syntipas copied at, 59
'Calenderer and his Son,' story of, 18, 25, 27, 30, 34, 35, 128
'Calila and Dımna,' Arabic version of, 52; Greek version of, 58; Hebrew version of, 64-65
Carmoly, translation of Sindibad by, 6, 23
'Chest, The Lover in the,' tale of, 34
'Child in the Cradle,' tale of, 31
China, mentioned in Sindibad story, 10
'Cloth, The Burnt,' tale of, 19, 25, 28, 35, 42, 46, 47, 141-143
Comnenus (Emperor Alexius), 58
Condemnation of hero to death, story incident, 17
Crier, proclamation of crime by, story incident, 22
'Cukasaptati,' Greek translation of, 27, 38
'Curiosity,' tale of, 30, 34

Dacier on Greek Syntipas, 53
Danger, prognostication of, to hero, story incident, 11
'Destiny,' tale told in Greek Syntipas, 24, 25

166　　　　　　　　INDEX.

Devil, tales of, 131-133, 147-148
'Disguise, The,' tale of, told in Hebrew version of Sindibad, 28
'Dog, The Go-between and the,' story of, 18, 25, 27, 31, 34, 46, 47, 48, 136-139
'Dog and the Snake,' story of, 19, 25, 28, 31, 140-141
'Dolopathos' of Herbers, French version of Seven Sages, 1, 37
'Druggist, The,' story of, 18, 25, 27, 28, 31, 34

East India Company Library, Persian MS. of Sindibad at, 6
Eberhard (A.), edition of the Syntipas by, 5, 63
Election, curious mode of, story incident, 11, 12
'Elephant, The Tame,' tale of, 30
'Elephant, The Young,' tale of, 41, 43, 146
'Erasto,' grouping of the text of, 1
European popular literature, 1-2

Falconer (Forbes), abstract of Persian MS. of Sindibad by, 6, 23, 32
'Father-in-Law,' tale of, 42
'Female Wiles,' tale of, 19, 24, 25-26, 31, 41, 43
Forty Viziers, connexion with Sindibad, 8
'Fox and the Ape,' tale of, 30
'Fox, the Wolf, and the Camel,' tale of, 30
'Fox, The,' tale of, 21, 25, 27, 28, 36
Fusion of different tales into one, 46-47

Gabriel (Duke), Syntipas translated by order of, 55-58
Galanos, publication of Greek text of Cukasaptati by, 38
'Go-between, The, and the Dog,' tale of. *See* "Dog."
Greek language of the Syntipas, 59-61
Greek Syntipas, tales told in, 24-26; text of, 5, 10 23, 51, 53-64
'Guests, The Poisoned,' tale of, 20, 25, 35, 153-155

Habicht's text of the Seven Viziers, 7
Hakim Azraki, 67
Hebrew version of the Sindibad, 5, 10-23, 27-29, 46, 64-67
Historia Septem Sapientum, 1, 47
'Honey, Drop of,' tale of, 18, 25, 34, 35, 133-134

'Hunchbacks, The Three,' tale of, told in Hebrew version of Sindibad, 28
Hungary, tradition in, derived from literature, 2
'Husband, The Libertine,' tale of, 41, 43, 49

India, mentioned in Sindibad story, 10
Indian origin of Sindibad, 3
'Infidelity,' story of, 18, 25, 28, 30, 34, 35, 41, 43, 130-131
Instruction given to hero, story incident, 12-15

'Janus in the Defence of Rome,' tale of, 47
'Jeweller, The,' tale of, 34
Joel, Rabbi, 64-66

'King of the Apes and the Burnt Elephant,' tale of, 30
Κῦρος, name of king in Sindibad story, 10

'Lamia, The,' tale of, 18, 25, 27, 31, 34, 35, 46, 61, 62, 131-133
Language of the Greek Syntipas, 59-61
'Liberators, The Four,' tale of, 31
'Lion's Track, The,' tale of, 18, 25, 27, 34, 35, 125-127
Literature, oral tradition derived from, 2
'Loaves, The,' tale of, 18, 25, 28, 34, 129-130
Loiseleur, upon Eastern text of Sindibad, 2, 3, 54; upon the Seven Viziers, 7
'Lover in the Chest,' tale of, 34
'Lovers, The Three,' tale of, 47
'Lovers, The Four,' tale of, 35

'Magpie,' tale of, 30, 35
'Man who understood Female Wiles,' story of. *See* "Female."
Manuscripts of Seven Viziers, Bengalee, 7; Tunisian, 7
Manuscripts of Sindibad, Greek, 5, 54, 63; Hebrew, 64; Persian, 6; Spanish, 8, 68-69; Syriac, 61
Manuscripts of 'Thousand and One Nights,' Arabic, 7
Mediæval popular literature, 1-2
Melenicus, castle or city of, 56
Melitene, government of, 57-58
Moral principles set forth, 22
Moscow MS. of Greek Syntipas, 54, 63

INDEX. 167

'Mother, The Careless,' tale of, 21, 31, 33
Munich MS. of Syntipas, 61
Musa, the Persian author of Sindibad text, 5, 51

Nachschebi's version of Sindibad, 6, 10-23, 37-52
Names of king in Sindibad story, 10
Neo-Grecisms in the Syntipas, 59-61
'Night of Al-kader,' tale of, 35
Nöldeke (Th.) on Dr. Baethgen's Syriac version of Sindibad, 5

Oral tradition derived from literature, 2
Oriental texts of Western tales, 1-3

Pancatantra, The, coincidences with Sindibad, 3, 13, 14
Parables of Sandabar, Hebrew version of Sindibad, 5, 66-67. *See* "Hebrew."
Paris, Imperial Library of, Greek text of Sindibad at, 5, 54, 59
'Parrot, The Woman and the,' story told by Vizier, 18, 25, 27, 30, 34, 35, 44, 127-128
'Partridges, The Two,' tale of, 31, 33
Persian version of Sindibad, tales told in, 6, 10-23, 29, 67
'Pig and the Ape,' tale of ('Ape and the Wild Boar'). *See* "Ape."
'Pigeons, The Two,' tale of, 19, 25, 27, 35, 145
Ploughing, 146
Prayer, birth of a son from, story incident, 11
Punishments allotted to the guilty woman, 22

'Ring, The,' tale of, 35
Rios (Prof. Amador de los), discovery of Spanish text of Sindibad by, 8
Rodiger, discovery of Syriac text by, 5, 61
Romaic version of Syntipas, 59

Scott (F.), 'Tales, Anecdotes, and Letters,' &c., 7, 35-36
Sengelman, translation of Sindibad by, 6
Seth (Simeon), 'Calila and Dimna' translated into Greek by, 58
'Seven Sages,' tale of, the basis of popular books, 1
'Seven Viziers,' tales told in, 34-36; versions of, 7, 10-23
'Sex, The Changed,' tale of, 18, 25, 27, 31, 34, 35, 46, 134-135
Silence imposed upon hero, story incident, 15-16
Sindibad, Indian origin of, 3; earliest mention of, 4; versions of, 5-8; form and contents of the story, 10-23
'Snake, Dog, and the Child,' tale of. *See* "Dog."
Son, birth of a, by prayer, story incident, 11
Spanish translation of Syntipas, 8, 10-23, 26-27, 64, 68-164
Syntipas, Greek version of Sindibad, 5, 51. *See* "Greek."
Syriac version of Sindibad, 5, 51, 61

Tales told to avert impending events, 17-21, 24-36
'Ten Viziers,' connexion with Sindibad, 8
Text of story of Sindibad, 10-23
'Thief and the Lion,' tale of, 19, 25, 28, 31, 45, 143-144
'Thousand and One Nights,' Sindibad tales told in, 7, 33, 39
Tradition. *See* "Oral Tradition."
Tunis MS. of 'The Seven Viziers,' 7

'Wife of the Seneschal,' tale of, 47
'Wishes, The Three,' tale of, 19, 25, 28, 31, 35, 147-148
Woman beguiles the hero, story incident, 16-17

LONDON:
PRINTED BY FRANCIS & CO., TOOK'S COURT, E.C.

GR   Consiglieri Pedroso, Zohimo
235   Portuguese folk-tales
C613

PLEASE DO NOT REMOVE
CARDS OR SLIPS FROM THIS POCKET

UNIVERSITY OF TORONTO LIBRARY